In The Grip of the Mullah

F. S. Brereton

[ZHINGOORA BOOKS]

This edition is published by
Zhingoora Books.

CONTENTS

CHAPTER I

THE CASTAWAY

"Perim!" shouted Colonel Hubbard, placing his hand to his mouth, and his lips close to the ear of his friend Major Bellamy. "The island of Perim, or I am much mistaken. It lies in the Strait of Bab-el-Mandeb, and has proved the destruction of more than one fine vessel. I can tell you that, on this dark night and with this fierce gale blowing, we are lucky to have caught even a glimpse of the light, and still more fortunate to have slipped by in safety. Now we leave the Red Sea, and run into the Gulf of Aden, where we shall feel the full force of the wind and waves. However, what does that matter? Better plenty of water all round, even though it is lashed into frenzy, than a lee shore close at hand, a dark night, and no bearings to steer by. Halloa, there's the flash of the light again!"

Clinging with one hand to the rail which ran round the saloon, the speaker pointed eagerly into the darkness. Aided by the faint gleam of the electric lamp which was suspended from the spar deck above their heads, his comrade, Major Bellamy, followed the direction of his finger, and having watched for a few seconds, suddenly exclaimed:

"Yes, colonel, you're right! I could have sworn that there was nothing but inky blackness over in that direction. But there's no doubt about the matter. The light is flashing in that quarter, I'll stake my word upon it. Won't our skipper be joyful! I heard him saying, an hour or more ago, that our safety depended upon his sighting the island; and there it is, sure enough. Well it's a great relief, and now I can turn in with some degree of assurance. I'm not nervous, you know, colonel, but, by Jove, a storm like this, and a pitch dark night such as we are experiencing, make one a little anxious in spite of one's self. Now, if it were on land, and we were in an enemy's country, I should feel far more at my ease. I'd double the pickets, of course, so as to give the boys a little more courage, don't you know; for even a soldier feels queer when posted a couple of hundred yards away from his fellows, especially if he knows that a score or more of niggers are probably crawling round like ghosts, ready to fall upon him at any moment. Yes, I've had experience of that, and I well remember how fidgety I was, for we were fighting on the West Coast, and knew well that the natives of Ashantee were as cruel and as cunning as they make 'em. So I'd double the pickets, colonel, and I'd make a point of going round to inspect them, and at the same time to encourage them, every quarter of an hour. Depend upon it, nothing like letting Thomas Atkins know that his officer is at hand, taking an interest in him, and ready to help him at any moment."

"Just so," responded the colonel, clinging the while with all his strength to the rail, for the steamer was rolling and plunging heavily. "Quite right, Bellamy; I'd do the same. But what can our poor skipper do? He can't send out sentries, and if he could they would be useless on a night like this. He must just trust to his eyes, and to his skill as a navigator. But, thank Heaven, we are out of the Red Sea and well on our way for India. Heigho! I'm sleepy, and, like you, want to turn in. Good-night! Let's hope the sea will have gone down by morning."

With a nod, they separated, and, still taking advantage of the rail, went along the slippery and deserted deck to their quarters. This was no easy matter, for every now and again their progress was impeded by the plunging of the vessel, which caused them to halt and cling frantically to their support till they saw a favourable opportunity to proceed.

"Good-night!" shouted the major, who reached the companion first, turning to wave his arm to his friend; but his words were caught by the wind and whisked into space. Then he dived below. The colonel never saw him again.

Colonel Hubbard and his friend Major Bellamy were on their way to India to rejoin their regiments, both having for the past two years been engaged in special work in South Africa. At another time the ship would have been full to overflowing with troops, going to the East to replace those who had completed their term of service there, but, owing to the fact that all Indian reliefs had practically been suspended during the South African war, there were only a few other officers on board.

The steamer had sailed from Liverpool ten days before, and had made a fine passage to the Suez Canal. But now a change had come over the weather, the glass had fallen with surprising swiftness, and a fierce gale had sprung up. Navigating his vessel with all possible care, the captain had at length the satisfaction of piloting her past the island of Perim, and had breathed more freely as he steered a course into the Gulf of Aden, *en route* for the Indian Ocean.

"We're safer here, at any rate," he remarked in tones of satisfaction to the first mate, as the two stood poring over a chart in the deck-house on the bridge. "We've our bearings, and can go straight ahead till dawn. But we shall have to be careful to take into account the set of the gale. I reckon that we are making a knot or more to leeward for every five we advance. So keep her helm well up, Farmer, and send to wake me if you have any doubts. If I were at all anxious, I'd keep at my post till morning; but now that we're in the open sea, there can be nothing to fear. A bright look-out, then, and good-night."

The captain gave vent to a loud yawn, and wearily left the chart-house; for he had resolutely kept at his station on the bridge ever since the ship entered the canal, and was now completely worn out. Groping his way, he descended to the spar deck, and disappeared into his cabin. Ten minutes later the gleam of light from his porthole was suddenly cut off, and the deck outside was plunged into darkness.

For three hours the fine ship plunged forward, ploughing deep into the waves and rolling heavily every minute. But no one suspected danger. Why should they indeed? What harm could come to such a powerful vessel in this open sea? Evidently the mate, as he kept watch upon the bridge, had no qualms, for he even hummed the refrain of a popular London air as he clung to the chart-house table, and pricked off the course run during the night. Danger! Why, not a soul expected such a thing, for if they had, would the passengers have been lying below in their bunks, vainly endeavouring to snatch a few moments' sleep? Certainly not. They would have been cowering in the open, a prey to terror, expecting every moment to bring some dire catastrophe.

"We're in the gulf, and safe," murmured the colonel, thrusting a pillow between his shoulders and the edge of his bunk, so that he might retain his position more easily. "We've a capable skipper and crew, and, so far as I can see, we have nothing to fear. So here's for a snooze till morning."

With that he turned on his side, and, covering his head with the clothes, settled himself for slumber.

Crash! The shock threw every sleeper from his bunk, and even brought the steersman to the deck. Crash! Suddenly arrested in her onward progress, the ship drew back for a moment, and then hurled herself with awful force against the obstruction. For the space of a few seconds she remained firmly fixed, and then, to the accompaniment of rending iron and timber, and the crash of the waves as they beat against her side, she slid into deep water once more, and wallowed there, as if undecided how to act. But there was no pausing with that sea raging all about her, and with such a gale forcing her onward. Heaving her stern high into the air, she rushed upon the unknown reef for the third time, seeming to leap at it eagerly in the vain hope of surmounting it. A moment later her keel fell upon the rock with a sickening bump, and breaking asunder in the bows, she disappeared in the raging sea.

It was a frightful calamity, and Colonel Hubbard, as he clung to a portion of the wreck, could scarcely believe that he was awake—could hardly realize that this was not some terrible dream, a nightmare for which the storm and its attendant discomforts was to blame.

"Wrecked?" he wondered, shaking his head to clear his eyes of water, and shifting his grasp so as to obtain a more secure position. "Am I awake, or is this only imagination? No; I am wet and shivering. It is all too real."

At this moment a monstrous wave bore down upon him, and clinging desperately to the tangled seaweed with which the rock was thickly covered, he braced himself to withstand the strain to which he was about to be subjected. Taking a long breath, he had just time to close his eyes when the mass of water was upon him. Clasping him in its cold embrace, it tore him from his hold as if he were weaker than a child, and then, bearing him onward, it hurled him against a piece of floating wreckage, and left him there, breathless, gasping for air, and almost unconscious. But the instinct of self-preservation soon asserted itself, and ere a minute had passed he was astride the floating woodwork, clinging to it with all his strength.

"If this is torn from me," he gasped, "I shall be washed away and drowned. But it shan't be, I'll see to that, for I don't mean to die yet. Things look black enough, but I won't give in."

Clenching his teeth, the gallant colonel clung to the wreckage gamely, and, though frequently submerged beneath the huge masses of green water which rolled and tossed about him, contrived to maintain his hold. Breathless, and shivering—for it was the winter season, and a piercingly cold wind blew through the gulf—he rode his strange steed through the remainder of the night, and just as the dawn was breaking, and the dark clouds in the east were beginning to light up with the rays of the rising sun, he espied a low bank of sand lying directly before him. Shading his eyes with his hands, he looked long and eagerly, and then gave vent to a shout of joy. Yes, though he had lost the best friend he ever had during the night, and had to mourn the death of every one of the crew and passengers of the ill-fated liner, yet so strong is the love of life to the average healthy individual, that Colonel Hubbard's spirits were raised to the highest by this piece of good fortune.

"Land, land!" he shouted excitedly, sitting up upon the baulk of timber to obtain a better view. "I reckon it is two hundred yards away, and getting closer every minute. I'm a bit done, or I'd make nothing of the swim. But I mustn't forget that the gulf has a reputation for its sharks; they are said to swarm everywhere, and to be only too ready to snap up everything that comes within their reach. Ugh, I won't give 'em a chance!"

Shivering at the thought, the colonel turned once more to the land, and watched it closely as the light of the dawning day disclosed its various features.

"A long rolling sandbank," he said thoughtfully, "with blue hills in the distance, and scarcely a patch of vegetation to be seen. Now, what shore can it be? The gale has been from the northeast, and therefore it must be the northern coast of Africa, and, I fear, a desolate, uninhabited region altogether. But I mustn't begin to grumble when Providence has watched over me so carefully. I must just make the best of matters, and be thankful that my life is saved."

Cheering himself with these thoughts, and with the reflection that, once ashore, the greater part of his troubles would be ended, the colonel began to paddle with his hands and kick out with his feet. By now, too, he had the satisfaction of finding that he was in smooth water, though a line of hissing surf in front of him, and the dull boom of breakers falling upon the sand told him clearly that he had still some danger to contend with. But what was it, after all, when compared with the storm he had outlived that night? He asked himself the question, and for answer prepared to leave the piece of wreckage which had proved his salvation, and strike out for the shore.

"I should be a fool to stick to it longer," he said. "Once in those breakers it would be twisted and turned in every direction, and if it did not stun me by a blow upon the head, it might very well roll over me and crush the life out of my body. So here goes!"

Slipping gently into the water, he struck out for the shore, firmly determined to do battle with the breakers. Almost before he thought it possible he reached the broad white line, and was engulfed in a moment. And now, indeed, his powers of endurance were put to the test, for whereas a green wave had frequently covered him for the space of a minute whilst in the open sea, now the seething water bubbled and frothed about his mouth and ears continually. Then, too, caught by the fierce wind which was blowing, a sheet of spray covered the tops of the breakers, making breathing almost an impossibility. But the colonel was no chicken, and now that he had come through so much danger, was determined to reach the shore alive. Undaunted, therefore, and with never a pause, he struggled manfully onward.

At length, worn out with his exertions, he reached shallow water, and though the receding waves did their utmost to drag him backwards, he contrived to escape their fatal embrace, and to reach a belt of dry and glistening sand upon which he threw himself at full length, for he was utterly exhausted. A quarter of an hour later he sprang to his feet, and, turning from the sea, set out for the interior.

"I shall starve if I stay here," he said, "for there's not a living soul in sight, and not a tree or green bush to be seen. I'm done, and I want food and drink badly. Perhaps I shall find both over that line of sandhills, and in any case by climbing to the top I shall have a better opportunity of looking about me to see how the land lies. Perhaps I shall see a village in the distance, or a shepherd's hut, and if so I'll go straight on and give myself into the hands of the inhabitants. It'll be risky, I know, but I must just chance it."

Trudging onward through the sand, which often rose above his ankles, he at length reached the summit of a low range of dunes which the wind, during centuries of ceaseless energy, had blown into position.

"Ah!" No wonder the colonel gave vent to an exclamation of astonishment, for when he reached the top he saw immediately before him a native camp. It was composed of numerous shelters of coarse linen or tattered camel-hide, which were dotted about the sand in regular order. Farther off were herds of sheep and goats and of camels, browsing upon the grass which here cropped out in every direction. There were also many horses, and natives were standing about, watching the animals as they fed. But what attracted his attention most and filled him with a feeling of dismay, was the sight of some thirty or forty armed men who sat on horseback in the midst of the camp. They were wild-looking natives, swarthy of feature, tall, and not ungainly, and clad from head to foot in flowing robes of white. Some were armed with guns, while a few carried long spears and shields, which they waved frantically above their heads. Then, at a shout from one of them who had suddenly caught sight of the colonel, they set their horses in motion, and came galloping at a headlong pace towards him. In a few moments he was surrounded, and very soon he was bound hand and foot, a prisoner of these fierce warriors of Somaliland.

Two hours later the camp was struck, and the natives began to march into the interior, driving their herds before them. The colonel's legs were freed, and he was ordered by signs to rise and follow his captors. To attempt to disobey was useless, and therefore, with downcast head and spirits at the lowest, he trudged onward beside the horsemen, a native with particularly brutal countenance riding close behind him. The colonel noted at a glance the long double-handed sword with which this ruffian was armed, and straightway he banished from his mind all thoughts of resistance or escape. For a week the caravan pushed onward, accomplishing, however, only short marches each day, for the pace was, of course, regulated by that of the herds which accompanied them. On the seventh day they reached their home, which consisted of a collection of mud hovels, and thereafter settled down to enjoy the loot which they had taken from the tribes inhabiting the coast. Colonel Hubbard was handed over to the wife of the Sheik, as the headman of the tribe was known, and at once became hewer of wood and drawer of water, a hateful and laborious employment for a man who had fought so well for his country, and who had commanded one of His Majesty's smart regiments.

Of the passengers and crew of the ill-fated ship which had come to grief in the Gulf of Aden not another soul escaped. The colonel, who was thus carried off into captivity, was the only survivor.

"Come in, my lad," said the head master of a large school situated in the Midlands, turning in his chair, as a knock sounded on his door. "Ah, come in and sit down there, Hubbard. I'm grieved, my boy, terribly grieved at this sad news. If only we knew for certain what had happened, it would make this trouble easier to bear; but the doubt, the hope that one dare not indulge in, is most trying. But you've come to see me. Have you any more news?"

As he spoke he sprang to his feet and crossed the floor to meet the youth, who was no other than the son of the officer whose fortune we have been following. Like his father, the lad was tall, and by no means devoid of good looks. His features, indeed, had a close resemblance to the colonel's. There was the same square chin, the same open, steady look, and a similar air of resolution.

"News, sir," responded James Hubbard, eagerly, declining the proffered chair in his excitement, "yes, I have; look at that!"

Thrusting his hand into his pocket, he produced a yellow envelope, and offered it to his master with trembling fingers.

"Good news, sir," he cried; "here is a telegram from my uncle which gives me more hope. After all, father may not have gone down with the ship. He may have been washed ashore. He may have had the good fortune to secure a life-belt, which would have kept him afloat. Why should this news not refer to him?"

Snatching the telegram from him with equal eagerness, the head master dragged the paper from the envelope and scanned the contents.

"More news to hand," ran the telegram. "A native arrived last week at Aden, having come from the Somali coast, and reports that, on the morning following the night upon which the station at Perim sighted a steamer passing east, a white man was cast upon the coast fifty miles east of Berbera. He was at once pounced upon by a marauding band of Somali warriors, despatched to the coast by the Mullah for the purpose of obtaining loot and prisoners. This is the only news, except that pieces of wreckage have been washed up close to Aden, while a homeward-bound steamer picked up a portion of a stern rail bearing the name of the ill-fated vessel."

"Hum, it is certainly news," said the head master, doubtfully. "This telegram proves beyond doubt that the ship upon which your father sailed met with a catastrophe. But, my dear lad, anxious as I am to give you hope, I feel bound to tell you that you must not jump to conclusions. This man who was cast upon the coast, and who fell into the hands of that fanatic known as the Mullah, may have been a stoker, a greaser, or an able seaman aboard the ship. I do not wish to discourage you, of course. God knows, if it were only possible, and certain news had been received that it was your father and no one else who reached the shore, I would rejoice with you, and do my utmost to aid you in obtaining further information. But it is hopeless. Whoever it was who lived through that night and safely reached the African shore, would have been far happier, far more fortunate, had he perished like the rest."

The head master paused for a few moments, and stood looking at the young fellow before him. There was no doubt that he was full of sympathy for his loss, and anxious to help him. But what could he do? To advise the lad to hope on would have been cruel in the circumstances. Better, far better, to put the facts plainly before him, even though in doing so he should cause him bitter grief. Yes, that was the best course to pursue, for to hold out the hope that his father still lived, simply upon the strength of this news just received, would have been madness—indeed, the greatest unkindness possible. Why, the man who fell into the hands of the Mullah was more surely dead than all those others who had sunk to the depths of the ocean.

"Don't think, my lad, that I am lacking in sympathy," he went on, taking a pace forward, and placing his hand encouragingly on Jim's shoulder. "I wish to help you to bear this trouble, and I feel that, when I tell you to extinguish all hope, I am giving you the best and the most considerate advice. There, tell me that you will take it in this way. Try to absorb yourself in work, and so forget your loss. Do not let this hideous uncertainty prey upon your mind, but banish it, for that is far the best course to pursue."

He pressed his hand more firmly upon Jim's shoulder, and looked earnestly into his face, as if to help him in coming to a decision. But the young fellow scarcely seemed to be aware of his presence. His eyes were fixed upon some distant object visible through the window, and his thoughts were evidently still farther away. His head was bowed upon his breast, and he looked for the moment as though this trouble, which had come upon him at such an early age, was crushing him. But suddenly his eye brightened, and a more cheerful expression overspread his face. He straightened himself, and, raising his head, looked steadily at his master.

"Thank you, sir," he said. "I know how kind you are, and that in speaking to me in this way, and in giving me the benefit of your experience and of your advice, you have acted with the sole purpose of assisting me. But I cannot believe that my father is dead; I cannot, indeed. Something tells me that he has survived the wreck, and that this white man referred to in the telegram is none other than he. Until I prove this or the contrary, I can never rest, and never settle to my work.

12

I am thankful now that my mother is not alive to feel this grief. I am an only child, and my father is my best and kindest friend. I cannot, and will not, forsake him. I don't know now how I shall act, but I feel that if the necessity arises, as, indeed, it must, I will willingly make my way into the heart of Somaliland, into the midst of the Mullah's bands, and there clear up this doubt. If I find that it was not he who was washed ashore and captured by the natives, then I shall be far easier in my mind, and besides, sir, I might have the good fortune at the same time to bring help to this poor captive. If he were only a stoker, it would be sufficient reward to have rescued him from such an horrible fate."

"But your examination, my lad. Will you permit yourself to miss it altogether?" exclaimed the head master. "Think what it means to you. You have now been reading hard for a year, and in two months, if only you are successful, as I fully believe you will be, you will have won a commission in the Army, and will be on the high-road to success, to follow in the footsteps of your worthy father."

"I will give it up, sir," replied Jim, emphatically. "Everything must be put aside for the sake of my father. I would rather lose this commission, and spend the remainder of my days upon an office-stool, than leave this doubt unsettled. It haunts me, and though I know how hopeless the matter is, I will go through with it till I am sure of my father's fate. But, in spite of everything, I feel that he still lives, and, perhaps, is even now wondering whether his son will take up his cause and set out for the purpose of rescuing him. There, sir, forgive me for saying that my mind is firmly made up, and that I must act contrary to your advice. In any other matter I would, as you know, have instantly fallen in with your wishes. But here it is different, for my father's life may be at stake, and both his happiness and mine depend upon my exertions. Therefore, I ask you to let me leave at once and go to my uncle. I will talk the matter over with him, and I feel sure that he will help me in every way."

Involuntarily Jim's hand left the pocket in which it had been reposing, and went out to meet his master's. And there together they stood for the space of a minute exchanging a firm and cordial clasp.

"You are a credit to me!" exclaimed the head master, enthusiastically. "A credit, I say, and your comrades here will be even prouder of you than I am. I have put the position plainly before you. And, without wishing to discourage you, have endeavoured to point out how hopeless it is. You must know as well as I do what dangers and difficulties will have to be faced in this undertaking, for your father and the many books you have read will have given you some idea of life in Africa. Knowing all this, and with a full knowledge that if you persevere in your search you must undergo privation and exposure, and may even lose your life, you tell me that you will sail for that country; that you have firmly made up your mind to go through with it all for the sake of your father? Then leave us, my lad, and may Heaven help you, for you are a brave young fellow, and deserve the utmost success. There, go to your room and pack your boxes. A cab will be at the door in half an hour; that will enable you to catch the next train for London. There, leave me now. I wish to think over the matter quietly before I say farewell."

Once more the two shook hands in silence, and then, turning about, Jim went hurriedly from the room, and hastened to prepare for his journey. An hour later he was in the train, and that evening had arrived at his destination, leaving his friends at the school to mourn the loss of as fine and good-hearted a young fellow as had ever entered its portals.

CHAPTER II

OFF TO ADEN

Jim Hubbard was a young gentleman of decidedly prepossessing appearance. Broad of shoulder, and particularly well set up for a lad of a little more than seventeen summers, he looked for all that far too young to have such troubles thrown upon his shoulders, to be called thus early in his life to face a difficulty which might well prove too great for a man of mature years and experience. But just as the colonel was endowed with the pluck and perseverance which had enabled him to live through that wild night in the Gulf of Aden, so also was his son gifted with a spirit and tenacity that helped him now to make up his mind to face any danger and difficulty in accomplishing the task he had set himself.

"It is clearly my duty," he said, as he trudged along from the London terminus of the railway to his uncle's residence in Kensington, "to see this matter through to the end. I have spent hours and hours in thinking about it, and have always come to the same conclusion. Until this doubt is absolutely settled, I can never rest, and never be sure that my father is not living. I will show him and all those who are interested in him that I am no fair-weather friend, and that I am prepared to stick to him and to his cause until further search is useless. I cannot imagine anyone placed in similar circumstances coming to any other determination, and if I were to hesitate now and allow imaginary dangers to frighten me, I should be a coward at heart, and unfit to bear my father's name. I'll put the facts before Uncle George, and I'm sure he will do his utmost to help me. Ah, there is his house opposite."

Crossing the street, James mounted the steps of a handsome dwelling, and pulled the bell vigorously. A moment later the door was thrown open by a footman, who had scarcely taken possession of his bag and ushered him into the hall before a short, stout old gentleman, with grey whiskers and hair and a florid countenance, bustled forward to greet him. Mr. George Hubbard was, in fact, some ten years the colonel's senior, and was of decidedly comfortable appearance. Indeed, whereas his younger brother had led an active life, going hither and thither to all parts of the world, wherever the duties of a soldier called him, George could scarcely boast that he had ever left the shores of old England.

"I'm a regular stay-at-home, and never feel better, nor more contented, than when I am engaged in my business in London," he had often said, with no small amount of satisfaction and pride. "I confess that a soldier's life never had any attraction for me, though, like all civilians, I can and do admire the man who goes out to face death at the call of his country."

As he advanced towards Jim with outstretched hand, his fat, good-humoured face showed the concern he felt for his young nephew.

"My dear, dear boy, welcome!" he exclaimed. "I don't know what to say to you, or how to help you in this distressing affair. Both your aunt and I have done nothing but talk the matter over, and have, indeed, spent sleepless nights in endeavouring to come to some conclusion, but without success. It is the most cruel, the most unhappy misfortune that I have ever experienced. But come upstairs. Your aunt would never forgive me if I kept her waiting."

Wiping the moisture from his forehead, and coughing as though the effort of speaking had been almost too much for him, George Hubbard turned and led the way upstairs. Jim followed him closely, and a minute later was in his aunt's presence. Then sitting down, the three discussed the matter fully, Jim telling his relatives to what decision he had come.

"You know the facts as well as I do, uncle," he said, "and I am going to ask you to do all you can to help me, and not to try and thwart me. I know how hopeless my mission must seem to you, and that many would think I was undertaking a wild-goose chase. But, as I told the head master at school, I feel sure that the man cast up upon the African coast was my father, and if that is the case, he surely needs my help. I have been thinking the matter over as I came up in the train, and bought a map specially to help me. By it I see that my best course will be to take a steamer direct to Aden, and from there I shall be able to get a trader to Berbera. Meanwhile, I shall telegraph to the News Agency which supplied the information sent me this morning, and will endeavour to arrange that the man who saw this survivor of the wreck land upon the coast, and afterwards fall into the hands of the Mullah's Somali warriors, shall be in waiting to receive me. Then, with him as guide, I shall make my way to the actual point where the incident happened, and from there we shall turn our faces inland. It may happen that I shall be able to join some shooting expedition, for one reads occasionally in the papers that English gentlemen take caravans into that part of Africa for the purpose of big game shooting. If not, I shall endeavour to hire a few followers, and take up the search alone. I know it sounds a big thing to attempt, uncle; but wouldn't you do the same in a similar case?"

George Hubbard gasped. He was a man of peace, and though well read and thoroughly sensible, he had, nevertheless, an exaggerated idea of the wildness and dangers to be met with in Africa. Nor could he be blamed for that, for weeks past the papers had been filled with accounts of Somaliland, and of the doings of the Mullah. And now to sit there in a comfortable armchair before his open hearth, and hear his young nephew calmly propose to sail for Africa, and make his way into the very heart of the Somali country, was quite enough to make a man of his disposition do more than gasp. He sat forward in his chair staring at Jim with a horrified expression on his face, and with eyes which threatened to fall out of his head.

"Go to Africa! March into the interior, and probably meet the Mullah face to face!" he exclaimed, mopping his forehead with his handkerchief. "Good gracious, you will be killed, you will lose your life to a certainty!"

"I may, uncle," responded Jim, calmly. "On the other hand, there is a possibility of my succeeding, for many men have made their way into Somaliland and returned to tell the tale. Think of the joy it would be to rescue father."

"But it is madness, Jim! Because one single white man out of some two or three hundred who left England on that unlucky ship contrived to reach the shore alive, you fly to the conclusion that it must have been my poor brother. It is utter folly to argue in this way, though I cannot help but admire the brave thought which prompts you. Still, I am a matter-of-fact man, and I say, without hesitation, that the dangers are too great, and the end too uncertain, to justify your taking the risks. However, no efforts and no money shall be spared to obtain further information, and should it turn out, as I trust and hope it may, that this survivor is indeed my brother, then you shall go. Indeed, so deeply do I feel his loss, that I am tempted to say that I, too, would join you in the search. But that would be foolish, considering what I am, and how utterly unfitted for such exertions."

He rose from his seat, and turning, stood facing Jim, with a comical look of despair upon his features. For some minutes there was silence, and then, just as he was about to begin a long and telling argument, with the object of dissuading Jim from an attempt which, to his uncle, appeared worse than madness, a knock sounded on the door, and a footman entered.

"A telegram, sir," he said.

With an agile spring, which was wonderful considering his unwieldy proportions, George Hubbard left his position by the fire, and darted across the room. Taking the telegram from the footman, he tore it open, and then began to read it aloud, while Jim and his aunt jumped to their feet and looked over his shoulder.

"From the News Agency!" he cried excitedly. "I gave them instructions to spare no expense in obtaining information, and here is the result."

"Read it!" exclaimed Jim and his aunt, impatiently. "What does it say?"

"Listen!" answered Mr. Hubbard, holding the paper so that the light should fall upon it. "'In accordance with your instructions, we have questioned native who gave information. He states that surviving white man was tall, with dark hair, getting grey at temples, grey moustache, and muscular body. Not quite certain, owing to distance, but thinks he caught a glimpse of a bangle about his wrist. If not that, it was a piece of cloth tied there, perhaps to cover a wound.'"

"That is father!" shouted Jim, unable to restrain his excitement. "I am certain it is he, for the description tallies exactly with his appearance, and, moreover, he was in the habit of wearing a watch bracelet upon his wrist."

"Tall, dark hair getting grey, and grey moustache," repeated Mr. Hubbard, as if to assure himself that he had read the telegram aright. "There can be no doubt that this is my brother. I quite agree with you, Jim, for, though it is possible, and even very probable, that many men aboard the ship would have answered to that description, the fact that the survivor wore a dark bracelet upon his wrist is, in my opinion, an absolute confirmation. I am glad, my boy—more than glad. Indeed, I cannot tell you how much this good news rejoices my heart."

Turning to his nephew, he grasped his hand and shook it till the lad's fingers ached, patting him meanwhile upon the shoulder with his other hand.

"Yes, delighted; pleased beyond measure," he continued earnestly. "Now you may rely upon the fact that your uncle is wholly on your side."

As for Mrs. Hubbard, she had a tender heart, and gently pushing her husband aside, threw herself into Jim's arms with tears of joy in her eyes.

"You deserve the good news, my dear boy," she said, kissing him affectionately. "It went to my heart to see your silent grief, and how bravely you had determined to clear up this uncertainty. It was horrible to feel that your father might be dead, and still more trying to hear that there was just a possibility that he was still alive, a captive in the hands of this man they call the Mullah. The uncertainty was more than I could bear, and I feel sure that, had I been a man, I should have followed the same course, and gone to Africa, so as to set the matter for ever at rest."

"And now let us discuss the question," interposed Mr. Hubbard, pacing restlessly up and down the room. "There must be no delay in setting out to rescue my brother, and as we in England can do little, seeing that we are so far from Somaliland, I advise that you at once take ship for Aden. It happens that my firm have business relations with a man living there. He exports camels to that part of Africa ruled over by the Italians, and gathers in his warehouses every description of merchandise which comes from the interior of the country. If anyone can help you he is the man. Now, let me see, a ship will leave the London Docks for the Mediterranean and Egypt to-morrow evening; we will telephone at once to obtain a berth for you. That done, we will set about getting you a kit, for it is absolutely necessary that you should go well provided, and in that respect the utmost attention must be paid to weapons. That reminds me, a gentleman of my acquaintance who has visited Africa for purposes of sport happens to live close at hand. We will go in and see him at once, for it is more than likely that he will be able to give us valuable advice."

It was wonderful to see the energy displayed by Mr. Hubbard. Now that there was no doubt that it was his brother who had survived the wreck, he was like a schoolboy in his eagerness to set about his rescue, and took the matter up in a manner which showed that he was determined to do as much for the cause in his own way as was his nephew. Hastening from the room, he and Jim quickly donned their coats and hats, and hurried to the nearest telephone station. As it was late in the evening, the instrument was disengaged, and within five minutes a passage was booked upon a steamer that was to leave England the following evening. Jim and his uncle now hailed a cab, and were quickly transported to the residence of the gentleman of whom the latter had spoken.

"Glad to be of service, I'm sure," he said, when Mr. Hubbard had explained the reason of his coming. "Indeed, had it been possible, I should willingly have undertaken to accompany your nephew, in which case my experience of life in Northern Africa would have been of some help to him. Aden is certainly his first point of call, and as you already have an agent there, the difficulty of obtaining a passage over to Berbera, and of getting together the necessary followers and camels for transport purposes, will be easily overcome. I strongly advise him to engage a 'shikari,' or head hunting-man, to accompany him and take charge of the natives; and if he applies at the British Consul's at Berbera, it is possible that he will be able to obtain the services of a man called Ali Kumar, a civilized Somali warrior, who accompanied me on an expedition two years ago, and who proved invaluable. Now as to kit. A couple of suits of rough cloth, with leather gaiters and good marching boots, will be the best. A felt hat would be worse than useless as a head-covering out there, for in the hot season the sun pours down with a fierceness that cannot be imagined, and can only be fully understood when actually experienced. Three or four water-tanks, so constructed as to be capable of being easily slung upon camels, should be procured, for this gentleman known as the 'Mad' Mullah has his happy hunting-grounds some two hundred miles inland, and to reach him it is necessary first to cross a range of hills, and then to face the Hoad, or waterless desert, which stretches for quite a hundred and fifty miles without a break. That is always a most trying ordeal, but you will have to face it, for, until the Hoad is passed, there will be no prospect of obtaining more than the most meagre news of your father."

"That will, indeed, be a terrible difficulty," interposed Mr. Hubbard. "One often hears of whole caravans lost in the attempt to cross these waterless tracts, and I suppose, in the case of this one which you call the Hoad, such a fatality is not unknown."

"I will not say that accidents have not happened," was the answer, in reassuring tones; "but so well is this desert known, and so accustomed are the natives to crossing it, that they think lightly of its dangers. But your raising the question reminds me to speak of animals. A good supply of transport camels will be required, and, in addition, a dozen or more of the trotting variety will be absolutely necessary. Then, supposing our young friend happens to obtain some piece of important news, he will be able to leave his caravan, and make a dash to any given point. Horses, too, he must have, and he will find no difficulty in getting as many as he requires. A small case of drugs is another item that should prove of use, and I strongly advise him to take some rolls of strong barbed wire. The additional weight that will have to be carried will be fully compensated for by the feeling of security that the wire will give."

"But how? I do not follow your point," said Mr. Hubbard dubiously. "I do not see how this wire will help my nephew."

"Then I will explain. He will march in the early morning, and if the sun is not too hot, will continue to do so for the greater part of the day. Sometimes he will cover only a few miles, and will then halt, for his powers of getting about the country will depend greatly upon the condition of his transport animals. Again, he will occasionally have to make forced marches, for the water-holes are often separated by long distances, which it is absolutely necessary to cover.

"But to come to the barbed wire. When he halts at night, he will form a zareba, sending out his followers to cut thorn-bushes with which to build a hedge. A few posts driven into the ground at intervals along the outside of the zareba, with wire stretched between them, will effectually stop a rush of the enemy, and will give timely warning in case of attack. In South Africa miles and miles were used between the blockhouses, and proved of great service."

"I see your point," exclaimed Jim, who had followed his words closely, "and I should imagine that if the posts and wires were hidden amongst the thorns, the surprise and alarm of the enemy would be even greater. Numbers might easily become entangled, and then we should be able to teach them a lesson with our rifles."

"Quite so. I fully agree with you," was the answer. "And, speaking of weapons, reminds me that I have not yet dealt with that subject."

For a few moments the speaker buried his face in his hands, and sat there thoughtfully.

"There is no doubt," he suddenly continued, "that this is a most important matter. I take it that you are not bent upon big game shooting, and that if you come upon lions or elephants you will leave them severely alone. For your purpose the Lee-Enfield rifle will be the best, and should it turn out, as it very well may, that you are attacked by the beasts I have mentioned, then you must trust to slay them by means of a volley, for it is hopeless to expect that a single one of these small-calibre bullets will prove fatal. If it were to strike a vital spot it certainly would, but that is a piece of luck which you must not count upon, for, remember, you cannot afford to take unnecessary risks. So you should equip your party with the rifles I have mentioned, and, in addition, a hunting knife and a brace of good revolvers would be useful possessions for yourself. A pair of field-glasses and a tin water-bottle should complete your equipment. I need hardly mention the advisability of carrying an abundant supply of ammunition.

"And now, my lad, it only remains for me to wish you the best of luck. I admire your pluck immensely, but I shall give you a few last words of advice. Be always cautious, never omit to post sentries at night and visit them yourself, and, above all, be ever on the look-out for treachery. The Somali natives have the reputation of being cunning rogues. Plunder seems to be their sole object in life, and camels have a peculiar attraction for them. They would think nothing of killing you, if by doing so they could obtain possession of your transport animals."

Thanking him heartily for his kindness, and exchanging a cordial shake of the hand, Jim and his uncle left their friend, and returned home at once.

"We shall have to be busy to-morrow," said Mr. Hubbard, as they took their seats once more in front of the fire. "In the first place, we must get your clothing and revolvers, with a few strong trunks in which to carry them. The rifles and any other items we may happen to think of can be purchased during the week, and I shall see that they follow you out to Aden. You will want to have means of drawing money, and for that purpose I shall write full instructions to our agent. His name, by the way, is Andrews, and you will find him an extremely obliging gentleman. I shall tell him to supply you with anything you may ask for, and I may say now that, though I do not desire that you should be extravagant, no expense that may help to the recovery of my dear brother shall be spared. And now to bed, my dear Jim, for to-morrow you have much to do."

Early on the following morning Mr. Hubbard's house in Kensington was astir. There was an air of subdued excitement about the servants, who in some mysterious way had contrived to hear full details of all that was occurring. Mrs.

Hubbard took her place at the breakfast-table, assuming as cheerful a look as she could, though her heart was full of misgivings for the safety of her nephew. But she was wise enough to know that he needed encouragement and help, and therefore determined that he should not guess what her thoughts were. As for Jim, he appeared with smiling countenance, for now that he felt sure that his father had really escaped the wreck, he was quite light-hearted, and though fully aware of the difficulties and dangers before him, was prepared to face them without hesitation.

"I know it's going to be a job," he had said to himself, as he lay awake during the night, "and I must be prepared to spend months, and even a year, in accomplishing it. But it has to be done, and if only I make up my mind from the beginning that nothing shall beat me, then my chances of success will be good."

Breakfast over, he said good-bye to his aunt, and then, entering a cab with his uncle, drove off to a firm in the city, from whom he was able to obtain a complete outfit of clothing. Trunks were bought at the same place, and directions given to have them packed at once.

"We'll call for them in an hour," said Mr. Hubbard, "and I shall be obliged if you will arrange to have everything ready for us, so that there shall be no delay."

Entering their cab again, they drove to a gunsmith's, where a couple of big Webley revolvers were purchased, together with a strong hunting knife contained in a sheath, which was so arranged as to be slung in a belt. A small case of drugs in tabloid form was obtained at another establishment, and then, armed with their purchases, James and his uncle returned for the clothing.

Within five minutes the luggage was on the cab, and they were on their way to Fenchurch-street Station. An hour later James was safely installed in his cabin, and shortly afterwards took leave of his uncle.

"You may rely upon my sending the other things promptly," said Mr. Hubbard, as he moved towards the gang-way. "They should reach you within a week of your arrival in Aden, and so that there shall be no difficulty about importing the arms, or about transhipping them to Africa, you had better go to the Governor at Aden, and tell him all the facts. I will visit the Foreign Office in London, and I am sure that every effort will be made to help you. Good-bye, and may you be successful."

That afternoon the steamer put out into the river, and by night was well at sea. Running down Channel, she made a good passage to Ushant, and was soon in the Bay of Biscay, which, to the delight of all the passengers, was comparatively smooth.

Jim was enchanted with this new experience, and before very long began to feel quite at home. Indeed, so quickly are friendships made upon an ocean-going steamer, that within a day or two he felt as though he had known all the passengers for quite a lengthy period.

After coasting along the Portuguese shore, the ship steered to the east, and entered the Mediterranean. Gibraltar was sighted, and signals exchanged, so as to let the folks at home know that a safe passage had thus far been made.

A week later they were in the canal, and in due time reached Aden. Here Jim's baggage was put ashore, and he himself followed, feeling somewhat forlorn amongst so many strangers.

"Mr. Hubbard, I think?" said a cheery voice at his elbow, causing him to turn round with a start, to find that a short, bearded man, with a pleasant face, was addressing him. He was clad in white from head to foot, and wore an enormous "topee," or pith helmet, upon his head. "I am making no mistake, I think?" he continued. "I am Mr. Andrews."

In a moment they were shaking hands, and then Jim's new friend called loudly to some Indian porters, and gave them instructions concerning the baggage.

"Everything here is done by natives from India," he said, noticing a look of inquiry on Jim's face. "In fact, Aden is, officially, part of our Eastern possessions, and boasts of no other coin than the rupee. But I will tell you all about that later. We'll drive to my place now. Hi! gharri!"

At his shout an open carriage, drawn by two "tats," as the small native ponies are known, dashed up to them, and when they were seated drove off along the main street of Aden at a pace which in London would have been considered furious. Leaving the town, they took another road which led to the right, into a part occupied by many bungalows, and at one of these they finally alighted.

"Aden itself is a horrible place," said Mr. Andrews, apologetically, waving his hand towards the town. "It is, as you see, little more than a wide volcanic plain, with nothing in the way of vegetation to relieve its barrenness. Out here, however, we have contrived to arrange a little oasis, in which we Europeans live. But come in, Mr. Hubbard, and I'll show you the room you are to occupy while staying with me. Then we'll have tiffin (luncheon), and afterwards we'll sit on the verandah and talk this matter over. I believe I've excellent news for you, which you shall hear in good time."

"About father? Does it concern him?" asked Jim, eagerly, pricking up his ears at the mention of news, for he had been without any for more than a week. "Perhaps he has been rescued? But that is expecting too much."

"No, it's not that," was the answer, in reassuring tones; "but it's remarkably good news, I can tell you, for I have ascertained that a certain gentleman is bound upon a similar expedition, or rather, is about to go into the Mullah's country for the purpose of obtaining intelligence of his movements. Hearing that you also contemplated penetrating into the interior, he asks leave to accompany you, and I have no doubt you will be delighted to take him."

"I shall, indeed," answered Jim, eagerly. "I was quite prepared to undertake the journey alone, but a companion will make all the difference, and I willingly agree to his joining my expedition."

"Then, that's settled; and now for tiffin."

Leading the way through a wide compound, laid out like an English garden, Mr. Andrews mounted the steps of a shady verandah, and entering a doorway in front of which hung a curtain of reeds, ushered his companion into a delightfully cool inner room, in which, on a table placed in the centre, was spread a snowy white cloth, littered with sparkling glass and silver. Silent-footed natives salaamed and prepared to wait upon them, and at once the two sat down and began their meal.

CHAPTER III

THE GUN-RUNNERS

"Now come out to the verandah," said Mr. Andrews, taking James by the arm as soon as tiffin was finished. "I have a couple of comfortable chairs there, in which we can lounge, for just now is the hottest part of the day, and no European ventures abroad unless compelled to by unforeseen circumstances."

Leaving the airy dining-room, the two stepped on to a broad paved verandah, which entirely surrounded the bungalow, and took their seats in a shady nook.

Above their heads was a thickly thatched roof, the eaves of which projected so far beyond the supporting posts as to make a broad stretch of shadow beneath. But as they lay in their chairs, Jim and his new friend could easily see beneath it. For the moment they sat there in silence. Indeed, Jim was lost in admiration, for Mr. Andrews had created for himself a perfect English garden. Glancing between the pillars, about which clung roses, jasmine, and honeysuckle, and many another creeper, he looked out upon beds of brilliant flowers, laid out in orderly array, and flashing gorgeously in the rays of the Eastern sun.

"I've only to forget the bungalow, and imagine myself in old England again," said Mr. Andrews. "That garden is just one of the luxuries I allow myself, and which helps to make life more pleasant here. Some day I hope to end my exile and return home, for, however fascinating bright and continuous sunshine may be, to return to one's native country is always a pleasure to which we who live out here look forward. But here is someone coming through the gate. Ah, I see, it's the gentleman of whom I was speaking."

He sprang from his seat and went toward the steps to greet his visitor. As for Jim, he watched with some interest to see what kind of man this stranger should prove to be.

"I hope I shall like him," he said to himself, "for it would be disastrous to our expedition if we were to fall foul of each other. But here he is, and—yes, he looks a good fellow, and I am sure we shall be excellent friends."

As this passed through his mind the visitor mounted the steps, and Jim obtained a clear view of his features. He was tall and thin, with fair hair and clean-shaven face, and, as far as one could guess, was about twenty-five years of age.

"Ah, how do, Andrews?" he exclaimed cheerily, springing with one bound on to the verandah. "Glad to see you, my dear fellow. I heard that the ship had arrived, and so came along to have a chat, and to meet the Mr. Hubbard of whom you were speaking."

"There he is, then," cried Mr. Andrews, turning to Jim; "and he, too, is anxious to make your acquaintance."

A moment later the two were shaking hands, each greeting the other with a steady look, which seemed to say, "I want to know what sort of a chap you are, and how we are likely to get along together."

"Glad to meet you, and I hope we shall be good friends. My name is Dixon— Tom Dixon; Tom for short."

"And mine is James—James Hubbard, you know," said our hero, with a friendly smile. "Mr. Andrews tells me that you, too, are bound for Somaliland, and have suggested accompanying me. I need not say that I shall be delighted, for it would be dreary work to go alone. But I would do it if necessary, for my father's life depends upon my going."

"Quite so, and that is just where we shall agree," was the ready answer; "for you must understand that I am a secret agent, an Intelligence officer, as we are often called, and——But one minute. Are we alone, Andrews? For my news is of great importance, and if your native servants were to obtain an inkling of it, the tidings would fly at once, and reach the ears of the Mullah in an incredibly short space of time. It is a fact," he continued, noticing the look of surprise with which Jim greeted his remark. "Our dusky friend has a perfect system of espionage, which would shame that of many a European country. Tales of a coming expedition told across the dinner-table in these bungalows are whispered in the native bazaars before a day has gone, and I speak only the truth when I say that the first ship for Berbera or the Somali coast, whether it be a steamer, a native dhow, or a rascally gun-runner, bears a man whose duty it is to pass on his information to the Mullah. Why, he knows well that the British Government is now buying camels here and training and equipping a native levy at Berbera. Our camp there is full of spies, and I do not exaggerate when I tell you that the movements of our troops are known by the Mullah almost before they are by our officers. So, take my advice, and go about with your lips closed and your eyes very wide open."

Tom Dixon spoke in the most earnest manner, and lifted his finger, as if thereby to impress Jim with his warning. And, indeed, he was making no erroneous statement, and telling only the truth when he described the extraordinary manner in which news is conveyed into the heart of Somaliland.

"Make your mind easy, Tom," said Mr. Andrews, reassuringly, stepping across the verandah to look into the dining-room. "The servants are all on the other side of the bungalow, and out of earshot, so that you may speak here without fear of the consequences, and chat this matter over to your heart's content. But your warning is a timely one, and, indeed, has only forestalled by a few minutes the advice I was about to give our young friend. Ever since this matter cropped up, I have kept it a dead secret between myself and the British Governor, you, of course, being also included. I have gone so far as to set aside a certain number of camels of the trotting and of the transport variety, and have also engaged some fifty followers. They were despatched from here a month ago for the service of the Government. But this is a more urgent matter, and, with the Governor's permission, I have arranged that you shall have them. When you arrive at Berbera, you will find them all encamped outside the town. Ali Kumar, a shikari of noted reputation, and a trustworthy fellow, will be there to head the followers and guide you through the country, while some twenty miles along the coast is a village in which lives the man who gave information about the survivor of the wreck. I have purposely refrained from engaging him in any capacity, but my agent at Berbera has seen him, and has informed him that a relative of the survivor will come to speak with him. That means reward, or 'backsheesh,' as these Somali fellows know it, and you may be sure that he will not fail you."

"Splendid!" exclaimed Jim. "Then, thanks to your kindness and forethought, there will be little or no delay, and, so far as I can see, the weapons and ammunition which are coming from England are the only things that can keep us waiting, and my uncle promised that they should be here within a few days of my arrival. What luck, too, to have got hold of Ali Kumar, for he is the very man I was told to engage."

"I know him well, and can tell you that he is a capital fellow," answered Mr. Andrews. "But to continue my story. All these preparations have been made in the quietest and most secret manner possible. Once you and Tom arrive at Berbera, you have only to ride out to this camp. Then, when night falls, you can slip away and march along the coast. There is a headland, forty miles east of Berbera, where you had better camp for a few days, keeping a bright look-out for a certain native dhow, which will bring you your rifles, ammunition, and stores. By acting in this way, you will be able to leave the coast for the interior without anyone being aware of your intentions—at least, I hope you may. Tom and I have talked the matter over, for he is as anxious as you to get away without the news reaching the Mullah's ears."

"Just so," interposed Tom. "You see, Hubbard, your search will carry you into the very heart of the Mullah's country, and as I am anxious to obtain full information of his doings, I, too, am bound in that direction. If he had the slightest notion of our intentions, you may be sure that he would do his utmost to murder the whole lot of us, and so it is of great importance to keep him in ignorance. This is your expedition, but I propose that we share expenses, and the command also, if you like. You see, I have spent many years on the coast, and speak the language like a native—a useful accomplishment for the job we have in hand. But I'm not a bit of a soldier, and when it comes to fighting I shall have to look to you to pull us through. Nominally, you will be in charge of the expedition, but I think that by putting our heads together we shall get along with greater success."

"I quite agree with you," responded Jim, thoughtfully; "the fact that you speak the language will be of the greatest service, and as this expedition is to suit your purpose as well as mine, I feel sure that we shall not fall out when difficulties arise. But there is one thing I wish to say. I must not have my movements hampered in any way, for it may turn out that news of my father will reach us as soon as we get into the interior. Perhaps, even, we may have the good fortune to rescue him at once, and in that case, my mission being ended, I should return to the coast immediately."

"And I should not attempt to dissuade you," said Tom Dixon, with a smile. "If by that time I had not obtained information of the utmost value, it would be my own fault entirely; and besides, supposing you were to rescue your father, I think there is but little doubt that we should find it necessary to retire at once—

in fact, to make a bolt for our lives, for the Mullah has a reputation for fierceness, and would not easily forgive our boldness.

"But I have something else to tell you, which may cause you to prick up your ears. It has come to my knowledge that a rascal here is about to ship a load of guns across to Somaliland. Would you care to join me in an attempt to capture him? It would be a risky business, I tell you candidly, but if we are successful, it would be a glorious adventure. You need not be afraid that it will delay us, for my plan is to ship aboard as a hand, and wait until close to the African coast. Then matters must depend upon circumstances. I shall endeavour to give warning to one of the British gunboats stationed in these waters, and in that case should allow myself to be taken prisoner without saying a word. But it is just possible that I may be unable to ascertain the exact destination for which we are bound, and in that case should have to take my chance of capturing the dhow single-handed, or of looking on quietly while the guns were handed over to the Mullah's emissaries. If you were with me, we could make a grand fight of it, for these dhows seldom have more than four men aboard. Sometimes, of course, they carry a bigger crew, and if it were to turn out like that, we should have to alter our plans."

"But how am I to be smuggled aboard?" asked Jim, eagerly, delighted at the thought of such an adventure. "I don't speak the language, and should certainly be spotted the very moment I set foot upon the vessel."

"I don't think so," responded Tom Dixon, emphatically. "The natives in these parts do all sorts of curious things, and it has just struck me that, by pretending that you have made a vow, you can get over this difficulty. We'll give it out that we come from some Somali tribe which is friendly to the Mullah, and that we are willing to lend a hand in loading and unloading the dhow in return for our passage. I shall say that you have sworn never to speak until you have made a pilgrimage to Mecca. That is no uncommon vow, and amongst these fanatical people will raise you to their highest estimation."

"It sounds a likely story," cried Jim, "and I'll come with you. When do you propose to start? And when are we likely to arrive on the Somali coast?"

"That I cannot say, but I believe the dhow will sail within a couple of days, and two more should take us across the water. Then much depends upon how matters turn out."

"It's a risky business," said Mr. Andrews, who had listened attentively all the while. "But I won't try to dissuade you, Hubbard, for the danger is no greater than you will encounter in Somaliland, and I think the experience you will get will help you in your search. It may turn out that by going upon this dhow you will come across a native who knows of your father. In that case the risk will not have been taken for nothing, for you can rely upon it that Tom will worm his secrets out. Our friend is a thorough native, and I only tell you the bare truth when I say that his get-up and behaviour are marvellous. You see, his father was stationed here for many years, and Tom has made the most of his opportunities."

"That is so," said Tom. "I used to be awfully fond of dressing up as a native and going down to the bazaar. Once or twice my disguise was discovered, and if I hadn't taken to my heels, I should have come in for some rough handling. But that is a very old tale, and I have played the trick so often now that, when in native costume, I feel and act the part with assurance. Indeed, I often forget that I am an Englishman, so absorbed do I become, and many and many a time have I come from the bazaars primed with a piece of information that has proved of service to our Governor. And it is on that account that I have been employed as an Intelligence officer. But you'll come, then, Hubbard? That is splendid, for, with you to help me, I shall hope to bag these fellows. I propose that you remain here till this evening, and then, when the servants have retired after dinner, walk down the garden to the gate. I'll be there to meet you, and together we'll go to my place. Mr. Andrews will look after your things here, and will send them over in the ship he spoke of."

Tom Dixon now rose, and, after chatting for a few moments with his friends, departed. For more than an hour Jim and Mr. Andrews sat on the verandah, talking in low tones, for there were many points to be arranged. Then Jim went to his room, and wrote a long letter to his uncle, telling him all that was about to occur, and describing the preparations which Mr. Andrews had made for his expedition.

"And now, as weapons will be required, I'll look to my revolvers," he said to himself. "I am very glad that I spent the time on board ship practising, for until then I had never fired anything but a toy pistol. Now, however, I can feel fairly sure of putting a bullet into a man at ten yards' range, and, as they are heavy revolvers, that should be quite enough to stop him. I have heard that these natives are very hardy, and will stand far more knocking about than the average individual, but I've a notion that if I were to hit the hardiest of them plump with one of these big bullets he would not require any more."

Unpacking his revolvers, he set to work to clean and thoroughly overhaul them. Then wrapping them in a towel, together with a small box of ammunition, he placed them in one of his trunks until it was time to join Tom Dixon. Then he set to work to look through his possessions, and so absorbed did he become in the occupation that he did not notice the time slipping by, and, when dinner was announced, could scarcely believe that it was already evening.

An hour later, having said good-bye to Mr. Andrews, he left the bungalow, with his bundle under his arm. When he emerged from the gate of the compound, he was joined by Tom Dixon.

"That you?" asked Tom, in a low voice.

"Yes; here I am," answered Jim.

"Then come along, old chap. We had better walk along silently, for I know these natives well, and caution in such matters pays. For instance, it's quite likely that someone is following you, just to see where you are going. The natives are the most curious people under the sun, and will take no end of trouble over a little matter like this. But we'll soon see. Come down here."

Catching Jim by the sleeve, Tom Dixon suddenly drew him into the deep shadow of a palm which grew close at hand, and whispered to him to crouch low upon the ground. Ten minutes later their caution was rewarded, for a dusky figure crept silently past them, and disappeared in the darkness.

"We'll give him five minutes to get well away," said Tom, "and then we'll move off in the opposite direction, and get to my place by a different route. I dare say all this secrecy seems unnecessary to you, but you've heard my warning."

"It does seem strange," Jim agreed, in a whisper. "Coming from old England, where everything is so free and open, one is at first at a loss to understand the need for all this secrecy; but after what you have told me, I can fully believe that our plans might easily be ruined, unless we kept them to ourselves. That fellow creeping after us just now is an object-lesson which I shall not easily forget."

When sufficient time had elapsed to make it certain that there was no fear of detection, the two rose to their feet again, and leaving the shadow of the tree, went off in the opposite direction. In some twenty minutes' time they arrived at the outskirts of the town of Aden, and, pausing to make sure that they were unobserved, entered a narrow doorway, which led to the interior of a native house.

"Ten paces to your front, and then stop," whispered Tom. "Now follow me closely, and take care that the door does not bang in your face."

There was the creak of rusty hinges, and the snap of a lock being pushed back. Then, guided by Tom's hand, Jim found himself descending a flight of rickety stairs, which groaned beneath his weight, and threatened to deposit him with more swiftness than was quite agreeable in the room below. A minute later a match flickered before his eyes, and he saw Tom applying it to a candle, which quickly burned up and allowed him to take note of his surroundings. To his astonishment he found himself in a comfortably-furnished room, with a tiny bed in one corner. There was a washhand-stand against the wall, and a couple of basket-chairs, while a big chest stood beneath a tiny window, which admitted light and air to the room during the day, but which was now curtained with thick material.

"Not exactly a model dwelling, or the kind of place that a European would choose for his residence in this hot climate," said Tom, with a laugh, "but it has the great advantage of obscurity. This is really part of a disused building, and it was whilst consorting with a gang of rogues, whose secrets I was endeavouring to ascertain, that I accidentally discovered it. I at once saw that it was the very place for me, and promptly set about putting it in order. You see, I am supposed to be a kind of clerk to the Governor, though my duties in that way are purely nominal. As a matter of fact, I turn up every now and again with bundles of papers in my hand, and have an audience with my chief. But the official-looking documents are a fraud, and my conversation has no reference to them. But to return to this room. I've the share of a bungalow elsewhere, and when about to undertake one of my spying adventures, I slip away from there during the night, for all the world like a thief, and find my way to this place. That chest is full of disguises, stains, and paints, and it takes but little more than an hour to transform myself into a worthy Parsee, a race of men engaged in trade in Aden. More often I leave this place as a simple coolie, and at times I have appeared in more disreputable attire, such as is worn by the budmashes, or criminal class of the town. Look here!"

Taking the candle with him, he went across the room to where the chest stood, and slipped in a key. Throwing open the lid, he disclosed a neatly packed interior, with a shallow tray at one end, which contained a number of wigs and hirsute adornments for the face.

"My stock-in-trade," said Tom, with some degree of pride. "It has taken me a long time to collect them, and so important do I consider the question of wigs, that I've gone to enormous trouble to provide myself with all those you see. After all, clothes are easily purchased. One has merely to go into the bazaars, and one will easily find every variety of garb worn by the natives in these parts. With the hair it is a different matter, and to obtain exactly what I wanted I have been compelled to make every one of those little articles myself, for the slightest mistake in get-up would lead to discovery, and most likely to death. But take a seat, and let us decide how we are going to act."

Throwing himself upon the bed, Tom motioned Jim to one of the chairs, and then lay at full length, his hands behind his head, and his eyes fixed upon a patch of dingy light thrown by the flickering candle upon the ceiling above. As for Jim, he sat back in his chair, lost in wonderment. Indeed, when he came to think the matter over, he could scarcely believe that less than three weeks had passed since the first news of the wreck had reached his ears. Then he was just a schoolboy, on the threshold of life, with no higher aim than to go up for his examination, and win a commission in the Army. In the meanwhile no worry troubled his mind, and all his spare hours were taken up in an endeavour to excel in games, for he was passionately fond of exercise in any form. And now, in a moment it seemed, he had been transported into a different life—into a different world indeed. Who could have dreamt that those few short days would have made such a difference to him, would have brought him all those miles across the sea, to face dangers and difficulties the extent of which he could scarcely conceive!

"And here I am, a regular conspirator," he said to himself, looking about the room, "and bound upon an adventure which, from all I can gather, will afford considerable excitement. But I've thought the matter out carefully, and believe that I am justified in entering upon it, for, who knows but that it may turn out an advantage in the end! If these gun-runners are in league with the Mullah, it stands to reason that they know something of his movements, and as white prisoners are seldom or never taken, the fact that the survivor of the wreck fell into his hands will have reached their ears. Perhaps, too, they are even aware of father's exact whereabouts, and if only Tom can worm the secret out of them, we shall be saved enormous trouble, and very likely a large proportion of risk; for, in that case, we should march into the interior as rapidly as possible, choosing night for our movements, and hiding up amongst the sand-dunes and hills during the day. Then, when we got within striking distance, we should mount our trotting camels, and make a dash for the place. If we were successful, I should abandon the transport animals and our baggage, so as to enable us to retire to the coast at all speed.

"But that is hoping for too much," he continued. "This business is going to be no ordinary affair, and before we are successful we shall be compelled to face no end of difficulties. But all the better, if in the end we are able to carry out our purpose."

For quite five minutes Jim sat there silently, lost in thought, while Tom lay upon the bed, still staring at the dingy ceiling, as if, indeed, he could see there a plan which would be likely to prove of service when endeavouring to capture the dhow.

"I can see my way quite easily," he said aloud, as if addressing himself to no one in particular. "At first, of course, I shall have to find out where the dhow lies, but an hour or two spent in the bazaar will soon set the matter at rest. That done, we shall have to obtain a passage aboard her, but there again I fancy things will be easily arranged. I'll get into casual conversation with some fellow who seems to know the destination of the craft, and I'll drop, as if by accident, a few words which will let him know that I am a friend of the Mullah. These natives are well aware of the risk they incur in these gun-running expeditions, and I've no doubt that hands are difficult to obtain. If that is the case, they will jump at our services, and we shall soon find ourselves installed upon the dhow. After that the outlook is uncertain."

"Bound to be!" exclaimed Jim, emphatically. "That's just where the risk comes in. But it would be a fine thing to hold them up, and to capture the vessel and its contents."

"By George, it would! You're right, Jim, and we will do it," cried Tom enthusiastically, swinging himself into a sitting position. "Look here, I've been going over all the points, and I've come to the conclusion that our best plan will be to do as I have just said. Just you lie down there and have a snooze, while I get into the proper togs and go out to the bazaar. Then we shall be able to start for the dhow to-morrow morning, without delay."

"I'd like to come, too, if it could be arranged," said Jim eagerly. "You see, I have to get used to the dress of a native, and shall feel far more sure of myself if my first attempt is made while it is dark."

"Then come along. Just hop out of your things as quickly as you can, while I do the same. Then we'll apply the stain to our bodies, and dress ourselves in the robes usually worn by natives from the interior of Somaliland."

Both at once proceeded to undress, and that done, Tom dived to the bottom of the chest, and produced a carefully stoppered jar, and a big brush, composed of the silkiest hair. With this he at once proceeded to paint Jim from head to foot, and when that operation was concluded, the latter took the brush and did the same for his companion. Another dive into the chest produced an earthen pot. This contained a dark, oily liquid, which was freely applied to the hair and eyebrows.

"Hum! Doesn't smell over-pleasant," remarked Jim, with a grimace. "It has a most peculiarly pungent odour."

"Oh, you'll get used to it in time," was the laughing rejoinder. "But I can assure you that it is very necessary, and quite typical of the Somali people. There are your sandals. Slip your toes into the tags, and walk across the floor. No, not that way, but like this, shuffling along."

Slipping a pair on to his own feet, Tom strode swiftly up and down the room, imitating a native, and would not be satisfied until Jim was able to do precisely the same.

"Now watch me put on this head-gear," he said, taking a long fold of snowy linen, and beginning to wrap it about his temples. He then produced a light belt of webbing, to which two holsters were made fast, and proceeded to buckle it about his waist, tossing a second to Jim for his own use. A minute or two later he had wound a long cloak of linen about his body, contriving, however, to leave one arm and half his breast bare, while his legs were visible from the knee downwards. Then revolvers were placed in the holsters, a small pouch filled with ammunition, and a long and spiteful dagger thrust through the belt, and arranged so that the handle just peeped out through the clothing. A second and shorter weapon was attached to the inside of the left arm, and thus equipped, Tom placed himself before a wide strip of looking-glass which was nailed against the wall, and having put the candle in position, so that its light fell full upon him, began to survey himself critically.

It was evident that he was satisfied, for he smiled at his own image, displaying a set of teeth which looked particularly white, now that his features were stained.

"And now for you," he said. "I want you to dress yourself from head to foot just as I have done, for, remember, you may have to do so before the natives, and if you bungled, then you would certainly be discovered."

Twenty minutes later the candle was extinguished, and the two crept up the creaking staircase and went out. Then, with long, shuffling strides, which carried them quickly over the ground, they made their way towards the native bazaar.

"Remember your rôle," whispered Tom, as they approached the line of squalid huts and booths which formed the native market. "Not a sound is to escape your lips. If you are addressed, make no answer, but turn away angrily, waving your arm. Should the man persist, turn upon him, but beware that you do not touch your weapons, for to do so would be fatal. Of course, if you are discovered, you must make a fight of it; but we'll hope that it is not coming to that."

Walking side by side, the two were soon in the midst of the bazaar, and Jim was interested to see how these Eastern people behaved. Lights twinkled in the various booths, and dusky natives were gathered in knots here and there. Some sat silently, but the majority were conversing in the most excited and voluble manner. Indeed, they might very well have been engaged in a squabble, so exaggerated were their movements. Suddenly, on turning a corner, the two adventurers came upon a circle of men squatting about a brazier, and singing a weird song to the accompaniment of a tom-tom. As they came into the firelight, one of the natives caught sight of them, and called loudly to them.

"Come hither and join us, brothers," he shouted. "Here we shall make room for you."

He shuffled to one side, those who were close at hand doing the same, until a sufficiently wide gap was left in the circle.

"Come on," whispered Tom; and straightway, shouting his pleasure, he went towards the place, Jim following closely upon his heels. To hesitate would have been to arouse instant suspicion, and therefore, watching closely to see how his comrade acted, our hero joined the circle and squatted in native fashion. It was a trying ordeal for a lad who had but recently left school, and though he fought against the feeling of excitement, almost of fear, which assailed him, he was nevertheless well aware that his heart was beating like a sledge-hammer against his ribs, and that his pulses were throbbing almost painfully. But he was not the lad to show the white feather, and remembering his determination to go through with the adventure, he sat stolidly, staring into the glowing brazier.

"A song, brother! Allah has willed it that you should join us this night, and we would hear your voice," shouted one of the group, stretching out a lanky arm and touching Jim upon the knee.

There was no answer, and, to the astonishment of all the natives gathered there, the stranger who had been bidden to join them as a guest still kept his eyes fixed upon the brazier. That he had heard they were certain, for an involuntary turn of the head had betrayed that fact. At once shouts of anger arose, and the man who had spoken sprang to his feet.

CHAPTER IV

IN DISGUISE

For the moment it looked as though the expedition upon which Jim and his friend had set out was doomed to early disaster, for there was no denying the fact that they had unwittingly aroused the anger of the natives. And yet, what could they do? Passing through the bazaar in their search for information, an evil chance had brought them into contact with this gathering, and they had found themselves compelled to accept the unwelcome invitation to join the circle which sat about the brazier. And now, at the very beginning, indeed, within less than a minute they were engaged in an altercation with them. Deeply did Jim regret the fact that he could not speak the language, for had he been able to do so, there would have been no need for silence, and no need to ruffle the feelings of the gathering.

It was a dilemma, and, puzzle his brains as he might, he could not come to any solution that would help him. Instead, therefore, he sat there stolidly, his eyes now fixed upon the brazier, and then turning for the space of a second to the man who confronted him.

"Insolent! How dare you to insult us so?" shouted the native, thrusting his hand into the folds of his waistcloth, to withdraw it a moment later clasping the handle of a dagger. "Dog!" he continued, springing forward. "Speak, or I will bury this blade in your flesh."

Meanwhile the other natives who formed the gathering had sprung to their feet, and crowded about the two young Englishmen with threatening gestures.

THE NATIVES CROWDED ABOUT THEM WITH THREATENING
GESTURES

"Yes," they shouted angrily, "answer, or we will kill you now, and throw your bodies into the gutter."

It was wonderful to see the coolness with which Jim and his companion acted. Had they lost their presence of mind, and sprung to their feet with the intention of escaping, they would have been instantly cut to pieces, for they were entirely surrounded. Indeed, there was no doubt that this was a situation demanding cunning more than anything else, and both recognized that fact fully. Seated, therefore, side by side, as if they were unaware of the commotion raging about them, Jim still looked nonchalantly into the flames, as if, indeed, he had no other interest in life, while Tom stared at the circle of angry faces with the utmost calmness.

"Are we, then, guests or dogs?" he demanded quietly, letting his eyes wander from one to the other. "Was it not you who bade us join your circle? Then why do you grumble if one of us is a man who will keep his vow, whatever befalls? My friend and I have come here from Somaliland, bound upon an expedition to Mecca. But ill fortune fell upon us, and now we return to our country to replenish our funds. For my part, I confess that I am disappointed, but my comrade is grieved beyond expression. His lips are closed, and his ears deaf, until the day when he completes his pilgrimage. He has sworn it by Allah, and by Allah he shall keep to his oath, even though thousands attempt to dissuade him. Take your places, then, again, I beg of you, and let us be friends, for we are deserving of your kindness."

The words, spoken quietly as they were, acted like oil upon troubled waters. Scarcely had they left Tom Dixon's lips, when the excitement of the angry natives disappeared even more rapidly than it had arisen. For a moment only they looked incredulously at one another, and then, saluting Jim with the utmost respect, they took their places again shamefacedly.

"We meant no harm, brothers," said the first speaker, apologetically. "Forgive us, if we spoke angrily and in some haste, but the occasion demanded instant explanation, and, now that you have given it, we are fully satisfied. More than that, it is an honour to us to know that there sits in our circle in friendship with us one who has made such a vow, and who refuses to break his oath in spite of any danger. I watched him carefully as I advanced upon him with my drawn weapon, but he did not flinch, did not even turn aside, or raise an arm to ward off the blow which might well have fallen. Moreover, he allowed no sound to escape his lips, and, true to his word, and to the holy task which he has set himself, sat there unmoved, prepared to die rather than cry out for mercy. It is marvellous the strength that Allah gives to such men."

"Yes, it is a great thing," chimed in an aged native, who sat crouching over the brazier, as if to absorb all its warmth; "and in Aden here not one in ten thousand is capable of making and keeping such a vow. It is only men from Somaliland who are brave enough to do such a thing. Our brother has just told us that we are honoured; we are more than that, for these guests of ours are friends of the Mullah, a holy man, who has made many pilgrimages to Mecca, and who will yet be king of the country which lies yonder across the sea."

He pointed towards the harbour, and looked round at his companions.

"Yes," they agreed in guttural tones, "the Mullah is a great man, and will be even more powerful."

"We can speak openly," continued the old man, "for there are none but friends here, and no Hindoos are within hearing. How thrives the Mullah?" he went on, addressing Tom. "Does he know that the English are preparing to march against him?"

"Yes, he is fully aware of it," answered the latter, quietly, "and will meet them in battle. But at present he is fearful of defeat, for though his soldiers are numerous, they are poorly armed, and for the most part carry only shields and spears. Guns are what he wants, and he is prepared to pay well for them. Indeed, he bade us on our return to make enquiries here, and endeavour to induce some of the wealthy merchants who are friendly to him to send him a ship-load of weapons and ammunition. We believe that such a ship has lately sailed, or will shortly leave this shore, but we are uncertain. We have been to more than one of those who live in this town, and are friendly to us, but they will do nothing until silver is placed in their hands, and of that we have absolutely none. However, once we can get a passage across to Somaliland, we shall be able to replenish our store, and shall return immediately."

"And how knows your friend of this arrangement?" asked the old man suspiciously, glancing sharply at Jim. "If he has made a vow not to speak, how can he have discussed this matter with you?"

The question was a shrewd one, and at once set the whole circle of natives staring hard at their guests.

"Yes, how can he have learnt of this plan?" cried another, rising to his feet, and waving his arms excitedly. "You say that you have been to many in the town, and have questioned them concerning arms for the Mullah. Then this vow of which your comrade boasts is one made to be broken or kept at will. Perhaps he is a spy come here to learn our secrets."

His words at once brought the whole gathering of natives to their feet, and again, such is the excitability of these Eastern people, they crowded threateningly about their guests, calling loudly for an explanation. But Jim and his friend were equal to the occasion. The former was certainly dumfounded at the sudden turn affairs had taken, for he had not understood a word of all that had been said. But he was fully aware that here again an attempt to escape would be worse than useless, and therefore, placing full reliance in his friend, he squatted there as calmly as before, prepared, however, to spring to his feet in a moment and join Tom in fighting for their lives. A hasty glance at the latter told him that there was still some chance of calming the natives, for Tom Dixon sat as if carved in stone. One hand was buried, as if accidentally, in the folds of his waistcloth, though Jim knew well that it grasped the butt of a hidden revolver; while the other was stretched out towards the brazier, as if to gather some comfort from its glowing embers.

"Did I say that I had discussed this matter with my comrade?" he asked sarcastically, looking round the circle with a contemptuous glance. "When I said that we had been to various merchants in the town, I thought that you were wise enough to understand my meaning. My comrade's vow is one which few or none of you would dare to take, and yet you do not hesitate to doubt it. It was sworn more than a week ago, and, by Allah, it has never been broken. But look at him? Do you not see him turn his head as each one speaks? He cannot help the words falling upon his ears, and hears and understands all that you say, without, however, deigning to answer. So it is with me. So that he should know what was to happen, I have spoken of my plans to him, but we have never entered into discussion on the matter. Come," he continued, "let us be friends, and treat us like brothers."

"We will," exclaimed the old man warmly. "We cannot venture to take risks, for were a spy to come amongst us, he would learn many things of value to the

Government. It was on that account that we tested you, and have proved you to be of ourselves. We are friends and brothers."

Each of the natives gave vent to a guttural exclamation of approval, and then, as if to forbid further altercation, the sharp notes of the tom-tom were heard, and the gathering began a chant, one of those peculiarly dismal dirges which seem to delight the ears of natives of the East. Then, when the song was finished, an earthen dish, containing slices of juicy lemon, was handed round, each man present helping himself.

"You spoke of a ship which might be sailing for Somaliland," said the old man, suddenly, awaking from a reverie into which he seemed to have fallen, and looking up at Tom. "You also told us that you and your friend were in search of a passage. Are you strong, and are you willing to work? For, if so, I will find places for you upon the dhow."

"It is a good offer, and we accept it gladly," responded Tom promptly. "As for strength, we are capable of hauling at the ropes as well as any man. Would there be much else to do? For I tell you honestly that we are unused to the sea, and are more at home when mounted upon horseback and galloping across the smooth plains of Somaliland."

"There is little else for you to do than keep watch upon the deck, and help to pull in the sails, for three men will go besides yourselves, as well as the master. But I warn you that fighting may fall to your lot, for a steamship flying the Government colours patrols these seas, and, should she sight you, will certainly endeavour to capture you. In that case your death would be swift and almost certain. If not, you would be thrown into prison, and would be a slave for the greater part of your days."

"Then the post will suit us well. If there is fighting we shall not grumble, for it is our trade, and as capture means death, you may rely upon it that we shall do all that is possible to defeat the enemy. But why should the Government fall upon this dhow?"

For a moment the old man scrutinized Tom closely, as if still suspicious of him, and as if doubtful whether he was to be fully trusted. But the latter returned his glance with one that was equally steady and unflinching, and, satisfied with this, the native at length answered:

"That dhow is filled to overflowing with guns and ammunition for the Mullah," he said. "If she reaches the Somali coast in safety, I shall have done well for myself, and shall have aided the cause of your master. She sails to-morrow at noon, and you will know her by the fact that she bears a red streak upon her bows, and has a large rent in her sail. When you see her, she will be lying some few yards from the shore, and any of the small craft in the harbour will put you aboard her. You must go below as soon as you get on board, and if any of the crew are there, pass them without a sound, but salute them in this manner."

The old man paused for an instant, and withdrawing his hand from beneath the blanket which covered him, placed two fingers upon his lips.

"That is the sign which you must make, and be careful that you do it exactly as I have shown you, for, if not, the crew will believe that you are spies, and will fall upon you as soon as you are below. To-day the Customs officer has been on board, inspecting the cargo. But the crew are even now busily employed in transferring it to another ship, and in taking in the guns and ammunition destined for the Mullah's troops."

"It is a good plan," said Tom, "and I can see the need for secrecy. To-morrow we shall go on board the dhow, and we shall be careful to follow your wishes. Can you tell us how long the passage will take, and where we shall be landed?"

Again the old man looked suspiciously at him, and then shook his head emphatically.

"No, I cannot tell you that. If Allah wills it, you shall land upon the coast and return to your people."

Some five minutes later Tom touched Jim upon the arm, and made signs to him to rise. Then, nodding to the natives, they left the circle, and went on into the bazaar. But they had already had one experience of native cunning and curiosity, and instead of turning their steps towards the room in which they had disguised themselves, they moved away in the opposite direction, and taking advantage of a narrow alley, which was filled with chattering natives, they mingled with the crowd, and sauntered on, now looking curiously at the wares of some Hindoo merchant, and then watching with evident interest the skill of a juggler, who sat in the middle of the street, with an admiring circle about him. Winding hither and thither, they at length came to a deserted part, and having hidden in the shadow of a booth for some ten minutes, so as to assure themselves that they were not followed, they took to their heels, and before very long had reached the dwelling in which they were to shelter that night.

"We're in luck," exclaimed Tom, in tones of satisfaction. "I must admit that at one moment I thought it was all up with us, for these natives are suspicious beggars, and would think nothing of killing anyone whom they suspected of spying upon them. If they had discovered us, you may take it for certain that we should have disappeared for good, and no amount of searching on the part of our friends would have led to news of our fate. There is no doubt that they are masters at the art, and no bribe will induce anyone to give evidence against his comrades."

"I can quite believe that," answered Jim, "and I agree with you that things looked very black. Of course, I didn't understand what was happening, and am puzzling about it even now. But the shouting and excitement, and the fact that that fellow drew his knife, told me that trouble was coming. It was as much as I could do to sit there quietly, but I took my cue from you, and I can tell you I was jolly glad when the squabble ended."

"You behaved like a brick, old boy. Considering that you are a novice, and quite unused to these natives, you showed no end of pluck. I admit that it was not without some misgivings that I allowed you to accompany me into the bazaar, for, you see, I hadn't an idea how you would behave. But I felt sure that the fellow who could come out here, and quietly make his preparations to face the dangers of an expedition into the heart of Somaliland, must be someone quite out of the ordinary. Of course, you might have been a thoughtless kind of beggar, who had no fear simply because you were unaware of, and had taken no trouble to find out, the difficulties and risks you were about to face. But I soon saw that you realized the gravity of your task, and, by George! I admired you for it, for there are precious few youngsters of your age who would have the grit to go on with the matter. But I am wandering from the subject. There's no doubt that if you had flinched, and shouted out when that beggar drew his knife, we should have been set upon by the whole gang of ruffians, and, though we were armed with revolvers, we should have had precious little chance. The whole row arose because you made no answer when they invited you to sing."

Throwing himself upon the bed, Tom Dixon gave his comrade a full account of the altercation, and then went on to describe how a passage had been offered them upon the dhow, which was to sail upon the following day, with arms for the Mullah.

"It will not do to take any risks," he said, "and therefore I vote that we practise going aboard and making the sign, for the slightest slip would mean ruin to our plans."

Accordingly, while Tom stood at one end of the room, Jim advanced from the other, and turning, raised his fingers to his lips as he passed him. Not till he had done it some half-dozen times was Tom satisfied, and then he, too, went through the process.

"The next thing will be to give news to the Governor," said Tom, "so as to make it possible for the gunboat to intercept us. She left Aden a couple of days ago, but was to return to-morrow night. If she slips away again at once, she should easily overtake us, and then I should give very little for the chances of the crew. There should be four on board besides ourselves, and if we cannot master them with our revolvers, I shall be greatly surprised. It will be a feather in our caps, Jim, to capture the dhow by ourselves and then hand her over to the gunboat."

"But you said that you had been unable to ascertain the destination of the dhow," interposed Jim. "Supposing the gunboat could not find her?"

"It would be very awkward, and that's where the risk comes in."

"Yes, it would be awkward," agreed Jim; "but then there would be all the more honour in capturing her. It would be grand to overpower the crew and compel them to sail the dhow back to Aden."

"Perhaps it will turn out like that," said Tom. "But you lie down on the bed and have a sleep while I go off to the Governor. I shall be back within an hour, and shall make myself comfortable in the corner there with a blanket as a covering. No," he exclaimed, seeing Jim about to remonstrate, "you are not yet used to sleeping on a hard floor like the natives. But I am, and even prefer it."

A few moments later Jim was left alone in the room, and blowing out the candle, at once lay down upon the bed and settled himself to sleep. An hour later his comrade returned, and threw himself down in the corner, where his heavy breathing soon gave evidence of the fact that he, too, had forgotten the adventures of the night and was lost in dreams.

Scarcely had the sun risen on the following morning when both were astir, and at once rearranged their clothing, so as to make sure that their disguise was satisfactory and would pass muster in broad daylight. Then Tom produced a small oil stove and a frying-pan, and began to prepare breakfast. Eggs were to be had in plenty, and as these were easy to cook, four of them were quickly spluttering upon the pan. Meanwhile a kettle of water was set upon a second stove to boil, and soon they sat down to a satisfying if not dainty repast. To a hungry man food, if clean and fairly well prepared, is always acceptable, and Jim and his companion were not the ones to turn up their noses simply because their eggs reposed on rough tin plates, and their tea was contained in mugs of similar material. Seated upon the two chairs of which the room boasted, and taking the plates upon their knees, they set to work with energy, and quickly caused the food to disappear. Indeed, so keen was their appetite, that they unanimously agreed to prepare a second relay of eggs, and partook of them with the same relish.

"And now to business," cried Jim cheerily. "I feel as fresh as paint, and quite ready for this adventure. Shall I do as I am?"

For the moment Tom did not answer, but pulling the curtain from the window so as to allow all the light that was possible to enter the room, he placed his comrade in the centre and walked slowly round him.

"The disguise is perfect," he said in tones of satisfaction. "I guarantee that you will pass muster anywhere, and, so long as you remember that you are never to open your lips, I have little fear that you will be discovered. Let me give you a little additional advice. As we go towards the dhow it is quite on the cards that we shall run across some of the passengers who accompanied you from England, and you may be tempted to renew your friendship with them, quite forgetful of your disguise. But you must not dream of doing such a thing, for sharp eyes are always watching in this town, and were the natives to learn that a spy is amongst them, your chances of success in Somaliland would be considerably diminished. Now, are your revolvers in position, and do you feel ready to accompany me?"

"Quite," exclaimed Jim, with emphasis. "I tell you that I feel as light-hearted as possible, and fully prepared for the adventure."

"Then come along."

Leading the way to the window, Tom Dixon threw it open, and placing a chair beneath it, stepped upon it and crawled through. Jim followed, without hesitation, and found himself in a narrow courtyard, from which a gate that was almost tumbling from its hinges led into a street behind. A glance showed them that the street was empty, and at once they stepped into it, and hurrying along, were soon in the main thoroughfare of Aden.

Had anyone taken the trouble to scrutinize them closely, he would have seen two stalwart and swarthy men, one somewhat younger than the other, and of slightly smaller proportions, but both evidently from the shores of Northern Africa. They strode along with that quick shuffling gait common to men of their race, and due, no doubt, in some degree, to the sandals which they wear. That they were strangers to Aden could be easily guessed, for they looked curiously about them, and stopped every now and again to look in at the shop windows. An Englishman marching along the footpath was obviously an object of interest and respect, for they turned aside to give him more room to pass, and gazed at him in wonderment. So cleverly did they act their part that no one suspected that they were not what they pretended to be, and even the natives, who swarmed everywhere, let them pass without a doubt. On one occasion a native arrested their progress, and would have entered into conversation with Jim, but a few words from Tom altered his intention, and he stood aside, allowing them to pass without comment. A few minutes later, when turning a corner sharply, they barely escaped running into a second Englishman, who was no other than Mr. Andrews. But he motioned them aside with a brusque "Out of the way!" and went on, without a thought of the two young fellows who had sat with him on the previous evening, and without a suspicion that the two Somali tribesmen whom he had met face to face were those whose interests he had so much at heart.

Half an hour's sharp walk brought Jim and his companion to the shore, where they paused for some minutes to gaze at a large steamer which was moored there, undergoing the process of coaling with the help of a perfect army of dusky figures who swarmed about her, shouting at the top of their voices.

From there they took their way to that part of the harbour usually allotted to native craft, and before very long had the satisfaction of noting that one which floated in deep water, and was of fairly large proportions, had a thin streak of red upon her bows.

Tom at once turned towards her, and, followed closely by Jim, went down to the water's edge. A number of flimsy native boats were drawn up on the mud, with their owners seated chatting beside them. As soon as they caught sight of the two strangers, the boatmen at once sprang to their feet, and, gesticulating wildly, offered their services.

"We want to go aboard the dhow there," said Tom shortly, selecting one of the boatmen. "What will you take us for?"

A price was agreed upon after some little haggling, and a few moments later a boat was run down into the water and pushed off. Taking his place in the stern, the oarsman paddled out into deep water, and quickly brought them alongside the dhow. Tom at once handed him his fare, and then, grasping the halliards, which were close at hand, swarmed up on deck, closely followed by Jim. As he did so he threw a glance aloft, and noted that the huge leg-of-mutton sail which was tied up to the mast had a large rent in one corner of it.

"We are on the right ship, at any rate," he said to himself. "And now for the crew."

Turning towards the stern of the dhow, he and Jim walked towards a narrow hatchway, which evidently gave admission to the hold. As they did so, three figures started up from behind some coils of rope with the silence of spectres, and gazed at them curiously and suspiciously; while a fourth, happening to thrust his head up at that moment, caught sight of the strangers, and, with a guttural exclamation, climbed out upon the deck. They were fierce-looking fellows, clad in scanty raiment, and undoubtedly armed, for, as the newcomers returned their glances and ran their eyes over them, they noted the handle of more than one weapon protruding from their waist-cloths, while the man who had just emerged from the hold bore a pistol of gigantic proportions.

"We shall have our work cut out to master them," Jim said to himself, "for they will fight hard and make a desperate resistance. However, so long as their suspicions are not aroused, and they believe that we are friends, and to be thoroughly relied upon, we shall have every opportunity of taking them by surprise. If we are successful in doing that, I think we shall be able to overawe them; and if not, why, they must look to themselves."

A movement on Tom's part now attracted his attention, and following him closely, Jim strode down the deck, taking little notice of the natives. Arrived at the hatchway, his companion paused for the space of a moment, and rapidly made the sign. Instantly the crew, who had stood there with menacing looks, evidently determined to attack them should they prove to be enemies come to spy upon them, sauntered away, watching, however, to see that Jim, too, lifted his fingers to his lips. A moment later both had disappeared into the darkness of the hold, and, creeping forward, sat down side by side.

"Guns!" whispered Jim, feeling about with his hands, and venturing for one second to break the silence which he had promised to observe. "Scores of them! They are all over the place."

"And precious uncomfortable to sit upon," answered his companion in husky tones. "The stock of one is digging into me. But, hush! We must not talk, for those beggars are certain to be curious about us, and we may take it for granted that for a day at least they will watch us like cats. No doubt, for the present, and until the dhow sails, we shall be left severely alone; but then will come the trial. Recollect, Jim, that we are landsmen, and don't forget to bungle when you hang on to a rope. I shall let them know of your vow, and you must act up to it by appearing morose and stupid. Hear nothing; say nothing; but wait until everything is explained to you by signs."

"Right, old man; you may rely upon me," was Jim's whispered reply; after which they both sat silently, neither venturing to speak nor move, but listening intently to every sound that reached their ears. Now and again they could hear the distant shout of some native boatman, or the howl of a cur prowling along the shore. Then, too, the voices of the crew could be occasionally heard as they chatted together on the deck, but the actual words could not be distinguished at that distance, though Tom would have given anything to learn what they were saying. And all the while the dhow rolled lazily from side to side, her mast creaking dismally as she did so, while the rigging rattled loudly against the woodwork. Occasionally, as a boat of large proportions passed, the sea would come with a splash against the side and drown all other sounds. But the noise soon quieted down, and Jim and Tom found themselves listening again, as if fascinated, to the distant shouts, the murmur of voices above, and the flapping of the sail.

Three long and weary hours passed—hours of suspense to the two young Englishmen seated below; and then, just as their patience was exhausted, they heard someone moving on the deck. There was a patter of bare feet upon the boards, followed by the noise of a rope passing through a block.

"Up goes the sail!" whispered Jim, in tones of delight. "Hurrah! We're off!"

"Then prepare to go on deck," answered Tom. "They'll wait until we're out of sight, and then will call us up."

"Ah, there she goes!" exclaimed Jim, as the dhow suddenly heeled over, and began to move through the water. A minute later she was driving along before a brisk breeze, and the two young fellows below realized that, at last, their adventure had begun in earnest.

CHAPTER V

A DESPERATE ENCOUNTER

Barely half an hour had passed from the time when the sail was unloosed, and the dhow cast off her moorings, before one of the crew knelt upon the deck, and, thrusting his head through the hatchway, shouted to Jim and his companion to come out of the hold.

"Now for it," whispered Tom. "Keep cool, and be perfectly unconcerned. If there is trouble, do not hesitate for an instant, but draw your revolvers and shoot. You've only got to look at those fellows' faces to see that we have to deal with desperate men, who would kill us if they had the slightest doubts of our good faith. Ready?"

"Quite," answered Jim with a calmness that surprised himself.

"Then up we go."

Rising to their feet, and bending low, for the cargo of guns left little space in which to move, they crept towards the hatchway, and in due time emerged upon the deck, blinking as the dazzling rays of the noonday sun fell upon their eyes. When they had accustomed themselves to the strong light, they became aware that three of the crew confronted them, while the fourth stood at the tiller, keeping the vessel to her course. Right astern, a dim blue line showed the position of Aden, while ahead, and on either hand, nothing but blue ocean could be seen. Not a sail was in sight, though Jim strained his eyes in every direction, and not a streak of cloud in the sky could, by the wildest flight of imagination, be interpreted as the smoke from the funnel of the gunboat. But at this moment one of the natives addressed him.

"You and your comrade can lie upon the deck for a while," he said, "but you must be ready at any moment to give us a help. Keep a keen look-out in all directions, and if you see a sail, shout so that I shall know. If we are pursued we must fly, and may Allah send a breeze to aid us. If not, we will fight, and in that we are told that you can help us."

"We hear what you say," answered Tom hurriedly, anxious to explain his companion's silence. "Take no notice of my friend, for, as those who sent us here may have told you, he is, for the time being, both deaf and dumb. Do not speak to him, I beg of you, for he will not answer, and will stand, as he does now, refusing to comprehend your words. If you have orders to give, I will hand them on to him by signs. As for fighting, what is that to us? In our country we are ever at war, and should be miserable without it. Make your mind easy, therefore, for we shall strike hard when the moment of danger arrives."

Apparently his words satisfied the natives, for they turned away, and walked towards the steersman. Tom at once grasped Jim by the arm, and pointing to the deck, strode across to the bulwark, and threw himself down there for an instant. Then he rose to his feet again, and placing a hand above his eyes, so as to shield them from the sun, stared long and anxiously across the sea. Again he threw himself upon the deck and repeated the process, but this time with a different result, for, apparently, he caught sight of some distant object, and giving vent to a shout, ran to communicate his news to the crew. Indeed, so realistic was his acting that they, too, imagined he had seen something of interest, and at once came crowding to the bulwarks, and stared eagerly across the water in the vain endeavour to discover some object between themselves and the horizon.

"Where?" shouted the man who had addressed Jim, and who seemed to be the master. "Where?" he repeated anxiously. "I can see no sail, though it is possible that one is hidden in the haze yonder. Hold out your arm so that I may follow the direction."

There was no doubt from the manner in which he spoke, and from the anxiety displayed by the remainder of the crew, that the prospect of discovery had filled them with alarm. They were conscious that they were engaged upon an unlawful expedition, and though that did not trouble them much, the thought of what would follow if they were captured set them trembling.

"Ah, what is that?" shouted one of their number. "I can see something which has the appearance of a bird, but which may well be a sail. If so, we are safe, for the Government would follow us in a steamship, if at all."

"It is nothing," replied Tom calmly, with difficulty keeping his features straight. "I saw nothing to alarm me, but was merely explaining to my comrade the duties he was to carry out. See, it is evident that he understands."

"Is that so?" was the grumbling reply. "By the manner in which you gave the alarm, I thought you had sighted a suspicious sail, and my heart leapt into my mouth at your shout. But it is well that there is nothing in it. Go to your places now, and do not forget to keep constant watch."

For a minute he stood by the bulwark, while Jim and his companion went forward and threw themselves upon the deck. Then he retired to the stern of the vessel, and sat down in the shade cast by the enormous sail.

For three hours the dhow kept steadily on her course, and then Jim, who lay upon the starboard side, suddenly caught sight of a speck of white coming from the opposite direction. Keeping his eyes fixed upon it, he noticed that it increased rapidly in size, and soon there was no doubt that it was another vessel. Giving a low cough to attract Tom's attention, he pointed towards the object, and then sprang to his feet. Walking along the deck, he approached the group at the farther end, and laid his hand upon the shoulder of the master, shaking him as he did so, for he had fallen asleep.

In a moment all were on their feet, and staring across the sea.

"It is a large dhow," said the man who commanded the crew, "and she is sweeping down in our direction. What do you think she is?"

"It is too early to say," answered one of the men, "but she is not a trader—of that I am sure—nor does she belong to the Government. It is possible that she comes from some African port, but until she is closer I cannot be certain. This I can say, she is larger than any dhow plying between Aden and the opposite coast, and therefore we shall do well to keep her at a distance."

For a few minutes the natives held a heated conversation, and a sharp order was given to alter the course. When that was done, and the dhow was holding along in a southerly direction, the crew gathered in the bows and stood there, gazing anxiously at the distant vessel. Cries of alarm escaped their lips when they noticed that her head came round, and that she, too, had altered her course so as to intercept them.

"She sails faster than we do!" exclaimed the master, with an oath. "We cannot hope to escape her, and therefore I advise that we resume our course, and make ready for an encounter, though it is more than likely that she will prove to be a friend. And if not that—well, we must prepare to sell our lives dearly. But I cannot believe that we have anything to fear, for none but peaceful traders sail upon this sea."

"That is so," agreed one of the crew. "But I have heard that, at times, piratical craft sail from the coast of Africa, and swoop down upon the traders. If that dhow is bent upon such an expedition, we are lost, for her owners care no more for the Mullah than they do for other people."

The news filled his companions with dismay. In a half-hearted manner they produced a number of guns from the hold, and proceeded to load them. Then they placed swords beside the bulwark, and motioned to Jim and Tom to select a couple.

"There is trouble before us, and we must fight for our lives," said the master, brightening up a little. "If you do not wish to be killed, you must join us, and help in the struggle."

"We shall do so gladly, if there is need," answered Tom. "But let us hope that the stranger will turn out to be a friend."

"I wish I could think the same," the master replied with a shake of his head. "It is more than likely that she is a pirate. But now we must separate. You and your friend go forward into the bows. I shall station two of my men in the centre of the dhow, while I and the fourth go aft. Then we shall be prepared at all points, and wherever they attempt to board us, we shall have men at hand to beat them back."

"If I were you I should order everyone to lie down," said Tom, thoughtfully. "At the distance they are from us now they cannot have ascertained how many we have on board, and will naturally keep away until they are certain. If they are bent on capturing us, and open fire when within range, we can all creep to the centre and give them a volley. Then we'll hasten to the bows, and fire from that quarter. You have plenty of guns, so that you have only to load a number, and pile them at various points along the deck, in readiness for our volleys. If we are quick, and take good care to keep well below the bulwarks, we ought to confuse them, and make them think that we have plenty of men."

"It is a good plan," the native answered. "I shall see that the guns are brought up at once, and the men warned. That ship will sail close up to us, expecting us to fall an easy prey. But we'll astonish them with our bullets, and will set them wondering, for it is unusual for a peaceful trader, as we are supposed to be, to carry any firearms. Go forward now, and explain to your comrade."

Tom at once ran to the bows, where Jim was reclining on the deck, watching the oncoming ship, and throwing himself down beside him, began to make signs to him, keeping a watch all the time, however, upon the other members of the crew.

"Ah, they've gone below for the guns," he said at last, "and there is only the man at the helm to be feared, and he is engaged in watching this pirate, or whatever she may be. Listen, Jim. We're in for a struggle, for that ship is an enemy, and is probably filled with negro cut-throats. I have advised the master of our ship to make a fight for it, but I doubt if he or his men have the necessary courage. What are we to do if that is the case?"

"It is hard to say, Tom. If the dhow over there carries a big crew, resistance would be madness, in my opinion. Better to give in and fraternize with them, if they will allow us, trusting to get away from them at some future date. That's the best advice I can give. But if you think we have any chance, I'm ready and willing to stand by you."

"I know that, old boy," answered Tom warmly; "but though I have advised resistance, I doubt whether it will be attempted. We'll just wait, and see how things go. This stranger may turn out, after all, to be a friend."

Whatever hopes they might have had as to the peaceful nature of the approaching dhow, they were quickly disappointed, for she was coming up rapidly, aided by a steady and brisk breeze. Almost before they thought it possible, she was within range, and then they saw that she was quite double the size of their vessel. Shooting up into the wind, she lay to dead across their bows, displaying at the same moment a broad expanse of white deck, which was thickly crowded with men. Almost instantly a puff of smoke belched from her bulwarks, and a ball came hurtling over the water.

"Caught, I am afraid," whispered Jim, peeping at the stranger. "We haven't a chance, Tom, for look at our comrades."

As he spoke the leader of the native crew rushed to the helm and waved his arm frantically in token of surrender, while his men threw themselves upon the deck, and grovelled there, in terror lest another shot should be fired by the pirate.

"Curs!" exclaimed Tom, angrily. "When there is no danger to be feared, they are fierce enough looking fellows. But now that we are in trouble, they show the real stuff of which they are made. But what are we to do?"

"Stay where we are till the enemy comes alongside," answered Jim, promptly. "If they rush on board with the intention of killing us, we must stand side by side up here in the bows, and keep them off with our revolvers. It is ten chances to one that they are only armed with swords, and in that case we ought to be able to make a good fight of it. Whatever happens, I don't mean to be killed without a struggle."

He spoke quite calmly, and thrust his hands into his waistcloth to make certain that his weapons were there. As for Tom, he looked at his young companion with amazement, and then, fired by his example of pluck, prepared to do as he had said.

"Then it's agreed that, if there is no hope, we fight," he said; "and if there is, we give ourselves up, and trust to better luck later on."

"That's it," replied Jim, shortly. "It would be madness to resist if they were inclined to spare our lives. But if they want to slay us, they'll find one here who strongly objects."

By now, the big native dhow had paid off into her course again, and, seeing that she had nothing to fear, came on till within easy hailing-distance. Then a huge negro, dressed in gaudy colours, and bearing a cutlass in his hand, sprang upon the bulwarks, and shouted to them.

"Who are you?" he cried. "And where do you come from?"

Shaking with terror, the master went to the side, and answered that there were five besides himself on the vessel, and that she came from Aden.

"Where for, and what cargo?" was the next question.

"For the coast, with arms for the Mullah."

"Then we are friends," came the answer. "The Mullah is our master also, and we sail the sea in his ship. All whom we capture we send to him to swell his forces, while the loot we keep for ourselves. Do you know of any trader about to leave the shores on the farther side?"

"Not one," shouted the master, scarcely able to restrain his joy. "But I can tell you that a British gunboat is on patrol, and you will do well to keep clear of her. Now, good-bye. We must press on at our fastest pace."

Going aft to the helm he brought the dhow round, and in another minute they were shooting away from the piratical-looking stranger, leaving her rolling gently on the water, with her bulwarks lined by a crew of natives, of all sorts of every race, who stood there watching the smaller vessel depart. Ten minutes later she, too, had turned, and was dashing away at a pace which showed how hopeless it would have been for the dhow to have attempted to evade her.

The delight of the master and crew of the smaller vessel was immense, and they could scarcely contain themselves for joy. They threw themselves into one another's arms, leapt high into the air, and shouted at the top of their voices. Then they produced a hubble-bubble, and, going aft, squatted down close to the steersman, and began to converse in loud tones. It was wonderful to see the change in their appearance. Whereas, a few minutes before, they had been shaking with terror, and prepared to accept their death without so much as a struggle, now they held their heads erect, and recounted to one another, in piercing tones, the brave deeds which they would have accomplished had the larger dhow turned out, after all, to be an enemy.

As for Jim and his friend, they lay full length upon the deck in the bows of the vessel, keeping a bright look-out over the bulwarks, and apparently undisturbed by the excitement of recent events. But, for all that, they were deeply relieved, for the situation had for a time seemed desperate.

"I am trying to think what would have happened," whispered Jim, taking advantage of the fact that the natives were fully engaged in conversation. "Suppose those pirates had compelled us to join them, and we had afterwards fallen in with a British ship, we should have been in a very awkward position, for we could not have refused to fight."

"We should have found a way out of it somehow, Jim. I noticed that, like this dhow, she carried a dinghy on her decks, and we could have taken advantage of that and slipped away during the night. But I am glad that things have turned out as they have, for now we have a better chance of capturing this vessel. Look out! Here's one of the beggars coming to talk to us."

As he spoke one of the men aft handed the stem of the hubble-bubble to his companion and came running forward.

"The chief bids you come and join us," he cried, and at once returned to his old position.

"You stay here, Jim," whispered Tom; "those fellows want a chat, so I'll go and smoke with them. If you were to attempt that you would certainly fail, for it requires a deal of practice to tackle a hubble-bubble."

Accordingly, leaving Jim on the look-out in the bows of the vessel, Tom sauntered aft, and was soon squatting beside the natives. The stem of the pipe was at once handed to him, and soon he was engaged in animated conversation. It was evident that something had aroused the suspicion of the master and his crew, for they questioned him closely. But his answers seemed to satisfy them, and in half an hour he returned to Jim's side, and taking advantage of the fact that the natives were still engaged in animated conversation, began to chat in low tones to him.

"They seem inclined to be very friendly," he said, "but I am not quite satisfied. Something—I don't know what it is—seems to have upset them. The fact of the matter is they don't quite believe in this silence of yours. One man declared that he had seen us exchanging words when the pirate bore down upon us. Of course, I said that that was impossible, and that he had imagined it. But he was positive, and, I could see, had been talking to his fellows. However, the subject dropped, and after a time turned to the Mullah. His position was mentioned, and, by pretending to know a great deal more about him than I really do, they became quite confiding, and told me the number of adherents of which he boasted. In the most unconcerned manner, I mentioned that a white prisoner had fallen into his hands of late, and I could see at once that they knew all about it. But I could get no further information from them.

"'Yes,' said their chief, 'a man was thrown upon the shore, and fell into the Mullah's hands; but he is only one, whereas, as soon as the foolish English advance, hundreds more will be made into slaves.'

"That's all I could get out of him, and so, after changing the conversation and having another turn at the hubble-bubble, I rose to my feet and returned."

"I'm not surprised to hear that they are suspicious, Tom. I saw one of the natives look at us while we were deciding what to do, and if he is quite certain that he saw us speaking, he will never be satisfied until he has found out all about us. You know what kind of men these fellows are, better than I do, and I have no doubt that, rather than run any risk in the matter, they would pounce upon us and throw us overboard. I advise that we keep watch in turn. It's already getting dark, and, if you like, I'll take the first watch. I'll wake you in a couple of hours, and you can do the same for me when you have had your turn. Hush! They are moving."

Turning his head, Jim saw the natives rise to their feet and disappear down the hatchway. Ten minutes later they climbed to the deck again, bearing a large dish and a gourd of water, and, having given the steersman a drink and placed a pile of food beside him, they advanced to the mast and sat down there, motioning to Jim and Tom to join them. Gladly did the young fellows obey the summons, for many hours had elapsed since they had partaken of any food, and their naturally keen appetites were sharpened by the sea air and by the excitement of the past few hours. Indeed, up to that moment, so much had occurred that Jim had had no time to think of food, for all his thoughts had been concentrated upon his surroundings. But the sight of it reminded him at once of his long fast, and he joined the group, feeling that it would require a large amount to satisfy his hunger.

Squatting around the bowl, they helped themselves to dates, of which there was an abundant supply. Simple though the food was it was satisfying, and Jim soon returned to his old position, feeling very much better. Tom remained for a short while chatting with the natives, and then rejoined his friend. It was now evening, and within a few minutes darkness fell, for there is scarcely any twilight in the Tropics.

"The night will be a cold one, and the dew heavy," said the master, coming up to them. "You had better go down into the hold and sleep there. I will post a man up here to keep watch."

"If it is the same to you, we would rather remain where we are," Tom answered promptly. "You see, we are not used to this kind of thing, and that stuffy hold makes us feel ill. We will ask you to lend us a couple of blankets in which to wrap ourselves."

"You shall have them, but you cannot sleep here, for the look-out man must stand in this position; but you can go farther along the deck, if you like. Come with me now, and I shall give you what you have asked for."

Ten minutes later Jim and his friend were wrapped from head to foot in thick blankets, and had taken their places close to the bulwark on one side, and about the centre of the vessel. As they did so one of the crew passed them and went to take his station forward, while the remainder proceeded aft, and throwing themselves down upon the deck, prepared to sleep. Two hours passed without incident, Tom's heavy breathing telling clearly that he was asleep. Then Jim, whose eyes had been wide open all the time, touched him gently with his foot, and had the satisfaction of seeing that he had awakened his companion. Then curling himself in his blanket, he closed his eyes. He could not sleep, however, for, though he was tired out with the long day of excitement, his novel position, and the thought that danger threatened them, kept him wide awake. He was, therefore, fully prepared when Tom stealthily stretched out an arm and tugged at his blanket, and at once sat up with his back against the bulwark. Once more it was time for his companion's watch, and Jim, who was now feeling decidedly drowsy, awoke him and lay down again upon the deck. A few minutes later he was fast asleep, and remained so for a considerable period. But a shout from Tom suddenly roused him, and, starting up, he saw that a struggle was taking place within a few feet of him. Dawn was just breaking, and the light enabled him to discover the fact that his companion was clasped in the arms of two of the natives, who were hustling him towards the bulwarks, and evidently endeavouring to throw him overboard.

Springing to his feet, Jim leapt across the deck at one bound, and sent his fist crashing into the face of one of Tom's opponents. Then, with a shout, he clasped the other by the neck, and, tearing him from his hold, sent him reeling across the deck.

"What has happened, Tom?" he asked. "What made them attack you?"

"I can't say," was the breathless answer; "but I deserved to be thrown overboard, for I believe I had fallen asleep. At any rate, they were upon me before I was aware of it, and, while one held me by the shoulders and placed a hand firmly over my mouth, the other caught me by the legs, and hustled me to the side. I fought like a cat, and managed to free my mouth. But you saved my life, old chap."

"Look out! They are preparing to rush again," cried Jim, in a warning voice. "I suppose we must make a fight for it."

As they were talking, the two men who had attacked Tom had picked themselves up, and had retired to their comrades, who stood close to the helm. That they were disconcerted by the sudden resistance was evident, but, seeing only two unarmed young fellows, they forgot their fear, and at once prepared to renew the combat. Snatching arms from a pile which lay beside them on the deck, they shouted to their comrades to join in the struggle, and then came rushing towards Jim and Tom at their fastest pace.

It was a critical moment, and might well have unnerved the bravest of men. Indeed, Tom was so shaken by the narrow escape he had had, that, for a second or two, he did nothing but stare at his opponents, as if fascinated. Jim, however, was fully alive to the danger, and promptly took measures to protect himself. Without taking his eyes from the natives he felt for and grasped the butt of a revolver, and, as they approached, presented it at their heads, hesitating to press the trigger in the hope that a sight of the weapon would overawe them. But they were maddened with rage, and, with shrill cries, came on boldly, waving their swords above their heads.

Crack! Jim pressed the trigger ever so gently, and, to his astonishment, the report had scarcely rung out upon the air when the leading man suddenly tossed his weapon above his head and fell to the deck with a crash. A second later, the native who followed him tripped over his body, and came sprawling upon all fours, where he lay, stunned by the fall.

"Now get ready for the other two," cried Jim. "Pull yourself together, Tom, and when they rush, leave me to manage the first one. You can put a bullet into the second, if necessary, but we don't want to kill them all, if it can be helped. Ah, here they come!"

Undeterred by the quick fate which had befallen their comrades, the master of the dhow advanced cautiously along the deck, accompanied by the steersman, and armed with an enormous double-handed sword, which he held well before him. The steersman snatched at one of the guns which had been loaded in preparation for the attack of the pirate on the previous evening, and sinking upon one knee, took steady aim in Jim's direction. He was in the act of firing it when Tom, who had suddenly come to his senses, took a snapshot at him with his revolver, in the hope of killing him before he could do any harm. But the bullet flew wide of the mark, and striking the bulwarks, buried itself deep in the wood. An instant later there was a loud report, and, to Jim's amazement, the folds of linen which were bound about his head flew high into the air, while he staggered back, feeling as though someone had struck him violently.

But he was not the lad to give way without a struggle, or to cry out before he was hurt. Starting forward a pace or two, he levelled his revolver at the man who had just fired, and who was, at that moment, engaged in reaching for another gun. Sighting carefully, and with the utmost coolness, he pressed gently upon the trigger, and had the satisfaction of seeing the native start to his feet with a shriek of pain, and then collapse suddenly upon the deck.

"And now for the master!" he said quietly, turning to Tom. "Tell him that if he moves a pace forward we will shoot him like a dog."

"Drop your weapon!" Tom at once shouted, advancing towards the man, revolver in hand. "We have already killed two of your number, and will shoot you also, if you show the slightest wish to continue the conflict. Drop your sword, I say, and hands up!"

"You are too strong for us," answered the native humbly, letting his weapon tumble with a crash to the deck. "Spare my life, and I promise not to attack you again."

"That's right! And now, wake this fellow up," continued Tom, pointing to the man who had been stunned, and who was now recovering consciousness. "When you've done that, go aft, and send him into the bows; but before doing so, you can repeat to him what I have said."

Meekly obeying these commands, the master of the vessel went to his fallen comrade and shook him savagely. Then he dragged him to his feet, and shouting words of warning in his ear, sent him forward, retiring himself to the helm.

"And now let us see to these other fellows," said Jim. "I expect the first is dead, for I fired at close quarters, and aimed plump at the middle of his chest. The second was a longer and more difficult shot, and may not have proved fatal."

Keeping their revolvers in their hands, in case of treachery, they crossed the deck to the fallen native, and turned him upon his back, Jim in vain attempting to disguise the horror with which the sight filled him.

"Dead!" he said in a whisper. "It's terrible to think that I killed him."

"I dare say it is, old boy," Tom answered calmly. "But then, you see, it would have been far more terrible if he had run you through with this murderous-looking sword, and had then thrown you into the sea. It's not nice, I admit, to feel that that ugly-looking wound is due to your bullet, but then, you know, he fully deserved it, for he had every intention of killing you, and, as you saw, did his best to rid the world of my presence. So, cheer up, Jim. It was a splendid shot, and I'm still marvelling at your pluck and coolness. If it hadn't been for you, I really believe that our bodies would have been floating a mile or more astern by now, a prey to the sharks, for I was completely unhinged by my struggle with them. You behaved grandly, I tell you, and you saved both my life and your own."

"I don't think so," replied Jim modestly. "You see, I couldn't very well have behaved in any other way. Your shout awakened me with a start to find you fighting with those two ruffians. Naturally, I went to your help, and as an Englishman's first weapons are his fists, I used mine with a result that fairly astonished me. After that, everything was, of course, plain sailing."

"There's no plain sailing at all about it, Jim, my boy," said Tom sharply, "and I'm not going to allow you to run down the share you took in the matter. You behaved splendidly, and with the greatest pluck, while I made a fool of myself. First of all, I fell asleep when I should have been keeping careful watch, and then I was so thoroughly upset by the attack made upon me that I was practically useless. But there, I can see you don't like the subject, so I'll say no more. Shake hands! That's right. I feel better now."

"Then let us look at this other fellow, Tom."

Walking along the deck, they knelt down beside the second native who had fallen, and turning him over, at once saw that he was dead, for he had been struck in the neck.

"A lucky shot," said Jim, looking pityingly at the man.

"And mine was an execrable one!" exclaimed Tom, in disgust. "It almost lost you your life. Let's look at your head."

"Yes, it was a narrow shave, Tom, but I was so excited that I forgot all about it in a moment. George! Look at that!"

Jim placed his hand to his head, and withdrew it with a long curl of dark hair, which had been neatly severed by the bullet.

"Yes," he repeated, "it was a close shave, and I never want another like it. Indeed, I have very much to be thankful for, for had the gun been aimed half an inch lower, my head would have been shattered, and I should be lying like that poor fellow there."

CHAPTER VI

ON AFRICAN SHORES

There was no doubt that Jim had good cause to be thankful, for his had been an extremely narrow escape; and as he turned away from his companion, he was quite overcome at the thought, for this was the very first time he had known what it was to be face to face with death. Burying his face in his hands, so that Tom should not see his emotion, he stood there, leaning upon the bulwark, for at least five minutes. Then suddenly he roused himself, and went to join his comrade, who respecting his feelings, had walked away to the other side of the deck.

"Well, Tom," he said cheerfully, "the expedition has so far proved an undoubted success, and this gun-runner is safely in our hands. The next question to be considered is what we are to do with her. You said that you would probably sail her back to Aden; but doesn't it seem a shame, now that we are almost within sight of Africa, to return to our starting-point?"

"It does, Jim; and I am in hopes that that will not be necessary. As far as I have been able to make out, we have held steadily upon our course since we left Aden; and in that case the gunboat should soon catch us up. I propose that we remain where we are until she comes up with us, and then we'll ask them to do us the favour of taking us on to Berbera. They'll be glad enough to help us, for this capture will appear in their names, and will be a feather in the captain's cap, though he will not fail to give us the credit that is due to us. You see, it wouldn't do to publish the full facts of the case, for, if the natives learnt that I had a hand in the capture, my life would not be worth an hour's purchase, and I should have to leave Aden for good and all. But, I say——"

"What?" asked Jim. "You were about to suggest something."

"About those fellows there, old man," Tom replied, pointing to the bodies of the natives.

"They're not very pleasant objects to look at, Tom; and if you think it right, I vote that we tie some weights to them and throw them over the side. Half a dozen guns should be sufficient if we cannot find anything better. What do you think of the plan?"

"It will have to be done sooner or later, Jim, and I think had better be carried out at once. Let's slip down into the hold and see what we can find. But—that would not do, for there is no trusting these native beggars; and it's more than possible that while we were beneath decks they would play a trick upon us."

"That has occurred to me, too, Tom; but from the look of them, I don't think we have much to fear. They are thoroughly cowed, and go in terror of our revolvers. I'll wait here at the stern while you go below. Just order the master to go forward, so that I can keep an eye upon both of them. If they show signs of wishing to attack me, I'll shout, and you can hop up to my help."

"That will do famously," answered Tom. "Look here," he continued, addressing the late commander of the dhow, who stood a few paces away, watching his captors through the corners of his eyes, "get away forward to your comrade, and sit upon the deck. If either of you attempts to move, you will be shot. So take good care to keep absolutely still, for my friend is a capital shot, as you have been able to see for yourself."

The precaution was a wise one; but a glance at the two prisoners showed that it was scarcely necessary, for all their courage had fled. Indeed, at the mention of Jim's prowess with the revolver, they shivered visibly, while their eyes wandered to the two figures lying upon the deck.

"You can trust us to be still," said the master humbly. "We have seen your bravery, and know that we are beaten. Promise that you will spare our lives."

"I can make no promise at all," answered Tom sternly. "You have been caught in the act of carrying arms to the Mullah, and in aiding the enemies of the Government, and to the latter you must answer."

"What is the talk about?" asked Jim at this moment; for, being entirely ignorant of the language, he could not even guess the drift of the conversation. "I hear you chatting away to these fellows, and long to be able to join in and understand what is said. I've quite made up my mind that, at the first opportunity, I shall begin to take lessons."

"He is asking me to promise them their lives," explained Tom, "and I have told him that it is impossible, and that someone else will have to do that for them."

"But you could say that you would speak for them," exclaimed Jim, a sudden thought occurring to him.

"And why? You seem to forget, old boy, that a few minutes ago these fellows were doing their best to kill us. And now you want to help them to escape the punishment which they have earned."

Tom became quite indignant at Jim's words, and turned away from him impatiently, as if it angered him to listen.

"Steady. Wait until you have heard all that I have to say," cried Jim, catching him by the arm and detaining him. "Did you not tell me that one of the crew knew more than he would admit about that white prisoner of the Mullah?"

"Yes, that is the case," answered Tom, unable as yet to follow his companion's meaning.

"Well," continued Jim eagerly, "these fellows deserve to lose their lives, but, you know, the Government are no more fond of hanging people than we are. You could, therefore, safely say to them that you would speak on their behalf on certain conditions. Don't you see my point now?"

"By Jove! Of course, I do, Jim! What a duffer I am, to be sure! I'll see what I can do at once."

They went along the deck towards the natives, who watched them furtively, fearful of what was coming, and expecting at any moment to be shot where they sat.

"I have talked this matter over with my friend," said Tom sternly, addressing the man who had commanded the captured dhow. "We both agree that we should be within our rights if we shot you. But you have asked me to promise you your lives, and I am inclined to do so on certain conditions. The first is that you solemnly promise to remain faithful to us until we hand you over to the Government; and the second, that you tell us all you know about this white man who recently fell into the hands of the Mullah."

"We shall fall in with your wishes gladly," replied the native, scarcely able to repress a shout of joy. "We solemnly declare that we will be true to you, and will not venture to attack you. As for the other matter, we do not know much, but we have heard that the prisoner was a soldier, what the Hindoos in Aden call a 'sahib.'"

"He says that the prisoner was an officer," explained Tom, turning to Jim, so that he should be able to follow the conversation.

"Ask him if he heard the name," was the eager reply.

"My friend wishes to know more," said Tom, continuing his interrogation. "What was the name of this prisoner?"

"That I cannot say; but he was 'sahib' and 'colonel,' so the man who told me of his capture said."

Jim was listening eagerly, vainly endeavouring to understand all that passed, and he could have leapt for joy when Tom translated the man's answer.

"That settles it, then," he said. "Up to this there has been some doubt as to whether my father was the man who reached shore alive, but now I am certain that it was he; for I have been through the list of passengers, and there was only one colonel on board, and he, of course, was Colonel Hubbard."

"I think you are right in what you say," answered Tom, after a pause. "I must confess that, until this moment, I have been very doubtful, far I happen to know that nine British officers out of ten wear a watch bracelet upon their wrists. It is a habit which seems to have become general during the Boer war. Still, the fact that this survivor was tall, and in other respects corresponded with your father, made it possible that it would turn out to be he. Now, however, the question is settled, for, no doubt, when the Mullah's men captured him he gave his name, hoping that that would cause them to release him. They know quite sufficient of the British to feel sure that a colonel is a man of some importance, and they must have boasted of it. That's how the news has got to this fellow's ears. Yes, I think you may take it as certain that your father is the white prisoner spoken of, for if not, who else could it be?"

"There is no doubt about it," answered Jim emphatically. "I was never very doubtful, and now any fears I may have had are absolutely set at rest. But ask him more, Tom. For instance, perhaps he knows where father has been taken, and whether he is being well treated."

Turning again to the native, Tom plied him with question after question, and was able to elicit the fact that the white prisoner was constantly with the Mullah, who often changed his whereabouts. Also that he acted as a slave, but was safe for the time being.

"How long he will continue to be sure of his life I cannot say," the master continued thoughtfully. "But I feel certain that if the Mullah suffers at the hands of the British troops, he will avenge himself by slaying the white man. Indeed, I wonder at his allowing him to remain alive so long, for all those who are not of his own colour and religion are his bitter enemies, and he slays them without remorse."

"So you can feel easy about his safety for a time," said Tom, as he discussed the facts with Jim; "we know that the Government is making preparations for a general advance, and that nothing can be done till all is absolutely ready. I should say that we have quite two months, and perhaps more than that, in which to effect his rescue."

"We must try to do it in two weeks, if that is at all possible," said Jim with decision. "You see, there is always an element of doubt, and until my father is out of the Mullah's hands, I do not think we can ever consider him out of danger. These native beggars are cruel and capricious; at least, so I have always been given to understand. He might order his prisoner to be killed in his rage at hearing that the British were preparing to attack him, and even might make the capture of these guns sufficient excuse to execute father. It is horrible to imagine such a thing."

"Don't be down-hearted, old boy," exclaimed Tom encouragingly. "If you allow yourself to think in that way, you will be miserable. Make up your mind that your gov'nor is alive and well, and badly in need of his freedom; and that you are going to bring it to him. That's the way to look at the matter."

"You're right," answered Jim with a sigh of relief.

"Better look at the bright side of things, and just put all one's back into the task. Yes, that is the way, I'm sure; and by Jove! I'll do as you advise, and what's more, I'll rescue father, or die in the attempt."

"Spoken like a man! If you say that you'll carry the job out successfully, I am sure that that is half the battle, and that you will get along ever so much better. I can tell you this, that I will help you to the best of my power, for this expedition has taken my fancy; and besides, Jim, I owe you something. Remember that half an hour ago you saved my life. I want to pay back the debt, you know; and how could I do it better than by standing beside you in this affair?"

There was no doubt that Tom was thoroughly in earnest, for he spoke with a vigour to which his companion was unused, and to show how deeply he felt, grasped him firmly by the hand.

"Thank you," Jim answered, returning the clasp with one as warm. "As to the debt, I fancy that we are quits, for, had you not stood by me, we should both have been like those two poor fellows there. Let's get rid of them. I cannot bear to look at them, for it reminds me that it was I who caused their death."

"Right. We'll set these two natives to work, for they will understand it better."

Tom beckoned to the master, and gave him instructions to tie half a dozen guns to each corpse, and then consign them to the sea. When that necessary but unpleasant task was satisfactorily accomplished, he ordered the two prisoners into the bows again, and retired with Jim to the stern, from which point of vantage they could keep a watch upon their prisoners. Not that that was necessary now, for the promise that he would speak on their behalf, made by Tom, had put the natives on their best behaviour. Indeed, unbidden, they began to sweep the decks, and then suggested that they should prepare some food.

"We have taken nothing to break our fast," said the master, coming to them as they sat by the tiller. "Is it your wish that I and my comrade should go in search of something with which to stave off our hunger?"

"You can go, certainly," answered Tom readily; "but one at a time. It does not matter what it is so long as there is sufficient, for we are badly in want of food."

In a short time the master returned and placed before them a plate of dried meat and some pieces of wheaten cake. This they devoured with the utmost satisfaction, completing the repast with a copious draught of cool water. Then both rose to their feet, and began to patrol the deck, for after having lived ashore for the greater part of one's existence, the craving for movement, for exercise of some description, when aboard a ship of such small proportions as the dhow, is very great. Half an hour later Jim gave vent to a sudden shout of joy and pointed astern.

"What do you make of that?" he asked in excited tones.

"No, not there, but more to the left."

Stretching out his arm so that his companion could follow the direction, he pointed to the horizon, where a faint streak of dark colour was visible. Tom looked at it for some minutes without answering, but at last he turned to Jim with smiling features, which told that he had guessed at the origin of the cloud.

"It's the gunboat, sure enough," he said, "and I tell you that it lifts a weight from my mind. You see, things have been rather uncertain, and there is no doubt that we have been in great danger. Of course, we came through this scuffle remarkably well, but if that pirate fellow had turned up again we should have been in a nasty mess. There can be no doubt that the patch of dark colour on the horizon is a steamer of some sort, and I fancy it will turn out to be the gunboat, for this is right out of the track of ordinary shipping, and though a few steamers are just now engaged in bringing stores to Berbera for the Mullah's expedition, I happen to know that none were leaving Aden during this week. So we can take it for certain that that is the gunboat, and I can tell you I am jolly glad. Won't it be grand when she comes alongside and finds the capture already made!"

"It ought to get you promotion, at any rate," answered Jim. "After all, when you come to look at the matter quietly, you must admit that it was rather a risky thing to do. Who else would have thought of making up as a Somali native and shipping aboard the very dhow upon the capture of which you were bent? Mind you, I take no credit to myself for that part of the adventure. It was you who planned the whole thing, and I think you deserve no end of praise. But, I say, look at her again."

By now the dark streak had developed into a low-lying hull, which was fast coming up from the horizon. Very soon a stumpy mast could be seen, poking up barely into the blue sky, and, within twenty minutes, Jim and Tom could even make out her guns, two of which stood amidships, and formed her only broadside, an amply sufficient one in such waters. Half an hour had barely passed before the gunboat came rushing alongside, surging through the swell, and sending the foam seething in a broad band of white from her cut-water. Then she put her helm hard over, and turning upon her heel in the space of a few seconds, and with a heave which caused her to roll her scuppers into the sea, she came up on the other quarter, and lay to, with the muzzle of one of her quick-firers grinning at the occupants of the dhow.

"Dhow ahoy!" came in stentorian tones. "Who's that?" shouted Tom in reply, springing upon the bulwark to obtain a better look. "Is it Humphreys?" "Yes; and who are you?" "Government agent from Aden," sang out Tom, refraining from giving his name, for, had he done so, the natives would have heard, and it would have become common property before very long. "I want to hand over this vessel to you. She's full of cheap guns, which were going to the Mullah. We've a couple of prisoners, too."

"Bravo! Congratulate you!" was shouted from the gunboat, while at the same moment a figure, clad from head to foot in snowy white, leapt upon the diminutive bridge and signalled to the dhow. "We'll come right alongside, and then you can slip aboard, and give us the tale. Any casualties?"

"None, I'm glad to say, though one, if not both, of us, was nearly killed. But we shot two of the crew, and threw their bodies overboard half an hour ago."

"Look out for us now," was shouted from the gunboat. "If you have a rope fender, or two, you might sling them overboard. Our plates are too thin to stand bumping, even against the wooden sides of your dhow."

Jim saw the commander of the gunboat grasp the handle of the telegraph, and, so short was the distance intervening between the two vessels, that he could actually hear the tinkle of the bell sounding down in the engine-room. Then the screws whirled around, the blades churning the waters of the gulf into white foam, which went hissing and frothing along the sides of the vessel as she ran astern. Five minutes later, she was securely fastened to the dhow, great care being taken to place several thick rope fenders between the vessels, together with some fibre matting which happened to be aboard the dhow. No sooner was all to his liking than the captain of the gunboat stepped on to the bulwark of his own vessel, and leapt lightly upon the deck of the one which Jim and his companion had contrived to capture. A particularly smart officer he looked, too, in his spruce and neatly cut white drill-clothing. Coming forward, with outstretched hand, he advanced towards Tom with a smile of welcome.

"Glad to see you—heartily glad to see you!" he said. "'Pon my word, when the Governor told me for what I was wanted, and packed me off post-haste last night, I quite thought I was on a wild-goose chase. It seemed to me that you and your young friend must have run your heads into a perfect hornets'-nest, and I tell you, had I come across your bodies floating in the sea, I should not have been by any means astonished. But I'm bound to say that the Governor, though fully realizing the extent of the danger, thought far better of your chances than I did. You see, I've often met you before and known you in the Club at Aden as a clerk in the Civil Service, and as a particularly good billiard-player. And to hear suddenly that you were an Intelligence officer, who was notorious for success in worming out the secrets of the natives, was quite astonishing, for you must understand that I always looked upon you as a peaceful sort of fellow."

"And so I am," laughed Tom. "You see, I've lived the best part of my life in Aden, so that to appear as a native is nothing out of the way for me. I am so thoroughly used to it that I run very little danger. But it's different with my friend here, for he is only just from school, and doesn't understand a word of the language, and yet he boldly came with me; and if it had not been for his help, I can honestly say that this would have proved my last adventure. But he turned out trumps, and proved to be as cool and steady as an old hand, and thoroughly plucky into the bargain. But, I say, let me introduce him. Jim Hubbard—Captain Humphreys."

"Glad to meet you, and I congratulate you on coming so well out of your first engagement," said the officer, gripping Jim by the hand. "Never been under fire before, I suppose, and never seen men fighting in real earnest?"

"Never!" answered Jim, returning the handshake with equal fervour; for the captain of the gunboat was an open-hearted, cheery individual, to whom one was bound to take on the instant. "I must admit, too, that the experience for the first time was far from pleasant; and if it hadn't been that the fighting came suddenly, and before I was really prepared for it, I am sure I should have been in a regular funk. You see, waiting always did upset me. I was the same at school when I was in for a licking, and had orders to attend in a few hours at the Doctor's study. I'm too impatient, I suppose, and employ the interval in imagining all kinds of awful things. But I'm sorry to say that I killed two of the natives during the struggle."

Jim looked the captain steadily in the face, and then flushed guiltily, for it appeared to him a terrible admission to have to make.

"I know what you feel, my lad," was the hasty answer, given with an encouraging smack upon the back. "But that's the fortune of war, you know, and everyone has the same regrets at first. Why, I remember how terribly upset I was when I sent a bullet into the body of a rascally slave-dealer. It thoroughly unnerved me when I looked at the fellow afterwards. But my chief took me aside, and just put the matter to me as I have to you. You may take it from me, that if you engage in adventures of this sort, you will kill more men before you have done, though always in self-defence. It's just that that helps one to get over the feeling."

"And now about the dhow," interposed Tom. "She's full up to her hatches with cheap guns and ammunition, and I now hand her over to you. In return, I ask you, if you possibly can, to take us to Berbera, for we are bound for Africa."

"So the Governor told me, and you may rely on it that I shall do as you ask, for I know how important it is for you both to make an early start into the interior. You say that the dhow is full of cheap arms. If that is the case, they are unlikely to prove of any use to the Government, and we should not be thanked for bringing them back. I'll just pop below, and look for myself, and then we'll put a charge of gun-cotton into her and blow her to pieces. It will be the cheapest and best plan in the end. But you may rely upon it, Dixon, that I shall make a full report to the Governor, and if there is no promotion in your particular branch, then I prophesy that your salary will be increased, for there is no doubt that this is a most important capture. Indeed, had all these guns reached the Mullah, so many more lives would be lost in the coming expedition. So you can see for yourself what good service you have done."

"It's very good of you to say so, Humphreys," answered Tom, "and I will only ask you, while mentioning the fact to the Governor, to be sure that my name is not published in connection with the capture, for it is important for me to continue to be known as a simple clerk in the Civil Service."

The captain of the gunboat readily assented to this proposal, and then, stepping along the deck, quickly disappeared through the hatchway. Ten minutes later he appeared again, and returned aboard his own vessel. An order was given, and within a short while a couple of seamen went into the hold of the dhow, where they remained for half an hour. Meanwhile, the lashings which connected the two vessels were cast off, the fenders and matting removed, and all aboard the dhow, except the men who were placing the fuse, were ordered to leave and take up their quarters upon the gunboat. Five minutes later the two British tars appeared, and when they had joined their own ship again, she sheered off from the low-lying gun-runner. When she had run a mile at the top of her speed, she went about, and stopped her engines. And there, with eyes fixed upon the distant vessel, all waited for the explosion that was to rend her to pieces and send her cargo to the bottom.

Bang! The roar of the bursting fuse could be loudly heard, followed by a spurt of fire which rose high into the air, accompanied by a dense column of smoke. As the latter cleared away, all looked to see what had become of the dhow, but not a vestige of her was to be seen.

"The Mullah will grieve for her, and will grind his teeth with rage when he learns that the freight of guns and ammunition is lost to him," laughed Captain Humphreys. "But we can smile, for we have done a good turn to those who are going with the expedition. And now, I want to ask you young fellows whether you intend to land as you are. If you would prefer to change into European costume, I have plenty of togs aboard which will fit you, and to which you are heartily welcome."

For the moment neither answered, but each looked at the other, as if awaiting a reply.

"I've been thinking the matter out," said Jim at length, "and I've come to the conclusion that we should be wise to make no alteration in our dress. Secrecy seems to me to be the object at which we particularly aim. Now, if we take advantage of your kind offer, and appear as Englishmen, our coming will certainly be noticed at Berbera."

"No doubt about it, Hubbard," said Captain Humphreys decisively. "Like Aden, Berbera has a very large native population, consisting, for the most part, of Arabs. The landing of a couple of Somali men would pass unnoticed, whereas it is perfectly certain that each white man causes a stir. He becomes the subject of conversation in the bazaars, and if his mission to the town is not perfectly clear, it sets every native wondering. Of course, if you were officers come to join the troops there, you would arouse no further interest. But as you are not that, and not traders, then for what reason have you come to Berbera? That's how these fellows look at such a matter, and they're cute enough and curious enough to go more deeply into it. Therefore, I think you will be wise to make no change in your dress."

"And I fully agree," cried Tom. "Our aim, as Jim has just said, is to arouse no curiosity, and to maintain our incognito. That can be best done by appearing as Somali natives. Once ashore, we can go to the Consul's to tell him our plans, and from there we shall strike straight away for the camp, where Ali Kumar awaits us with the followers. The same night we shall disappear, and when we have received our baggage and stores, and put a day's march between ourselves and the coast-line, we can get rid of this paint and these long white robes, and reappear in our ordinary costume."

"And now for a meal!" interposed the commander of the gunboat. "I expect you two fellows will be glad of one, for the grub aboard that dhow must have been of the coarsest. Let me see, it's a hundred and forty miles from Aden across to Berbera, and I reckon we have already steamed the greater part of the distance. By the time we come on deck again the coast should be in sight, and shortly after noon we should be at our destination."

Accordingly, the trio descended to the tiny cabin, where they did ample justice to an excellent luncheon. Then they chatted for an hour before going on deck again. When they did so, it was to discover a low-lying coast before them, with purple headlands, and a long range of hazy blue hills in the distance. Indeed, at the first glance, it was a hospitable-looking coast, for the sand-dunes and the desolate, treeless wastes were not visible. Soon Berbera itself was sighted, and the gunboat was headed for the harbour, which seemed to be filled with trading dhows, and with a few steamers of small size, which had come there with stores for the troops. Half an hour later they were safely moored inside.

Jim and his companion took farewell of the captain, and watched him as he was rowed to the tumble-down pier which did duty as a landing-place. Then, as the dusk of evening fell, they put off in a small dinghy which the gunboat carried, and were landed at a deserted part of the town. Stealing away in the darkness, they were soon lost among the Arab streets, and had the satisfaction of feeling that their expedition was to begin under the best auspices. For who would take the trouble to enquire about them? Captain Humphreys had impressed upon his men the need for silence, while the two prisoners who had been captured with the dhow could do them no harm, for they were at that moment in irons beneath the deck of the gunboat, and likely to remain there until they were thrown into prison at Aden.

It was, therefore, in the highest spirits that they sauntered through the town, and made their way towards the British Consul's.

CHAPTER VII

THE "MAD" MULLAH

"You'll know the house where the British Consul lives immediately you set eyes upon it," Captain Humphreys had said, when giving directions to Jim and his friend. "It's a long, low-lying bungalow, surrounded by quite a little forest of trees, and has the reputation of being one of the coolest in Berbera. As soon as you are ashore, you must pass through the Arab town, and bear towards the harbour again. I shall go to him at once, and will tell him that you are coming, and arrange for the door of his sitting-room to be left open. Of course, it gives entrance from the verandah, and all you will have to do will be to walk straight through the compound and into the room. I leave it to yourselves to get there without being seen."

Accordingly, acting upon this advice, they made their way slowly through the narrow and dirty streets of the town, remarking how clean the white-washed houses looked in contrast with the filth and squalor around. Here and there a smoky oil-lamp glimmered, allowing them to catch glimpses of huddled figures sitting in the doorways, swathed from head to foot in robes of white. At length they reached the outskirts, and seeing a belt of trees before them, at once turned in that direction. Nestling in the centre of this plantation was a low building, the windows of which were brightly illuminated. For a minute or more the two stood in the deep shadow cast by the trees, and took careful stock of the dwelling.

"There's the room which we must aim for," said Jim, in a whisper, suddenly pointing to the farther end. "Look! you can see that the door leading on to the verandah is wide open. Let us creep along in the shadow until we are directly opposite; then we shall be able to see whether there is anyone waiting in there for us. If none of the native servants are to be seen walking about, we'll cut straight across and slip in. After that we'll ask the Consul to draw the blinds, and shut out the light, for it would look funny, and would certainly give rise to a good deal of chatter, if we were observed in conversation with His Excellency."

"I follow. It's very good advice; and, upon my word, you are becoming a regular conspirator," laughed Tom. "I quite thought when we started out upon this expedition that I should constantly have to warn you to be cautious; but really, you seem to have taken to your new *rôle* as a duck does to water, and I am sure that no one could lay his plans with more care and discretion than you do. Come along. I quite agree that the room yonder is the one in which we are to have our interview."

Stealing along in the dense shadow cast by the thick growth of leaves overhead, Jim soon reached a point exactly opposite the farther end of the building, and at once threw himself upon the ground, for a dusky figure suddenly appeared between himself and the brilliantly lit window beyond. It was a native servant; of that there was little doubt, for he stood there, leaning against one of the verandah posts, sharply silhouetted against the rays cast by a tall standard lamp.

"Hush, Tom!" Jim whispered, turning to find his comrade close beside him. "Lie down, for I can see someone over there."

"And there's a man in the room," was the answer. "See, he's getting up now and coming our way."

As he spoke a tall figure, clad in white, and with a red cummerbund about his waist, suddenly appeared at the open window, and catching sight of the native, addressed him angrily.

"Be off!" he cried sharply. "Have I not frequently given the order that no one is to come upon this side of the verandah at night? Be off, then, I say, or I shall find a means to sharpen your memory."

The words had effect at once, for the servant salaamed, and retired hastily.

"Now is our time," said Jim. "Let's walk quickly across."

Leaving the shadow of the trees, the two started across the open space at a sharp walk, and mounted the verandah. A few steps forward took them into the room, when they at once crossed to the farther side, so as to be well away from the window.

"Excuse me," said the gentleman who was present, and who had betrayed no astonishment at their sudden entry. "I'll just shut the window, and let down these thick rolls of matting, for, you know, it wouldn't do quite for the Consul at Berbera, the representative of the great 'Sirkal,' as the British Government is known, to be seen engaging in an animated conversation with two of the very tribe against which our forces are about to march. It would look queer, particularly at this time of the day, and would set the town agog."

Gently pulling the sash to, he lowered the blinds, and then turned with smiling face to his visitors.

"Very glad to see you," he said, coming forward, and shaking both by the hand. "I have already had a communication from the Governor of Aden, who writes to me that he has had orders from the Foreign Office to help you as far as is possible. Short of providing you with troops, or an armed following, I am prepared to do anything that lies in my power, for, Mr. Hubbard, I have the pleasure of your father's acquaintance. But putting that aside altogether, it is the nature of Englishmen to stand by one another, whatever the trouble, and this, I think, is just the case in which we should do our utmost to give assistance. Now, sit down there, and tell me what I can do for you."

"I hardly know," answered Jim, after having thanked him for his kind offer of assistance; "but if you will allow the dhow which is to bring our guns and baggage to land her cargo without question or molestation, we shall be greatly obliged. We have decided to go straight from here to the camp in which our followers are quartered. To-morrow morning we hope to have disappeared, and a week from this we should be in the heart of Somaliland. Should you obtain news of us after we have gone, will you kindly forward it to Mr. Andrews at Aden, who will telegraph home to my uncle?"

"Make your mind easy about the dhow," said the Consul. "The Governor at Aden gave his authority for it to sail, and the gunboat which blew up that rascally vessel which was carrying weapons for the Mullah has been quietly warned to look the other way. As for news of you, it is quite probable that I shall occasionally hear some, for we have many spies in various parts of the country, who are well paid to bring in information. Thanks to them, we know a good deal about the Mullah and his movements, though I am bound to confess that their word is not always reliable. But Mr. Dixon and yourself will have excellent opportunities of obtaining an insight into the true condition of affairs, and I may tell you that we are hoping to derive great benefit from your expedition."

"You shall have all that we can get," exclaimed Jim, "but I must admit that at the present moment I have only the haziest idea of this gentleman whom you call the 'Mad' Mullah. In fact, until a month ago, I should have found it very difficult to explain precisely the whereabouts of Somaliland."

"In that you are like the majority of people, I fancy," laughed the Consul. "Hitherto the minds of the public have been fully occupied with other parts of this huge continent. First, there was Egypt, with the campaign which ended at Omdurman, and resulted in the reclaiming of the Soudan. Then the Boer war began, and whereas scarcely one in ten was aware of the position of the two Republics a couple of years ago, now everyone could point them out on the map with the greatest ease. You must recollect, too, that the Niger, the West Coast, Abyssinia, Coomassie, and other parts, are forever engaging public attention, and consequently, this strip of country which occupies the north-eastern angle of Africa has been overlooked. Suddenly, however, the rising of this Mullah and his bands of desperadoes has filled the papers with long and interesting articles, and bids fair to arouse as much enquiry as did the rising of the fanatics who met our armies at Omdurman.

"But—look here—you're just bound for the interior, and it is as well that you should have all the news I am able to give you. Sit down, do, and make yourselves quite comfortable. You may feel quite certain that we shall not be interrupted, for I have given strict orders to my servants that I am not to be disturbed."

The Consul, who was a man of middle age, dragged a chair into a convenient position, from which he could easily observe the faces of his listeners. Then, seating himself, he gave a preliminary cough.

"Let me see," he said, "I think, then, I had better begin by giving you some idea of the class of men you are likely to meet with. Of course, I understand that Mr. Dixon is well acquainted with them, in fact, better even than I am, for his long residence in Aden has given him many advantages. But to you, Mr. Hubbard, the news will be strange, no doubt, and may be of service."

"I'm sure it will, and I am eager to hear all about these Somali people," exclaimed Jim.

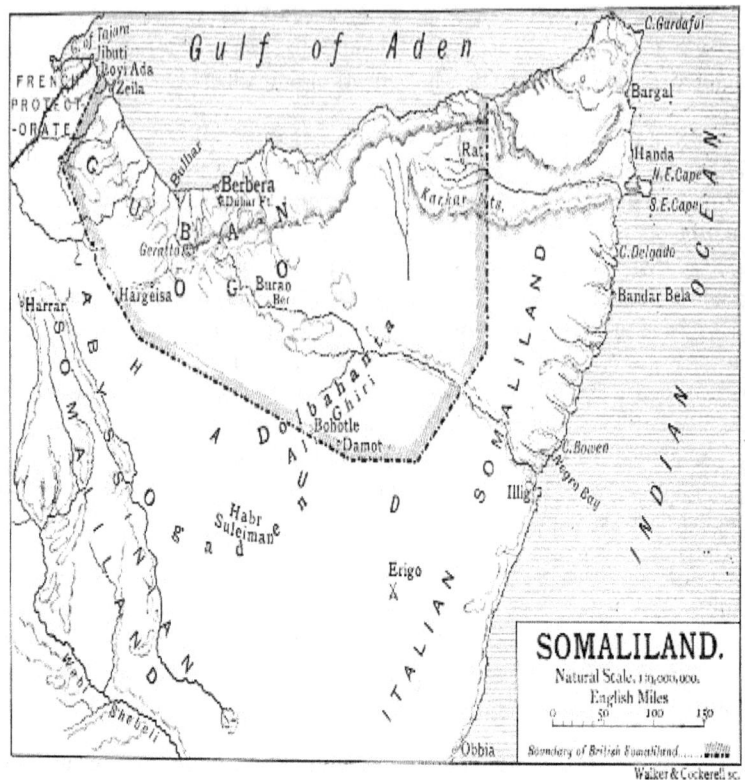

SOMALILAND.

"Well, I will tell you what I know about them. Up to recent times they have been known to us as friendly and harmless people. Many of our countrymen have made shooting expeditions into the interior, and all have reported that they have met with kindness and courtesy; that the natives are intensely fond of sport, and enjoy the pursuit of wild game, with which the country abounds. I remember having a long chat with one of these great hunters, and he told me that the Somali people are entirely different from the 'Fuzzy-Wuzzy,' as the natives of the Soudan are jocularly known. They are more like playful children, and are extremely excitable. If suddenly thrown into a position of danger, they will face it boldly, and are reliable fighters in such circumstances. But they are afraid of uncertainties, and that being the case, are of little use as soldiers. Then, as I dare say you have already heard, they are a scheming and cunning race, so that it is always well to be on the best terms with them, for then one has nothing to fear. On the other hand, if you incur their hatred, you may look out for squalls, and you will find it a wise precaution to put an extra guard over your camels. Indeed, the one serious occupation of the Somali is to keep his own beasts safe from marauders, and to rob his neighbours of as many as possible. Sometimes a few of the men will band together and raid a neighbouring tribe. If they are discovered, they fly for their lives; for camel-stealing, though a recognized crime in the country, is one which is not easily forgiven by those who are attacked, and capture means certain death. But the narrow escape is never taken in the light of a warning, for, on the very first opportunity another raid will be planned and carried out.

"There, I think that will give you a fair idea of the men you will meet during your march; but, because I have described them as a friendly race, you must not on that account omit to take every precaution. You will meet many different tribes, some of which are still friendly to the British, but others which have gone over to the Mullah, whose emissaries are busily at work stirring them up against the white people.

"As for this man, whom we all speak of as the 'Mad' Mullah, he is, I have little doubt, an unscrupulous ruffian. To the Somali he is known as Hadji Mahomed Abdullah. He belongs to the Habr Suleiman section of the Ogaden tribe, who have their hunting-grounds in the southwest of the country. He married into the Ali Ghiri, a Dolbahanta tribe, and is, therefore, connected with a great number of people. But what has given him such a powerful position in Somaliland is the fact that he has made several pilgrimages to Mecca, and, consequently, is considered a man of deep wisdom, and 'hadji,' or holy, as the word is understood here. For some time he has travelled about Somaliland, pillaging the various districts and attacking the peaceful tribes. But it was not until he quarrelled with a certain tribe living in our Protectorate that we took any notice of him. Then we began to gather troops, so as to attack him. Having pillaged the land in this direction, he struck off towards the Abyssinian frontier, and flung himself and his hordes of desperadoes upon the men of that race who happened to be stationed there. I am happy to say that they beat him handsomely, so that he was forced to fly. For some time we heard little more of him, and, no doubt, during all that while he was busily collecting men and arms, the latter being considerably harder to obtain than the former. But there are some rascals who will do anything for money, and amongst them, I regret to say, are a few white people, who, at considerable risk, run cargoes of inferior guns to the coast, and sell them at an exorbitant price, careless of the consequences to the peaceful nations who live within touch of the Mullah.

"In due time his preparations were completed, and he then began to give us further trouble. First, it was by raiding a tribe who lived under our protection, and then by stealing camels from Berbera itself. In one way and another he has steadily made himself a pest to the country, and as he is as cruel as he is unscrupulous, the people have suffered terribly at his hands.

"And now to tell you why Britain should concern herself with the Mullah. The Italians, the French, and ourselves, each hold a Protectorate over a large tract of country along this northern coast of Africa, and there is really no more reason why we should take up the quarrel any more than the others. But then, you know, Britain has always been the one friend of the oppressed. It has been our policy for generations, and we are known the world over as a fighting race who love freedom and hate the oppressor. Look at the manner in which we subdued the Soudan at enormous cost to ourselves, and yet without benefit to our country. This is a sample of the work we do, and we are about to repeat the same process here. Indeed, we have already made one successful attempt, during which we beat the Mullah with heavy loss to himself, and caused him to retreat. But a holy man, in a country like this, has extraordinary power, and the Mullah rapidly took advantage of that fact. Within an incredibly short space of time he gathered together the remnants of his following, and at once began to march through the country preaching a holy war. Those tribes who were reluctant to join him, and who preferred a peaceful existence, were compelled to throw in their lot with him or take the consequences, which meant that they would be robbed in a most scandalous manner, and, possibly, would run the danger of being altogether exterminated. And so the host of warriors marching beneath the banner of the Mullah has steadily and rapidly increased, so much so that they have become a menace to us, and forced us to take action.

"The Foreign Office, which governs this Protectorate, gave orders that a field force should be prepared for service in Somaliland. In January, 1901, the force did not exist, but, by dint of superhuman exertions, fifteen hundred natives were got ready for the fray at the end of May. They consisted almost entirely of Somalis from the neighbouring friendly tribes, and they were trained and taught to use the rifle by a select band of British officers, than whom there are none more expert at this class of work. A score of non-commissioned officers from India helped them, and together they built up a very creditable following. At length, when all arrangements had been made for transport, and sufficient drivers had been engaged, the force marched for Burao to cross the waterless Hoad. Crossing the range of mountains known as the Gobik, they entered the Geratto pass, which leads from the Guban, or low country, to the high country, which is known as the Ogo, and which is very much healthier. From there the troops safely crossed the desert, and entered the Mullah's country. And now, for the first time, they met with opposition, for stragglers hung upon their flanks, sniping at the caravans, and flying whenever an attempt was made to come to close quarters. At length information came to hand that the enemy was a couple of days' march away, and at once it was decided to attack him. Leaving his baggage and the greater part of his camels to the care of a handful of the Somali levy, with Captain McNeill in command, Colonel Swayne, who had charge of the whole expedition, marched forward with the bulk of his men, hoping to come upon the enemy unawares and teach him a lesson.

"You will remember that I mentioned to you a certain characteristic of these people. I told you that in certain circumstances they were bold and reliable, and that, if they were unfriendly to you, it was wise to watch them with the utmost care, on account of their cunning and treachery. The Mullah speedily gave an example of this, and made a crafty move, which might have proved disastrous had it not been for the soldierly qualities and the bravery of Captain McNeill. You may be sure that if we had information of the Mullah's whereabouts, he, also, was well aware of our movements, for his spies and scouts were in all directions. Waiting until Colonel Swayne and his men had marched well away from the camel zareba, this leader struck his 'karia,' or camping-ground, and travelling in a roundabout direction, so as to evade the main column, threw his thousands upon the tiny garrison which was left to protect the camels and baggage. It was a splendid move, and was most successfully accomplished, so far as eluding the main army went. But the Mullah was not to have it all his own way, for he had, as I have just said, a man to deal with who had studied his profession. Put yourself in Captain McNeill's position for one moment, and imagine what you would have done. Knowing that the greater part of the force had marched against the enemy, many men would have put aside all thought of danger, and would have been content with the ordinary precautions which are necessary when campaigning in an enemy's country. But Captain McNeill thought otherwise. It occurred to him that, with a crafty man such as the Mullah was known to be, this was a splendid opportunity for him to fall upon the weaker portion of the force which had come to attack him, and after disposing of that, to march swiftly upon the other part, and take it by surprise. Therefore, he at once made preparations to meet an attack in force. Selecting an excellent site, upon a raised plateau, so situated as to be unapproachable from one side, and altogether cleared of the scrub and undergrowth, which could be so useful to an attacking enemy, he built two zarebas of thorns, strengthened with long stretches of barbed wire, and between the two a third, into which he drove the camels. At the highest point he built a mound, and placed upon it a Maxim, which, owing to its elevation, could command the plateau in all directions, firing over the heads of the defenders when necessary. That done, he sent out scouts in all directions, and having appointed each man to a post and given him precise instructions as to his part in the coming battle, he sat down to await, with as much patience as he could, the appearance of the Mullah and his rascally gang.

"Never before was there such an uneven contest, for you must recollect that in this case the commander of the British zareba had only Somali natives to depend upon, and they were so little trained that they could only be termed raw recruits, while their reliability was a matter of pure conjecture, for they had never yet been called upon to show the stuff of which they were made. In addition, there were a few Indian non-commissioned officers, and one lieutenant from an English line regiment. In all, their numbers were extremely small, while the Mullah would have at least five thousand troops.

"Well, thanks to the foresight of Captain McNeill, all that experience could suggest had been carried out, and, satisfied that this was the case, the garrison waited. They were not to be disappointed, for, scarcely was all in readiness, when quickly moving dots in the distance told them of approaching horsemen, and very soon scores of the Mullah's followers came clambering over the distant sky-line and dashed down into the wide sweeping plain which surrounded the zareba. Evidently with them it was a foregone conclusion that this weak party left in charge of the camels was to be annihilated, and then, what loot there would be! At the thought of the hundreds of camels there, and the huge stores of baggage, their delight was intense, but it was as nothing to their pleasure when spies reported to them that the reserve ammunition of the whole force lay in that zareba, ready to be taken. And what a prize that and the rifles of the defenders would prove! Guns were difficult to obtain at any time, but of late, since the British Government had sent its torpedo-boats to patrol the coast, it had become almost an impossibility to get them, while, in the case of ammunition, it was difficult to lay hands upon the smallest supply of powder.

"No wonder the Mullah, as he looked down from the surrounding heights upon that solitary camp, gave vent to an exclamation of satisfaction. He was exultant, and almost shouted for joy.

"'They are mine!' he shouted; 'the hated foreigners will fall into our hands, and Allah will punish them as they deserve. Press on, my men, and fear not the bullets of the enemy, for I swear to you that they shall do you no harm; and, even though they strike you, they shall melt upon your bodies as the snow turns to water. Rush on them, then, and slay every living man within the zareba.'

"By now, some thousands of dusky warriors had descended into the plain, and while those who we're unmounted pressed forward at their fastest pace, the men who had horses and camels to help them came on impetuously, and it seemed, indeed, as though they would venture alone to attack the tiny garrison. Such, no doubt, was their intention, for, carried away by their fanatical hate, and shrieking loudly so as to encourage one another, and with weapons waved high in the air, they charged at the lines of thorn-bush which surrounded the zareba.

"Were they to break in without opposition, and without losing a man? It looked as though this was to be the case, for not a gun flashed, and not one of the defenders could be seen, save a group of five or six, who stood immovable upon the mound where the Maxim was placed. But the defenders were acting under the orders of their commander, and resolutely held their fire, though the temptation to open upon the oncoming horsemen must have been great indeed. Lying behind the thick thorn-bushes, with rifles in readiness, all in the upper zareba kept their eyes upon that tall, khaki-clad figure standing beside the Maxim. Would he ever give the word? Were they to lie there and suffer death at the hands of the Mullah's soldiers without even attempting to defend themselves? It was a sore trial to untrained troops, to men who up to this had done little else but occupy themselves in agricultural work, broken here and there by a camel raid, the excitement and danger of which was as nothing to that which they were now experiencing.

"'Fire!' The command rang out sharply in the crisp, clear air, and almost instantly the clatter of the Maxim awoke the echoes. Glad to be doing something, the remainder of the defenders joined in the fusillade, and, encouraged by the calmness of their officer, emptied their rifles without throwing away a shot. Scarcely a cry escaped them, for their attention was far too much engaged in the business of exchanging full cartridges for empty ones, and of discharging them against the enemy. And still the latter came on in their hundreds, undaunted as yet, reckless of the consequences, and careless of the numbers killed, so long as they could gratify their hate and slay these insolent invaders. Falling by ones and twos, and very often in groups of five and more, the adherents of the Mullah pressed on with a courage which was truly wonderful, and which was, no doubt, due in part to their leader's promises that no harm should befall them.

"Then, too, these Eastern people have a childish belief in fate. To them Allah's will is everything, and if it is decreed that they shall die, they will meet death boldly. Therefore, though scores of their comrades had already fallen victims to the Maxim, or to the rifle-bullets, the horsemen still dashed forward, while the footmen, coming upon the scene at this moment, rushed to join them, undeterred by the bodies which lay scattered everywhere upon the plain. Armed with Sniders, with elephant-guns, and with cheap muzzle-loaders, which no sane man would have dared to fire, they went bounding forward, shrieking at the top of their voices, and waving their weapons madly in the air. A few of the more cautious ones halted at times, and, dropping upon one knee, discharged a load of slugs at the defenders. But they were up again in a minute, and this time, with sword in hand, flung themselves against the zareba. Leaping upon the thorns as if they did not exist, they hacked desperately at them, endeavouring to force a way through. Coming in contact with the wire, a few became hopelessly entangled, and in due time were killed. And all the while, without cessation, without a moment's pause, the rifles of the defenders flashed forth revengefully, and the Maxim scattered its volleys into the masses of the enemy.

"'They give way, they fly!' shouted the British commander. 'Hold to it, my men! Let them learn that we are not to be so lightly attacked, and that when the time for fighting comes, they have soldiers here to deal with who will make them pay dear for their boldness.'

"At his words the defenders redoubled their efforts, and so fierce and well-aimed was their fire, that at last the hordes gave way. Panting with their efforts, shattered by the terrible hail of bullets which poured continuously amongst them, they turned their backs to the zareba, and, taking to their heels, or applying spurs to the flanks of their animals, fled in dismay. Yes, bleeding and breathless, some of them so grievously wounded that they could not look to live, they raced away across the plain, followed still by those scathing volleys, and when they were out of range, threw themselves upon the ground, cursing their fate, cursing the day on which they had thrown in their lot with the Mullah, and the leader who had betrayed them with false promises. Then, when they had regained their breath, they retired sulkily to the hills, and were quickly lost to sight.

"Not till then had the gallant defenders time to look round and ascertain the losses they had suffered, but it was with a feeling of relief and gratification that their young commander learnt that he had few to mourn, and that in no case had the enemy been able to force a way into the zareba. Had they done so, there is little doubt that their swords would have given them a great advantage, and they would have quickly despatched every one of the defenders. But the thorn-bushes, strengthened as they were by the barbed wire, had effectually kept the enemy out, and the check given to their first rush had enabled the garrison to pour in a stinging fire which, as I have told you, proved sufficient to drive them back into the plain again.

"It was a glorious success, but as yet it was not sufficient to teach the Mullah that he was beaten. His surprise and anger at the result can be imagined, for he had expected to find an easy prey, and had already counted the huge stores of baggage and ammunition as his own. And now, instead of victory, he had to mourn the loss of numbers of his men, and, what was worse, a fall in his own prestige, for he had sworn to the tribesmen who accompanied him that this was a holy war, and that the bullets of the infidels could not possibly harm them.

"However, this 'Mad' Mullah has always been a man of resource, and quickly recovering from his depression, he gathered his followers about him, and harangued them, as he alone knows how to do. A few words from his lips were sufficient to revive their courage and hate, and before very long they were ready to make a second attack. You will remember that I told you that no warning is taken to heart by these people, and that life is held but cheaply in their efforts to obtain camels. This, of course, is no matter for surprise, for in this world men will do much for money, and the beasts I mention are practically the only currency with which the Somali people are acquainted. They pay their debts with these animals, and their wives are bought at the cost of so many camels. If they are engaged as followers on a shooting expedition, the promise of a camel or more proves a far more tempting bait than does the rupee, particularly to the tribesmen who come from the interior. The men hereabouts are, perhaps, a little more civilized, and are always eager for the large silver coin.

"Can you be surprised, after what I have told you, that the sight of that small British zareba, with its piles of baggage and its hundreds of beasts, proved a tantalizing object to the Mullah's followers? From their position of security in the hills they looked down at the three circles of thorn-bushes, and saw the defenders moving busily about, saw their scouts leave their comrades and ride out into the plain, and watched with longing eyes as the camels were driven down to the river, which formed one side of the zareba. Then, forgetful of the reverse which they had recently suffered, they swore that they would not leave the place until they were conquerors.

"A few hours later, therefore, they stole down from the hills, and separating so as to approach the zareba from every available point, crept softly towards it, hoping to take the defenders unawares. But, again, they were bitterly disappointed, for scarcely had they sprung to their feet and begun to charge, when the rattle of the Maxim set the hills echoing again, and the angry snap of the rifles told that the defenders were fully awake, and ready to receive them, I will not describe the contest to you, though it was even more severe and exciting than the first. It suffices to say that the Mullah and his followers were driven off with heavy loss, and that so great was their consternation, that they at once left the neighbourhood of the zareba and fled towards the interior. Meanwhile news had reached Colonel Swayne, and promptly facing about, he marched to intercept the enemy. Meeting him in his flight, his horsemen quickly scattered his Somalis, and chased them for miles, killing and capturing large numbers. But the Mullah, unfortunately, contrived to escape, and galloped away into the desert with a few of his followers.

"From that date nothing was heard of this fanatic for many weeks. But in time he re-established himself in the favour of the people, and, collecting a band of desperadoes, began his old tricks again. Soon there were tales of him from every part, and such a pest did he become that another expedition was decided upon. It proved a failure, for, meeting the Mullah and his forces face to face, our Somali levies showed the white feather, and bolted, leaving the expedition to its fate. Fortunately, however, the greater part of it contrived to escape, and to reach Berbera in safety. It was now apparent that operations on a larger scale must be contemplated, and as the Somalis had shown themselves to be unreliable, it was determined to employ native troops from the West Coast of Africa, and Indian soldiers. If you were staying here to-morrow, you would see these men about the town, and would obtain some idea of the preparations we are making, but I understand that you are pushing forward at once, a plan which I think is advisable. However, it is more than probable that you will meet with the troops later on, and who knows but that they may even prove of service to you? And that reminds me of my instructions. If you are in need of help, and our troops are within reach of you, do not hesitate to send word to their officer, who will hold out a hand to you, if it is possible."

CHAPTER VIII

PREPARING TO ADVANCE

"I think I have now given you all the information I possess," continued the Consul, after a pause, "and at the risk of appearing anxious to be rid of you, I suggest that you should lose no time in going to your camp. It is already upon nine o'clock, and you will scarcely reach it within an hour. After that progress will be very slow, for marching at night with a convoy of camels is no light undertaking. And now it only remains for me to wish you all success in your enterprise. May you, Mr. Hubbard, return within a short period with your father, and you, Mr. Dixon, reach us once again primed with information concerning the Mullah. Good-bye, and good luck!"

Rising from his seat, the Consul advanced towards Jim and his friend, and shook them most warmly by the hand. Then thrusting the roll of matting, which did service as a blind, on one side, he opened the sash of the window, and stepped out upon the verandah. A hasty inspection satisfied him that there was no one about, and he returned to communicate his news to his guests. Five minutes later the two friends were racing across the compound. When they reached the shadow of the belt of trees, Jim halted, and gripped his comrade by the arm.

"Let us wait here for a few minutes, as we did before," he said, "for it might happen that one of the servants overheard our conversation, and is waiting somewhere near at hand to catch sight of the Consul's visitors."

"Right," his companion answered promptly. "I was thinking just the same, and I know the precaution is a wise one."

Accordingly they lay down upon the ground, and remained in that position for nearly a quarter of an hour. Then they rose to their feet again, and moved away like ghosts, for their sandals made not the slightest noise as they walked. When they had put some three hundred yards between themselves and the bungalow, they halted again, so as to make certain that they were going in the right direction.

"Through the town, and bear to the left, away from the sea-coast, the Consul told us," said Jim, whose spirits were now roused to the highest by the prospect before him. "Ali Kumar has been warned to be prepared to meet us, and, I hope, will have quietly made arrangements to move away. If that is the case, and no one happens to be near, we ought to disappear without exciting curiosity, and without arousing the suspicions of the Mullah's spies."

"After that, we'll strike along the coast-line," broke in Tom, "and march until we come to some wells of which I have been told, and with which our shikari is certain to be acquainted. The following day we shall ride over to the village in which the man lives who gave information about your father. That done, we have only to collect our stores when the dhow arrives, and march straight for the interior. It's going to be a risky business, Jim; and I tell you plainly, that the more I think of it, the more do I realize the danger and difficulties we have to face. Don't think I am getting nervous, old chap," he continued hastily, "but we shall have to be extremely cautious, for this Mullah has just obtained a victory, and that fact alone will make him even more audacious, and will obtain for him the help and support of many who have hitherto held aloof."

"I agree with you, Tom, and I am quite sure that we shall find it well to steer clear of all these encampments. If we march into the interior, demanding of all we meet whether they have heard of a white prisoner who recently fell into the hands of the Mullah, I am quite sure our doings will be reported, and that we shall call down upon our heads the wrath of this fanatic. I have been thinking the matter out as we came along, and have hit upon a plan which might serve us. Let us tell anyone with whom we come in contact that we have been in the service of the 'Sirkal,' or the Government, but that we are tired of them, and have decided to throw in our lot with the Mullah. The fact that I do not speak the language will not matter greatly, for, you see, I can be put down as from Aden, where all sorts of nationalities are to be found. But I shall contrive on all occasions to keep my mouth closed."

"It sounds well," answered Tom thoughtfully; "but what about our men? Knowing that we are Englishmen, they will quickly spread the news abroad, so that everyone will know."

"Much depends upon Ali Kumar," replied Jim decisively. "If he has told them that they are in the employ of Englishmen, a portion of my plan will fall through, but otherwise, we shall adhere to it, if you are agreeable."

"Perfectly! And now let us push on."

Accordingly, walking side by side, and taking no notice of those whom they occasionally passed, save that Tom returned their salutation, the two pressed on, and passed rapidly through the Arab town. Then they bore to the left, and within half an hour came in sight of a zareba. By now a small crescent of the moon had risen in the sky, and its light enabled them to see that some sixty camels lay stretched upon the ground, while close at hand were other smaller figures, the followers who had been engaged to accompany them into the interior. Standing in a listening attitude, a few paces away, was a tall man, dressed in white robes. He bore a lantern in his hand, and every now and again lifted it so as to throw the light farther afield, as if he were expecting someone. Suddenly he had heard Jim and Tom advancing, and recognizing them, even though they were disguised, he came towards them, salaaming deeply.

"Welcome, my masters," he said eagerly. "I am Ali Kumar, and I was warned to be ready for your coming. Here is the camp, with thirty men lying there sleeping, but prepared to march at any moment. Give your orders, and I will see that they are obeyed."

Again he salaamed, and, lifting his lantern, looked long and closely into Jim's face, as if he were anxious to ascertain what sort of lad he was to follow.

"Good!" he exclaimed at length. "You are young, full young for this enterprise, but you are brave—that I can plainly see in your eyes. And how could you be otherwise, for no one who was not possessed of courage could go upon this expedition, even for the sake of his father."

"Have you heard news of him?" asked Jim eagerly, taking no notice of his remarks.

"None," was the answer. "I have but lately arrived, and know little more than I did a week ago. But to-morrow, when we meet the man who saw your father, we shall obtain all the information that is possible. Is it your wish that we march at once?"

"Yes; for the sooner we are off the better I shall be pleased. Do you know the direction to take? We are informed that there are wells within twenty miles of here, where we ought to halt."

"I can follow the road in the dark as surely as in broad daylight," was the reassuring answer. "Stay here, masters, and I will send camels to you. You could have had horses, had the saddles arrived, but at present we have not received them."

Leaving the lantern with Jim and his companion, Ali Kumar went across to the sleeping men and gave a quick order. Then he returned leading two enormous camels, which grunted and grumbled at being disturbed, as only animals of that class can.

"Keep a strict watch upon their heads," said Ali, in warning tones to Jim, "for these beasts are as treacherous as the followers of the Mullah, and love nothing better than to seize with their teeth anyone who may be passing. Then, too, they will kick out with their feet when people pass too close behind them. I have seen more than one man killed in that way. Hau! Lie down!"

He shouted the words in the native tongue, and at once, obedient to the command, but still giving vent to extraordinary grunts, the two camels sank to the ground, and waited there to receive their riders.

"Sit sideways," said Ali, taking Jim by the sleeve; for he saw that his young master was wholly unaccustomed to such a steed. "Now put your right leg round this piece of the saddle which sticks up in front, and hook it there. That is the way; and now you can slip your foot into the stirrup which dangles here, and will feel safe even when the animal begins to trot."

Jim carefully followed the instructions given to him, and was surprised to find that, though intensely uncomfortable at first, his seat was secure, and allowed him to turn freely, and without the fear that he was about to fall from the saddle. Having settled himself, and watched Tom take his place with the ease obtained from long practice, Jim gave the word, and at once, on a sharp command from Ali, the camels rose to their feet, swaying wildly from side to side as they did so, in a manner which threatened to throw their riders to the ground, and groaning in such loud and guttural tones that one would have thought the effort was a severe one.

Meanwhile the sleeping camp had suddenly awakened into bustling life. Men hurried here and there, and the camels were forced to their feet by a succession of loud shouts, and often, too, by means of the free application of the haft of a spear, for they disliked this sudden disturbance. But at last all were ready, and, at a sign from Ali, the cavalcade streamed off into the night, the animals looking decidedly ghostly in the uncertain light. In twos and threes, and sometimes in bigger groups, they took the direction of the wells, leaving the neighbourhood of Berbera without a soul being the wiser.

"No one will know what has happened to us," said Ali, forcing his beast up to the one which Jim was bestriding. "We have given it out that we are in the service of the Governor, and as it is quite the custom for camels to be sent on to one of the advance stations up-country without warning, the natives will think that nothing out of the way has happened."

"But what about the men?" asked Jim. "Do they think that they, too, are hired by the Sirkal?"

"That is the case, master; but I have quietly sounded them, and I have learnt that they are willing to go anywhere, so long as good pay is promised them. Half of these followers were with me once before in an expedition, and I can fully trust them; the remainder are, however, strangers to me. But I think you will find them brave and reliable."

"I want to ask another question," said Jim, as they rode along. "My friend and I think that if we go into the interior disguised as we are, we shall arouse no suspicion, and shall have a better chance of evading the Mullah. What do you think of the plan? And, is it possible to keep our nationality from the followers?"

Ali Kumar did not answer for some moments, but bent his head upon his breast, as if lost in thought. Then he looked across at Jim and shook his head emphatically.

"No; it is not altogether a good plan, and not a bad," he said. "If you attempt to deceive these men who act as followers, they will certainly discover your secret before many days are past, and will think the worse of you for not taking them into your confidence. Besides, some of the men who went with me before already know of your mission. But they are to be fully trusted, as I said. To hoodwink the Mullah and the tribes with which we happen to come in contact is, however, a ruse which carries great weight with it, and I think with you that it will be well if you and your friend go dressed as you are. If we are questioned, you can stay in the background while I do the necessary talking, and if strangers insist on speaking with you, you can freely admit that you are

English, and that you have found it more convenient to travel in the guise of a native.

"That would probably lead to trouble; but, then, you are sure to meet with some, however cautious you are. And now, master, I will go to the head of the cavalcade, and will lead them, for, though the moon is bright, it is easy to lose the way at night."

Salaaming to Jim and Tom, he spurred his camel forward with his heel, and was not seen again till the following morning. Just as day was breaking he came to the rear again, and reported that the wells were at hand, and that the camels and men were already settling in the camp.

"And now, if the masters are ready, we shall ride on to the village of which you have heard. It is only an hour from here, so that we shall be back before the sun is overhead."

"We are ready. Show us the way," answered Jim promptly; "and let us hope that this fellow will have good news for us."

Accordingly, waiting for one minute to watch their followers, who were preparing to water their beasts, they turned their faces towards the east, and, with the sun striking full into their eyes, pushed on through beautifully green country, dotted in all directions by trees. This was, indeed, a small oasis, surrounding the wells, which, by the many footprints that could be seen indenting the ground, was evidently frequented by numerous animals, which, no doubt, came there to obtain water. Farther on, however, as they increased their distance from the camp, the stretches of closely cropped grass gave place to an interminable sandy waste, devoid of all vegetation, and obstructed here and there by enormous dunes of glistening sand, which had been built up by the wind. An hour's ride brought them to a tiny village, and soon they were conversing with the man who had given the information of Colonel Hubbard's capture. But he had no further news.

"It chanced that a beast of mine had strayed from its feeding-ground," he said, "so that, mounting my pony, I rode into the desert, hoping to discover it. Suddenly I saw a group of tents beyond me with armed men about, and caution prompted me to watch ere I approached them. It was not long before I had every reason to congratulate myself upon my care, for they proved to be a marauding expedition sent down to the coast by the Mullah. As I lay behind a hill of sand, keeping my eyes upon them, I observed a man struggling wearily towards the shore, through the surf which was breaking heavily upon it. Creeping nearer, I watched him, and soon made out that he was a white man. Then, as I was about to run forward to warn him, the Somali warriors suddenly espied him, and, shouting to one another, galloped in his direction. For three hours I watched, and saw the camp break up and the expedition ride away with their prisoner, and then I learned by questioning a follower who had been left behind, having broken a leg, that the prisoner was a colonel, as you speak of the leaders of your soldiers. More than that, I do not know, save his looks, which I will describe to you."

The native then gave a description of the appearance of the Mullah's prisoner, and as Jim listened with all his ears, any doubt that he might still have had as to the identity of the man who had reached the shore was set definitely at rest, for it was beyond question that it was his father. Having assured himself that no further information was to be obtained, he made the man a handsome present, and then the party turned about, and retraced their steps towards the camp. On the following day they pushed farther along the coast, and, when the next morning dawned, had the satisfaction of observing a dhow beating in for the shore. It proved to be the one which they were expecting, and before the day had passed she had safely discharged her cargo.

"And now to begin our work in earnest," said Jim, surveying the piled-up baggage. "I propose that we issue rifles at once to those who can use them, and that we give them a preliminary training. That done, we'll appoint certain of the men to act as scouts, while others will be in charge of the baggage-camels. I should say that if we march with five men thrown well forward and on the flanks, and another five in the rear, we ought to feel secure from a sudden rush. What do you think, Tom?"

"That the plan is an excellent one, old boy, and shows that you have your wits about you. As an additional precaution, I suggest that one or other of us should always ride with these scouts, Ali Kumar accompanying the one who goes in front, for it is from that direction that danger is to be expected. Then, I think that we ought to make up our minds what action we are to take should we be suddenly attacked. You see, it wouldn't do to be thrown into confusion and have these followers of ours firing wildly in all directions."

"Quite so, Tom, and for that purpose I propose a preliminary training. We've a couple of hours of daylight left, and we know that there is no one to watch our movements, for Ali Kumar posted half a dozen of our men this morning right away on the hills over there. Let us give the order to strike camp; and, by the way, what about mounts for ourselves?"

"For the purpose of the march we shall find ponies far more useful than camels," answered Tom promptly; "for the ponies can carry one at a swift gallop for a few miles, and will enable us to keep easily in touch with our front and rear guards. For longer stretches, however, for instance when we desire to reach quickly a spot some twenty miles away and return with equal despatch, the camels will prove most valuable, for, once fed and watered, they will go on for hours at a steady swinging pace, which soon gets over the distance. No wonder they are called 'ships of the desert,' for, with their extraordinary powers, their spider-like legs, and their broad, soft feet, they are eminently fitted for such a country. But can you ride, Jim?"

"I've been on a horse several times in my life, Tom, but I can't say that I ever felt very comfortable. But if it is necessary to ride, I will learn, whatever it costs me."

"Then we'll give orders for a couple of the ponies to be saddled and bridled," said Tom, "and for the camp to move on."

Accordingly they called for Ali Kumar, and directed him to see the baggage loaded. Then, for half an hour, they toiled with their followers, struggling in the midst of a group of recumbent camels, busily lashing burdens on the animals' backs. That done, all the natives were gathered together, and fifteen of them, who professed to be able to use the rifle, were supplied with weapons, the remainder continuing to carry swords and spears only. Then ten of those who were provided with firearms were mounted upon the best ponies, and given strict orders as to their behaviour.

"They are terribly excitable people, these Somali races," said Tom, "and I have often been told that when employed as scouts they are continually giving the alarm. Perhaps they see a buck in the distance, or the peak of a mountain comes into their line of vision, and at once, turning about, they gallop furiously back to the column behind them, shouting at the top of their voices, and waving their weapons above their heads. Then they pull up in a matter of two yards, and express their astonishment at finding a hasty zareba formed, and preparations already made for an attack. It is all done to show off, for they are just like children, and love to attract attention to themselves. But as we cannot afford to be in a condition of constant alarm, we had better warn them that they will meet with our displeasure if they behave in such a way."

Tom's words were communicated to Ali Kumar, who, with Jim beside him, at once began to address the followers, impressing their duties upon them, and making them repeat the instructions. Then they were dismissed, and at once mounted, the men who were to look after the camels clambering into their seats. At this moment three spirited-looking native ponies were brought forward for the use of the leaders of the party. Giving them a hasty inspection, and pausing for a moment to see that the stirrup-leathers were of the right length, Jim selected the one nearest to him, and at once proceeded to mount.

"Hold the reins like this," said Tom, coming to his side so as to show him. "Now, while you grip them with your left hand, catch up a wisp of the mane with your right, and twist it round the spare fingers of your left. That's the way. Now put your foot in the stirrup, and up you go!"

Following these instructions carefully, for hitherto he had had very little acquaintance with horses, Jim was quickly seated in the saddle, and feeling the opposite stirrup dangling beside his sandal, thrust his foot into it. Meanwhile the pony had made no objection, but had stood there, with ears thrown back, and eyes cast suspiciously at his new master. Then, probably realizing that he had a more or less new hand to deal with, he gave vent to a loud squeal of anger, and started away with a bound which almost shook Jim from his seat.

"Keep his head up, and your knees well pressed into the saddle!" sang out Tom. "Now, watch him, for he's going to play a trick upon you."

That this was the case was quickly evident, for, finding that his first efforts to dislodge his rider were unsuccessful, the pony went off at a furious gallop, kicking his legs high in the air as he did so. Then, when in the very midst of the loaded camels, he suddenly ducked his head between his forelegs, and, arching his back, sprang high into the air. It was a fatal movement for Jim, who at once shot forward into space, and, turning as he went, landed full upon the broad of his back. In a moment he was on his feet again, gasping for breath, but determined not to be beaten. Fortunately he had been thrown upon a sandy patch, and though shaken considerably, he was by no means hurt. As for the pony, now that it had accomplished its purpose, it stood there unconcernedly, as if it were incapable of such behaviour. Jim at once walked up to it, and gathering the reins in his hand as Tom had shown him, thrust his sandalled foot into the stirrup, and was in the saddle again in a twinkling.

"Well done!" shouted Tom; while the natives, who were all looking on in the most interested manner, gave vent to exclamations of approval. "Well done! Stick to him like a leech, and show him that you mean to be his master!"

"I will, even if I'm thrown twenty times," answered Jim, setting his teeth, and sitting down closer to his saddle. "Now then! On you go!"

The animal needed no second bidding, and at once set off at a rapid pace. But this time, when it attempted to go through the old movement which had proved so successful, Jim gave a sharp jerk to the reins, and kept its head well up. Again it made the attempt, but without success, and then, unable to get rid of its rider by means of bucking, the spirited pony suddenly darted to one side, and Jim, losing his balance, was deposited upon the ground once more. Four times in succession was he thrown, but in every case he clambered into his seat again, and finally, after the animal had bolted with him at its topmost speed for a mile or more, he managed to quiet it down by patting it upon the neck, and talking to it in a soothing voice. Then he turned it about, and with the beast well in hand this time, came trotting back into the camp, with flushed face and dusty garments, but triumphant and elated. As he did so, Tom gave vent to a cheer, while the natives hammered their spear-heads loudly upon their shields in approbation.

"You have done well, master," said Ali Kumar, coming forward as Jim dismounted in their midst. "These men already know that you are an Englishman, and that you are their leader. They have been waiting to learn what manner of man you are, and whether you are bold enough to ride into the Mullah's country. It was easy to see that you were no great horseman, and, believe me, your courage in mounting again and again, and in laughing at your falls, has raised you high in their estimation. They will now obey your words far more willingly than they would otherwise have done. But we are ready; shall we move on?"

Jim agreed with a wave of his hand, and at once the cavalcade was set in motion. Forty of the camels, which were laden with every variety of bale and box, marched in the centre, while close behind them came twenty others, which could be relied upon to trot for many hours together, all roped to one another. Near them were the followers who were not to act as scouts, keeping an eye upon them lest they should attempt to stray, and prepared to make secure any bundle which showed signs of breaking loose. Spread out like a fan, a mile ahead, were five well-mounted men, while a similar number stood by their horses at the camping-ground, waiting until the column moved well away. And in this order, with Jim and Ali Kumar walking their ponies in company with the front guard, and Tom with the rear, they pushed on in a southerly direction, their faces turned towards a distant hazy blue line which showed the position of the range of hills they would have to cross before reaching the highlands, and the broad stretch of desert which intervened between themselves and the Mullah's country.

Jim was in the highest spirits, and delighted to feel that at last the search for his father had begun. For a time he rode beside Ali Kumar, conversing with him, and then he trotted back towards the camels. Having assured himself that all was well with them, he was about to return to his post, when suddenly one of the scouts, stationed away on the flank, came galloping towards him at top speed, shouting and waving frantically. At the same moment, catching sight of him, the other scouts retired upon their centre.

"Probably a false alarm," Jim told himself; "but I shall take every precaution. Down!" he shouted, signalling to the followers to stop the camels. Then, remembering the native word used on such an occasion, he repeated it loudly.

Collecting their beasts together, the men quickly had them lying upon the ground. Then, obedient to Jim's signs, they left two of their number to guard them, and separating, ran forward some fifty yards. There they halted, and knelt upon the ground, ready for anything that might turn up. A few minutes later Ali Kumar and the scouts joined them, and the former at once sharply interrogated the man who had given the alarm.

"What did you see?" he asked.

"A group of camels three miles to the right," was the answer. "As far as I could see, they were browsing quietly, and had no attendants."

The words were interpreted to Jim, who immediately gave orders for the column to move on again.

"We'll send a couple of our scouts over in that direction," he said to Ali Kumar, "and you must tell them that they are to ride near enough to be able to obtain full information, without themselves being seen. Let all these fellows know at the same time that they are to investigate anything which may turn up within a reasonable distance, and that they are not, on any account, to come galloping back until they are sure that there is real danger. Let us have a signal in a case like that, so that all may understand."

"That is a first-rate idea," cried Tom, who had been listening to the conversation. "If we are certain of danger, we need not fear making a noise, and, therefore, it would be as well to fire a rifle. A shot out here, in this atmosphere, will be heard for a couple of miles, and will give due warning to all of our men. Immediately they hear it, they can turn and gallop back to the centre."

Ali Kumar gathered the scouts about him for the second time, and, having again impressed the caution upon them, despatched them to take up their posts. Then the camels were ordered to rise, and once more the column took the road. Shortly after darkness fell a bright moon climbed into the sky, and, aided by its light, they kept on steadily. At nine o'clock they halted, and at once the followers were sent to cut thorn-bushes, which grew in profusion everywhere. With these a thick wall, or zareba, was formed about the camels, which meanwhile had been relieved of their burdens. A second hedge was constructed near at hand, and in this the two young leaders and their following took their places. Very soon a fire was burning brightly, and an hour later they were all seated at their evening meal.

Two days passed uneventfully, and then, one evening, as the column rested at the foot of the hills, Ali Kumar slipped away from his companions, who were already fast asleep, except for the few who were stationed some fifty paces off as sentries, and creeping to Jim's side, touched him gently upon the shoulder.

"Hush, master!" he whispered. "Awake, and listen, for I have news of treachery for you. Within an hour, at any moment, indeed, we may be attacked, for I have discovered that one of our followers, who was a stranger to me until a few days ago, has been in conversation with some wandering natives, and has even now stolen away from the zareba so as to join them and lead them to the attack."

CHAPTER IX

AGAINST HEAVY ODDS

Worn out by a long day's march in the sun, Jim had wrapped himself in his blanket at an early hour, and had fallen into a heavy sleep. It was with a start, therefore, and with an involuntary clutch at the rifle which lay beside him, that he suddenly raised himself into a sitting position, to find Ali Kumar beside him.

"Treachery!" he whispered, as if dazed. "What news have you to give to me?"

The leader of the native followers repeated his words in low tones, and again warned him to keep silent.

"I have watched the man of whom I speak for these two days past," he said. "And I have learnt that he is a traitor. Three times I have seen him conversing with natives when supposed to be watching the camels which were out grazing. Creeping towards him like a snake, I hid in a thorn-bush, and listened with all my ears, but they whispered to one another, so that I could not make out their words. This evening, after our zareba was formed, I followed him again, and saw him meet two men, who, by their dress, were the chiefs of a neighbouring tribe. He pointed to the camels, and counted their number upon his fingers. Then I saw them turn towards the entrance of this pass through which we are to go on the morrow."

"'We will meet you there,' cried one of the chiefs, 'and perhaps even attack before you enter. But my men do not like the darkness to fight in, and besides, in the confusion and alarm, the beasts might be slain or scattered. But we shall see; Allah will help us in this enterprise, for are not the followers in the zareba servants of the infidel?'

"That, master, is what I overheard," continued Ali, "and returning to the camp, I made plans to give you the warning; but there were many eyes watching me, and so I waited until now."

"You did wisely," said Jim quietly, now sitting bolt upright, and fully awake. "We'll get my comrade to join us, and then will decide what is to be done, for this is a serious matter, and, unless we take instant steps to protect ourselves, may lead to disaster."

Accordingly, he stretched out his hand and shook Tom gently, explaining to him as soon as he was awake the reason for his doing so.

"And now we have to decide what is to be done," he said. "If we sit here, and take no measures to protect ourselves, it is probable that this scoundrel who has betrayed us will induce the tribesmen to attack to-night. The moon is full, so that they would have every advantage, for our zareba lies bathed in the light, while they would be hidden in the crevices of the rocks."

"I don't see that we can do much else than awake our followers and warn the sentries to be alert," Tom whispered in reply. "If these fellows do attack us, we must lie down and answer their fire; but I fear that our camels will suffer heavily."

"Where are these men likely to come from?" asked Jim, suddenly, turning to Ali Kumar. "If they live in the highlands, and march upon us by way of the pass, I think we ought to arrange a trap for them. If it were carefully laid and proved successful, the lesson might be a warning to them, and teach them to leave us alone."

"They will descend from the hills, master, of that I am sure; for the chiefs whom I observed in conversation with our follower were men from the highlands, without doubt."

"Then I propose that we divide our forces," said Jim, after a thoughtful pause. "Will you, Tom, stay here, and defend the zareba with one half, while I take the other? Then, with Ali Kumar to help me, I shall creep up the pass, and select a spot where the road is narrow and difficult. There we shall lie down and wait for the tribesmen. If they come down in force, and do not turn back when we call to them, we will empty our rifles into their midst; and I think that if we are careful in choosing the site, we ought to be able to do a large amount of execution. That, I take it, is the only way to persuade those people to leave us alone."

"I'll willingly do as you say, Jim, old boy," Tom answered readily, wondering as he did so at the coolness and foresight shown by his young companion. "Your plan sounds an excellent one, and the only suggestion I have to make is that you should shout loudly as you return, or you may be drawing our fire upon you. You see, these native followers of ours are excitable fellows, and hearing the sound of people approaching, and being in fear of an attack, they would blaze recklessly into the darkness."

"Then I'll be careful to call out your name, Tom, and you will be able to explain to the men that all is well. Now I'll be off, as these tribesmen may appear at any moment, though I fancy it is too early for them yet. They will probably wait till the early morning, when we ought to be in our deepest sleep, and should therefore fall easy victims. But, thanks to Ali Kumar, we have been warned, and if we do not take advantage of that fact, we shall have only ourselves to blame. Good-bye, and don't get fidgety if I do not return for some hours, for, as I have just said, we shall probably have to wait a considerable time before they put in an appearance."

Nodding coolly to his companion, Jim rose to his feet, and silently crossed the zareba to the spot where the followers lay sleeping. One by one, those who were armed with rifles, and could be trusted to stand by their master in a position of danger, were aroused and cautioned to keep silent. At length fifteen were collected, and with these and a sufficient quantity of ammunition Jim stole out from the zareba, and took the narrow and rough road which led to the pass. He left Tom busily engaged in instructing the remainder. These were also armed with rifles now, though they were less expert than their comrades. Still, at close range they could be trusted to give a good account of themselves, and to aid in keeping the enemy at a distance. Then the sentries were brought in closer to the wall of thorns, and ordered to lie down, so that they should be invisible to the enemy, for while they were standing the rays of the moon falling upon their tall figures threw long shadows, which would soon have drawn the fire of the tribesmen.

Thanks to the brightness of the night, Jim and his little party had no difficulty in picking their way, for every boulder, and each nullah, or ravine, stood clearly outlined. They were soon at the bottom of a gentle ascent, which marked the beginning of the pass. But here the road was broad, and would have been difficult to defend.

"They would manage to slip round us," said Jim in Ali Kumar's ear, taking note of the surroundings. "I want to get to a part where the pass narrows to a few yards only. If we can find such a position, we shall pile boulders across the road, and post our men behind them. Then every shot we fire will tell, for these Somalis who are about to attack us will certainly come in force, and as they will not be expecting danger until they reach the bottom of the gorge, they are likely to be marching in close order. That will be our chance, and if it occurs, we will make the most of it."

"I know of a position which will suit your wishes, master," answered Ali. "Often have I made my way by this road, so often indeed that I could find the path during a darker night than this is. We must keep on for another quarter of a mile, as you English people speak of distance, and then we shall find that the hill to the right and left of us closes in suddenly, as if about to obstruct our further progress. I think that, at some time, years ago perhaps, a river must have forced its way from the highlands through these hills on its way to the plains below and to the sea. Whatever the cause, the crags are cleft in twain a little way above us, so that a road is possible. Half a mile farther on the land recedes as suddenly as it runs together here, and by marching for an hour one finds one's self again in the midst of a sweeping plain, but this time far higher than before."

"It sounds as if it would prove a likely place," said Jim, eagerly, "so let us push on, I am in a fever to get our men into their positions, for if these tribesmen happened to advance now instead of later on, our plans would be ruined, and we ourselves should be in a very dangerous fix."

Striding ahead through the darkness, Jim encouraged his followers to greater exertions by the example which he set them. So rapidly did they walk, that barely ten minutes had elapsed before he became aware that the gorge in which they were was narrowing. Soon he could see black walls of rock on either hand, and a moment or two later it seemed as though the road itself had suddenly come to an end. Nothing but pitch black darkness could be seen before them, while the path at their feet was buried in obscurity, the rays of the moon having been cut off by the steep cliffs. But a careful search revealed the interesting fact that there was a broad cleft in the wall in front of them, through which the road passed on its way to the highlands.

"The very place for us," whispered Jim, almost giving vent to a cry of exultation, so great was his delight. "This gorge cannot be more than five yards in width, and will suit capitally. You say that it continues for another half-mile at the same width?"

"No, master, I said not at the same," answered Ali Kumar hastily. "From this spot for twenty paces perhaps, it is as narrow, while the road is littered with big rocks and boulders, which are difficult to cross. Farther on, however, it widens gradually, and then, at the distance you mentioned, suddenly, till one finds one's self in the open again."

"If that is the case, these men who are coming to steal our beasts will crowd together without meaning to do so," said Jim thoughtfully.

"That will be the case, master. They will descend the pass without great caution, for the traitor who was of our number will have told them that our sentries are never posted more than a few yards from the zareba. Therefore they will have no need to observe much stealth till they emerge lower down. They will walk together or separately, knowing that the difficulty of the path at this end of the gorge will impede the progress of those who are in front, and allow all the stragglers to come up with them. After that, no doubt, they will send scouts ahead, and follow like ghosts, hoping to take us unawares."

"We shall have something to say to that, I think," Jim answered, indulging in a chuckle at the thought. "I've been busily making plans, Ali, and I have decided to act in this way. We have fifteen men with us, and our two selves. If more than a third of that number attempted to hold the bottom of the pass, it would lead to certain confusion, for the space is very small. Now, it has occurred to me that the surprise would be far greater if we were to separate a little. For instance, we will give five of the natives orders to remain here, and let them set to work at once to pile a ridge of rocks across the path. Then we will climb the cliff on either side, and if we can find ledges big enough for the purpose, we will send the remainder to them."

"It is a great plan, master," said Ali, salaaming to Jim in his enthusiasm. "A truly clever one with which to entrap these people, and it shows that our leader is not only brave—as we clearly saw when he first mounted his horse—but wise and far-seeing also. We are fortunate indeed, for it sometimes happens that the lives of all in such an expedition as this are sacrificed because of the want of discretion in the one who commands it. Yes, it is a good plan, and it should prove successful. There are surely ledges above us to which active men such as we have could climb, and from which they could pour a scathing fire into the enemy. Perhaps, even, they might be posted farther up the gorge, with a pile of boulders at their feet. There is nothing that strikes fear into the hearts of those who are unaware of danger as the sudden descent of rocks upon their heads. They fly in terror to right and left, but cannot escape, and if they turn with the hope of retreat, it sometimes happens that the road is blocked by their comrades. Then, indeed, is the time when men become wild with fright, and suffer defeat at the hands of a few."

"Perhaps it may turn out in that way to-night," Jim said thoughtfully. "I do not wish to harm a single one of these tribesmen, but if they really mean to attack us for the sake of the loot which they would get, then they must take the consequences. Of course, we might retreat, but if we shirk this danger and difficulty now, we shall never succeed in reaching the Mullah's country. We should be laughed at by everyone, and should have cause to be ashamed of ourselves. No, I have decided to go on with my undertaking, whatever happens, and if these fellows interfere with us, they must look to themselves. I shall get you to warn them, and if after that they still come on, hoping to overpower us by numbers, then I shall blaze into the middle of them, and the severer the lesson they are taught, the better it will be for us in the future, for the other tribes will hear of the conflict, and will take the warning to heart. And now let us place the men."

Anxious as he was to get all in readiness for the expected attack, Jim would not allow his fears to hurry him unduly, for it was important to obtain the most advantageous position. To allot five of the followers to the mouth of the ravine was an easy task, and very soon those who had been selected were busily engaged in preparing a low breastwork which would give them shelter should the tribesmen possess firearms, as was very likely, and discharge them in that direction. Jim waited patiently beside them, directing their operations, and was not satisfied till a wall some four feet high was erected, with niches cunningly left near the base through which the muzzles of the rifles could be thrust. Then, accompanied by Ali Kumar alone, he scaled the steep cliff on the right, and set to work to look for a ledge which would do for his purpose.

"Here is one," he exclaimed at last, when after a very difficult piece of climbing they had ascended some twenty yards or more. "This piece of rock juts out from the face of the ravine, and will allow the men to fire down into it, while the edge will protect them."

"It is well chosen," agreed the native headman, creeping to the edge and looking over. "Standing here, we are in deep shadow, but in an hour, when the moon has risen higher into the sky, the light will fall full into the gorge, and every object will be visible. Yes, master, it is wisely chosen, for how can the enemy return our fire when it comes from the darkness of the rocks?"

Bidding Ali call gently to five more of the men, Jim waited to see them take up their appointed posts, and left them there with strict orders that they were not to make a sound, and were not to attempt to open fire until the word was given. Then he and his companion descended, and made their way up the face of the opposite cliff. It was even a harder climb than the other had been, but after winning their way up for a distance of a few yards only, they had the good fortune to strike upon a narrow ledge which seemed to wind up the face of the rock. At the best of times it offered but a precarious footing, but now, when it was attempted in darkness, it was a hazardous undertaking. But Jim made light of the danger. Indeed, he gave no thought to it, for all his attention was occupied in the search for a favourable and commanding site. Thanks to the soft sandals which he wore, he was able to obtain a firmer footing than would have been possible had he been shod with boots, and taking advantage of the feeling of security which this gave him, he clambered steadily upwards, Ali following closely behind him, and giving notice of his presence by his hard breathing. Suddenly the tiny ledge broadened out, and on halting for a few seconds to rest, Jim became aware of the fact that the cliff had receded, leaving a small shelf, capable of accommodating thirty or more men.

"We are in luck!" he cried joyfully. "This part of the cliff overhangs the gorge below, and is some yards from the entrance. I can feel boulders everywhere, so that our fellows will not have to search far for missiles. Then, too, there is no danger of their dropping them on their comrades, for they will be well out of range. Yes, it will suit very well; let us call up the men."

Once more the process of giving directions to the natives was gone through, this time orders being issued that they were to rely upon rocks instead of upon rifles. Then, satisfied that everything was in readiness, Jim sat down upon a boulder at the entrance of the gorge, and waited there with what patience he could command. It was exciting work sitting there in the darkness surrounded by precipitous walls, and without a sound to break the silence save the occasional jar of a rifle as it was struck against a piece of stone. All sorts of thoughts and fancies passed through his mind during the hours of waiting. He wondered whether his school-friends were thinking of him, what time it was in old England at that moment, and whether the boys were even then engaged in battling with the same tasks which he had so lately forsaken. Yes, it was strange to reflect that barely a month ago he was a mere boy, acting a boy's part, and with scarcely a thought for the future. And now he was the recognized leader of a real expedition, about to invade the country of the Mullah, as fierce a fanatic as had ever sprung to power to be a scourge to his neighbours. It was strange indeed. It was almost beyond belief that it was he, Jim Hubbard, sitting there upon that rock, listening to the beating of his own heart, and straining his ears for the sounds which seemed as though they would never come. Supposing this tribe did not attack after all. Supposing Ali had made a huge blunder, and was the victim of too vivid imagination. Supposing——Hark! What was that? A stone falling from the cliff away above his head, or a footfall upon the road which led through the gorge?

At this sound, faint though it was, each man who lay there in ambush became alert, while Jim sprang to his feet and peered into the blackness.

"The enemy!" whispered a voice in his ear. "Did I not tell you rightly, master? After all, the sheiks have decided to attack during the hours of darkness."

It was Ali Kumar who had slipped up to Jim's side without making so much as a sound. Then, together, they stood listening, bending their heads towards the gorge, as though that would help them.

Ah! There it was again. Was it a man walking, or was it the sound of a voice?

For some minutes there was silence, and then the mystery was cleared up to everyone's satisfaction, for down the rocky sides of the ravine came the noise of men talking. Almost at the same moment a thin streak of the moon climbed up above the highest edge of the cliff, and shot rays of brilliant whiteness down upon the road.

One, two—why, the gorge was packed with figures clad in white and bearing every sort of arm. They might have been bound upon a friendly visit so far as precautions went, for they talked without restraint, but in low tones; while their leader, happening to strike his foot against a boulder of unusual size, gave vent to a loud cry of pain, and stood there, with one hand upon the mass of rock, and the other chafing his injured limb.

But however friendly their appearance, the object of their midnight wandering was quickly apparent, for, as he rubbed his damaged foot, the sheik called to his followers to gather about him, and proceeded to harangue them, Ali Kumar interpreting his words to Jim as he did so.

"Stand as near to me as the gorge will allow," said the leader of the tribesmen, "and I will tell you what course to take when we have descended to the plain. There, as you well know, lies the zareba of these unbelieving dogs, and with them are many camels, and loot sufficient for us all. I command you to keep together until you are almost upon them. Then you will divide, and while one half march so as to gain the farther side, the other will rest where they are, taking pains to preserve the greatest silence. When all are ready, I will fire my gun, and then let every man fall upon the dogs. Allah will strengthen our arms, and will give us the victory."

"Allah is great, and we are his chosen," murmured his audience. "Lead us, and we will slay these unbelievers."

"Let them come a few paces nearer, and then shout to them to return home," said Jim sternly, whispering the words in his companion's ear. "Tell them that we had news of their intended attack, and that we will fire upon them if they come any nearer."

Striding to the barrier of stones, Ali called loudly to the sheik, who was in the act of moving forward again.

"Halt where you are!" he cried. "My master bids me tell you that he is aware of your treacherous plans, and that he is prepared to punish you for them. But he does not desire to shed blood, and therefore gives you the choice of returning in peace to your homes. If you refuse, he will open fire."

At the words the sheik and his following came to an abrupt stop, and stood there silently, dumfounded by the news. It seemed impossible that their intention should have been discovered by the leader of the expedition, and still more unlikely that he had the power to do them any but the smallest harm.

"Why, they are but thirty all told," cried the sheik, with a scoffing laugh. "And yet they come here to meet us and to threaten us with death should we persist in our plan. It is ridiculous! It is a child's plot, made to frighten us. Do not listen, but press on, my men."

With a shout the tribesmen at once started forward, and, drawing their weapons, rushed at the entrance of the gorge. But they had not counted on the fact that it was plunged in darkness, and obstructed with numerous boulders. Running forward upon a pathway which was, just there, lit by the rays of the moon, they stumbled blindly against the rocks, and, one of them happening to fall, a dozen or more of his comrades had tripped over him, and were grovelling on their faces before a minute had passed. But the remainder pushed on without a pause, and, closely packed together, and shrieking threats at the top of their voices, endeavoured to reach the spot where their unseen opponents were.

"Fire!" shouted Jim, seeing that the moment for action had at length arrived. "Empty your rifles into them."

"FIRE!" SHOUTED JIM. "EMPTY YOUR RIFLES INTO THEM."

Leaning upon the breastwork of stones, he took steady aim with his own weapon, directing it at the sheik, who was to be seen wedged in the middle of his men, and frantically struggling to push them back so as to allow him to bring to his shoulder the gun which he bore in his hand.

Bang! The report set the rocks ringing on either hand, and was at once followed by a volley from the breastwork and from the ledge to the right. Shooting out the empty cartridge, Jim looked eagerly to see what success he had had, and was astonished to find that the sheik still occupied the same position. But he was hit, and mortally, too, for a moment later he suddenly threw his hands into the air and fell backwards. Another moment, and he was beneath the feet of the tribesmen, who trampled upon him without hesitation.

But now another feature was added to the scene. Struck by the volley aimed at them, the attackers had drawn back in consternation, but, quickly recovering, they answered the shout of another leader, who at once came forward to replace the sheik, and again dashed headlong for the entrance of the gorge. As they did so, a series of loud and sickening thuds told that the men who had been posted above were carrying out their orders. Indeed, a glance at the cliff overhead showed clearly what was happening; for the rays of the moon had now penetrated to the shelf, and each follower, as he rose to lift a boulder and cast it over the ravine, stood clearly outlined against the dark rock behind.

Shouts and screams soon told that their efforts were not in vain, and just as Jim was about to order another volley to be poured into the gorge, the enemy turned, and now fighting fiercely with one another to get away, fled from the scene as rapidly as the circumstances and their crowded condition would admit.

"Let us hope that that will be enough for them," said Jim, leaning over the barrier and staring along the ravine. "I can count twelve bodies lying amongst the boulders, and there are others beneath the rocks farther on. I am glad now, Ali Kumar, that you advised that these boulders should be thrown down upon their heads, for it was that that caused them to fly. What do you think will happen now?"

"They will retire into the plain beyond, and perhaps even farther, before they recover their courage," answered Ali thoughtfully. "Then they will look amongst themselves to discover who is dead. When they find that we have killed their sheik, and that they have suffered heavy losses, they will be mad with anger, for all will know of their disgrace. Before setting out this night, you may be sure that they held a feast, and called all their women folk to it, boasting that to capture the camp was but a simple matter, for it contained few men, and would certainly be taken by surprise; and now they will reflect that they have been beaten by a mere handful, and that their prey is about to escape them, and even to laugh at them. I know these people well, master, for I am one of them by birth; and I am sure that the succeeding sheik will harangue his followers, speaking as I have just told you. Little by little he will rouse their anger, and when he reminds them of the booty to be obtained, I feel sure that they will again advance to the attack."

"Then we had better prepare for them," said Jim sharply, "We have given them one surprise, and I propose that we arrange another, for that is the only way in which we can attempt to make up for the great difference in numbers."

"But what can you do, master? You have made all the plans and selected every position that it is possible to think of, and now all that you can do is to remain as you are."

"I fancy that we can manage more if we try," answered Jim with decision. "You see, if the fellows attack again, they will know exactly where our men are posted, and will certainly open a hot fire upon them, telling off so many of the tribesmen to keep it up and make it impossible for them to show themselves, or hurl rocks down into the ravine. At least, that is what I should do if I were their leader. In that case, the remainder would have an excellent chance of getting to close quarters, which is what we want specially to avoid, for if that were to happen, numbers would certainly tell upon us."

"But you cannot think of retiring, master!" exclaimed Ali hastily. "To do so would be to sacrifice all your following. Stay here, then, for to reach the zareba the tribesmen must pass through this gorge, there being no other way round."

The native headman grasped Jim by the arm in his anxiety, and looked into his face, fearful lest he should decide to take a step which would end in their ruin.

"You may banish that from your mind," said Jim sharply. "I am not going to retire for any man, but what I propose to do is to push on till near the other end of the ravine. There, we will make the same plans as we carried out here, and when the enemy advances, will have another surprise in store for them. But, tell me, supposing we creep along, and build a barrier farther on, can the tribesmen climb the cliffs and treat us in turn to a shower of rocks?"

"You are safe from that, master. It is true that there are ledges at the farther end, but they are narrow and short, and do not come far this way. Were it otherwise, the sheik would already have sent his followers to occupy them, and by now we should have a storm of slugs and bullets pattering upon us. No, we have nothing in that way to fear, while as for your ruse, it seems to your servant that it is as wise as that which you planned before. To find us at the other end, and come upon us long before they expected to do so, will, indeed, be a surprise, and, as you say, that is the only way in which we can make up for our small numbers."

"Then we'll move ahead at once," exclaimed Jim. "Call to the men to come down, and warn them that they are to keep perfectly silent. Tell them what we propose to do, and say that after the enemy have attacked us, they are to remain in their new positions till I shout. Then they are to retire to this post again at their fastest pace, and lie down as before. In that way we shall have an excellent chance of withdrawing, should the contest prove too uneven for us."

Acting upon his orders, Ali soon had all the native followers gathered at the bottom of the ravine, and a glance at their faces as they were outlined in the rays of the moon was sufficient to show that they were to be relied upon, and that the success which had already attended them had filled them with elation and determination to fight to the end.

"Good!" exclaimed Jim, surveying them critically; "they will do. Now let us get ahead, and, Ali, come with me in advance. It will be as well to make sure that none are watching us."

Creeping along the rugged road which threaded the gorge, Jim and his men soon reached the opposite end. Not a soul was met, and though they lay down for some minutes, not a sound could be heard. Then a scout was sent away into the plain, and while he was gone, the remainder took up their positions much as before, for numerous rocky ledges were to be found. Half an hour later a barrier was erected across the ravine, and behind it lay Jim and five of his men.

"Hush!" exclaimed Jim suddenly. "I hear someone coming. Perhaps it is our scout."

A second later the bleat of a sheep was heard, and before long a dusky figure rose up before the barrier.

"They are coming," said the man. "I went far out into the plain, and came upon them talking and shouting. They were drinking the wine of the country, which is made by melting the fat which comes from the tails of young sheep, and were crying upon their sheik to lead them forward. As I left them they were setting their faces this way, with the determination to slay us all, for they are angry, and their bitterness is great at their defeat."

"Then let them come," said Jim doggedly, when the words had been interpreted to him. "They have had their warning, and this time I will not spare them as I did before."

Standing behind the wall of loose stones, he waited in silence for the enemy, and within a few minutes saw a large force of men streaming across the moonlit plain on their way to the ravine. Very soon they were close at hand, and, gathering together, came walking forward without a thought of guarding against surprise.

CHAPTER X

FIGHTING THE TRIBESMEN

Standing in the shadow cast by the cliff on his right, Jim looked out upon the brightly lit plain, and watched the tribesmen coming to the attack. There was no need for them to remain silent, for they already knew that their design of capturing the zareba was known; and, therefore, they marched forward, shouting loudly to one another, and brandishing their weapons above their heads. A few, carried away by their excitement, even fired their guns, as if already in sight of their opponents, as indeed they were, if only they had known it. Nearing the entrance of the gorge, they gathered together, and then, at a shout from their leader, halted for a minute.

"We must slay the infidels this time," he called out. "Let each man prepare now for the fight, and when I give the word, rush forward at his fastest pace. In that way only can we hope to escape the shower of rocks from above. Some I have already told off to climb the cliffs and pick off the defenders, and they will carry out their commands at once. Are you ready? Then, in Allah's name, forward!"

At his words a storm of cries and of fierce shouts burst from the Somalis, and some three hundred of them came rushing towards the ravine, eager to be the first to reach the farther end and come to close quarters with the men who had given such a bitter blow to their pride. Well might the little band of defenders tremble at the sight and at the noise, for on the former occasion the tribesmen had advanced in comparative silence, and their defeat and subsequent retreat had been swift and but the matter of a few minutes. Now, however, it was a different matter. Here were the enemy rushing upon them in numbers sufficient to overpower them, indeed, to sweep over them and trample them underfoot without feeling their presence. For the moment the hopelessness of their case appealed to Jim, and he felt as though all were lost, and that his hopes of saving his father from slavery, or worse, were destined to be shattered at the very beginning. Then a sudden determination to conquer came upon him, and he turned quietly to Ali.

"Call gently to the men, and tell them to hold their fire and keep well under cover until they hear me shout," he said. "I shall wait till the enemy is within fifty yards, so that our volleys may have good effect. Let them know also that they are to reload at once, and that if the natives do not retire after the first volley, they are to open upon them with the magazine, and continue firing till they fly. How thankful I am that we took the precaution two days ago of showing them how to manage their rifles."

Ali at once carried out his master's orders, first telling those who lay behind the barricade of stones, and then going to inform the remainder who had been posted upon the ledges. That done, he returned to Jim's side, and stood there awaiting the attack, determined to help him as far as in him lay, for the bravery of this young Englishman appealed to him. Indeed, he was lost in wonderment to find this lad, who had had no experience of this sort of life, and who had had no dealings with natives, so calmly placing himself at the head of his followers, and leading them against odds which would have appalled many a grown-up man.

By now the tribesmen were within eighty yards from them, and, led by their sheik, they came rushing pell-mell towards the entrance of the ravine, expecting to find it open, and never dreaming that the enemy whom they were bent on attacking already occupied it. All their thoughts and all their energies were occupied in the race to reach the farther end, each one striving to be there before his fellows, to strike one of the few blows which they told themselves would be necessary to conquer these impudent people.

"Death to the infidels!" shouted the sheik. "Fear not their bullets, but rush upon them and slay them ere they can lift their weapons to do you harm."

Crowded together in a surging mass, his followers advanced towards the gorge, shouting defiance. A minute more and they were within the distance which Jim had mentioned, looking as though nothing could stop them, so great was their eagerness, and as though they would overrun the wall of stones and scatter it to right and left in their impetuosity.

Clash! Bang! At Jim's order, a stream of flame spurted from the ambush, and from the ledges to right and left, as the men opened fire, sending a hail of bullets into the centre of the mass. At such a short range, and with these modern rifles which threw bullets of the smallest calibre and of the greatest penetrating force, every missile flew on till it was stopped by the sheer weight of the mass before it. Not one, but many men were struck down by the shower of lead, and falling headlong upon the ground, lay there sprawling in all directions and in every attitude, a trap for the feet of those who followed. But if the surprise of the tribesmen had been great during their first attack, when they discovered that the opening from the ravine had been closed, it was now more than doubled. They were dumfounded at the trick played upon them, and as the rifles flashed out vengefully, they came to an abrupt halt, as if by mutual consent, and stood there, breathless, their weapons still held above their heads, staring into the darkness beyond them, as if they wished to penetrate into the depth of the gorge and learn what was happening. For more than a minute they paused, while the defenders, taking advantage of the breathing-space, opened the breeches of their weapons. Shooting out the empty cartridges, they replaced them with fresh ones, and closed the locks with a snap and bang which told, as plainly as if they had mentioned the fact, that they, too, meant business, and that nothing but the absolute defeat of their enemies would satisfy them.

"They give back! They fly! Death to the dags!" shouted Ali Kumar excitedly, at this moment, noticing that a few of the leaders had suddenly turned, and were endeavouring to thrust their comrades aside and find a means of escape. "See, master, you have already taught them the lesson of which you spoke."

"Wait!" answered Jim sharply. "It is only those who have no stomach for the fight who are returning. The majority will fight it out; of that I am sure. Ah, here they come!"

As he spoke, the sheik, whose astonishment had at first been overpowering, suddenly recovered his wits, and, rendered desperate by the position in which he found himself, and fearful of losing credit with his following, suddenly sprang to the front, and, turning towards his men, shouted loud words of encouragement.

"Are you then afraid?" he cried. "Shall these few infidel dogs turn us from our purpose? On! Let not the flash of their weapons terrify you and rob you of your bravery. Forward! Death to the enemy!"

Swinging round until he faced the gorge once more, he levelled his gun at it, and pulled the trigger. Then he tossed it to one side, knowing that it would be useless in a hand-to-hand conflict, and drawing a long, double-handed sword from his waist with the quickness of a flash, he charged at the defenders.

Taking encouragement from his words and action, the tribesmen at once sprang forward and joined him, following close on his heels, and setting up a fierce shout which awoke the echoes, and almost deafened the defenders. "Kill them!" they shouted. "Slay the infidels!"

Pressing forward at their fastest pace, they were soon within some twenty yards of the barrier. But at that moment the rifles flashed out again, and a storm of bullets was poured into their midst. Throwing out the catch of their magazines, Jim's followers sent missile after missile into their midst without cessation, and, pausing only to replenish them, opened again, rising in their excitement from behind their shelter, so as to obtain a better aim.

Three times did the tribesmen win their way to within a few paces of the wall of stones, but on each occasion the rifles of the defenders beat them back. Then they retired sulkily, and, taking up their posts behind boulders and scraps of cover, which existed here and there, open a stinging fusillade upon the ravine.

"Order the men to lie down behind the rocks!" cried Jim; "and tell them that they are to reserve their shots until they are certain that they can see one of the enemy. They are then to take careful aim, and pick him off without wasting a cartridge. Let them show these tribesmen that recklessness will not pay, and that the instant one rises from his shelter he will be slain."

Obedient to the orders which were repeated to them by Ali Kumar, the native followers lay down upon their ledges, and kept a careful watch upon the tribesmen. But all the while each held his rifle to his shoulder, and closely scrutinizing the moonlit plain beyond, endeavoured to discover the whereabouts of lurking tribesmen. Then, taking careful aim, and waiting till the man he covered rose to empty his weapon in the direction of the ravine, he pressed his trigger gently and sent his bullets home. Not once, but many times, did the defenders pick off one of the enemy, and, when an hour had passed, quite twenty had paid the penalty for their boldness.

"Their volleys seem to be getting heavier," remarked Jim, some twenty minutes later, when a perfect storm of slugs whistled and shrieked through the entrance of the ravine, striking against the rocks on either side to glance off them and ricochet into space with a characteristic note to which an old soldier would have been quite accustomed. Others struck the hastily built wall of stones, and, smashing to pieces there, sent a shower of fragments in all directions. Indeed, so heavy and well-aimed was the tribesmen's fusillade, that a number of the small garrison were wounded, but only to a slight extent, thanks to the nature of the missiles used.

"Yes, it is certainly becoming heavier, and I should not be surprised if they made another rush before very long. Sing out to the men to be prepared, Ali, and tell them that on this occasion I shall not give the command to open fire until they are considerably closer, for they will have had their warning, and will most likely come on in open order, in which case we could not hope to inflict much loss, for the light is uncertain, and makes accurate aiming difficult. But they are bound to come together within a few yards of this, and that is the moment we must select for blazing into them."

"The advice is good," was Ali's answer. "These men who have so rashly attacked us are burning to avenge their defeat, and they will not rest until they have slain us, or we have chastised them so severely that they recognize the hopelessness of their cause. Therefore, if ten, if twenty, fell to the earth, shot down by our bullets as they rush to the attack, the remainder would not pause, would not hesitate for a moment, but would come on at their fastest pace. It is a clever plan, therefore, to wait until they are within easy range and packed close together, for, seeing that our guns are silent when they had expected them to open heavily upon them, they will, perchance, imagine that we have retired, and have prepared another ambush for them. I should advise, master, that you order the men at once to lie down, for they are now having little success, as the tribesmen have been warned by the death of their comrades, and are careful not to expose themselves."

"You can do as you suggest, Ali, and I feel sure that our silence will make them wonder. Perhaps they will hold a council of war, and then come on warily, imagining that we have retreated to our old barricade. Call to our followers, and explain the situation to them. Then let them know that they are on no account to make a sound until I give the signal by firing my rifle."

Ali at once turned to the natives, who had so gallantly supported their young English leader, and hastily communicated Jim's words to them. Then all knelt, or lay at full length behind the cover each one had selected, and remained there, eyes fixed upon the plain beyond and upon the figures of the tribesmen which flitted hither and thither, now rushing from one thorn-bush to another, and now creeping along some shallow trench cunningly scooped from the sand with their hands, to reach a site which seemed more favourable. It was evident that all had taken the lesson to heart, and had felt the bullets of the defenders, for up to a little while ago they had, in the manner of Eastern people, recklessly and defiantly exposed themselves, standing fully erect to discharge their weapons. But as many of these bold men had fallen, shot through the head or chest, the remainder began to learn that the sight of a shoulder or of a head peering from behind a boulder was the signal for the instant snap of a rifle and the swish of a bullet close at hand. And now their crafty sheik had had time to recover his self-possession, and from his position in the centre of his men, sent messengers crawling to right and left with instructions for the next attack.

"I fancy I can see something moving over there," said Jim, some ten minutes later, as he stood behind the barricade, silently looking out upon the plain. "Is it the moonlight which alters objects or are those thorn-bushes getting slowly nearer to us? Look! There is a large one out there in the very centre, and I declare that, five minutes ago, it was twenty paces or more from the rock close beside which it now stands."

He stared anxiously over the sandy waste, and pointed with his finger to indicate the bush to which he wished to draw Ali's attention, quite forgetting that he himself, together with all the defenders, were shrouded in the inky darkness with which the entrance of the ravine was clad. But Ali's eyes were as sharp as a ferret's, and long residence amongst the natives had given him powers of sight far more acute than those usually possessed by more civilized people. A glance into the open showed him the large bush, and instantly his attention became riveted upon it.

"It moves!" he whispered breathlessly. "See, master, a moment ago it was beside the rock of which you spoke, and now it stands in front of it, so that I can scarcely see its outline. And—look! There are others to right and left which are creeping forward. It is a ruse, a cunning plan to get close to us before making the final rush. Each one of those thorn-bushes conceals one or more of the tribesmen, all with their eyes fixed upon the central bush, and all slowly, steadily, but insensibly, drawing nearer. Soon they will have approached as close as they deem possible, and then casting the cover aside, they will spring to their feet, and come rushing upon us. What shall we do?"

For the first time since the tribesmen had attacked Ali showed some symptoms of fear. His lips trembled involuntarily as he asked Jim the question, and unconsciously he grasped the lad by the arm.

"What shall we do, Ali? Why? What else but watch them carefully, and send our volleys swishing into them when they do rise for their attack? I've been thinking the matter out, and I feel sure that the plan we have agreed upon is a wise one. For ten minutes not a shot has been fired from our side, and though they have certainly been listening with all their ears, they have not heard a sound. But still they creep forward, only half suspecting at present that we have withdrawn. Soon, however, they will begin to think that, if we are still here, we are blind, for we could not fail to have discovered the moving bushes. That will set them wondering, and it will never cross their minds that we have chosen to prepare another surprise for them. They will be quite sure that all their trouble in creeping forward in this way has been useless, and they will rise to their feet and advance towards the ravine, fully expecting to find us gone. But we will teach them to be more sensible. Now is our time to give them a blow from which they will never recover. Cheer up, Ali! Things are not half so desperate as they seem."

Jim's words had the desired effect upon his native follower, for the latter at once straightened himself, and, standing erect behind the barricade, looked out upon the enemy with far more determination and courage than he had shown before. As for Jim, though he leant there apparently unmoved and unconcerned, he was far from feeling as sanguine as he had expressed himself, for there was no doubt that he and his little band of followers were in an extremely precarious situation, from which they could not hope to escape without severe and desperate fighting. Indeed, when he considered the odds, and remembered the fierce shouts with which the enemy had previously attacked, he was bound to confess to himself that the position was almost without hope. Could he and these few men, well armed though they were, expect for the third time to beat back a crew of fanatical tribesmen who were bent upon slaying them, and who, taught to think that they were the only true believers, considered that death earned in slaying an infidel was well earned indeed? Against such men effectual resistance was difficult, and, unless reinforcements were at hand, or great success attained at the beginning, could not possibly be continued for very long.

"But we'll do it," said Jim doggedly, to himself. "I've come out to this country for a certain purpose, and have done no harm to these people. Indeed, I was prepared to be the best of friends with them. But they have thought fit to attack me in the hope of obtaining loot, and must just take the consequences."

With that his lips closed firmly together, and, lifting his rifle once more, he felt softly at the lock to see that all was in readiness.

"Nothing but the magazine this time," he murmured. "We must sweep them away, and mow them down before they can get within reach of us."

By now the line of moving bushes had drawn sensibly nearer, and as each man of the garrison kept his eyes fixed upon them, he was able to observe figures crawling behind them. To those of Jim's followers who lay upon the ledges above, the whole plan was now quite evident, for from their elevated position they could easily see over the tops of the bushes, and could even count the number of the enemy. In such circumstances the temptation to select some individual, to raise the rifle ever so quietly to the shoulder, and gently to press the trigger when certain of the aim, was great indeed. Breathlessly, with fast-beating hearts, and hands glued to the stocks of their weapons, they stared out from the darkness into the space lit up by the rays of the moon, and longed for the order to fire, for to lie motionless, without attempting to defend themselves when they knew that men were there hungering for their lives, was a sore trial to all of them. Impetuous and excitable by nature, they would, had they been alone, at once have emptied their magazines, and then either fled down the ravine, or died fighting where they were. But they had confidence in their young leader, who had already shown his fitness to command them, and, in spite of their longing to begin the engagement, remained in absolute silence.

"They have stopped!" whispered Jim some few minutes later, noticing that the line of thorn-bushes had come to a halt. "Look! There is a man creeping from the right-hand side towards the centre, and another is following him. They are going to have a talk, and decide upon some action."

"Others are coming from the left, master," added Ali, catching him by the sleeve; "and now someone has risen from behind the bush which stands in the middle. It is the sheik, for I know him by his great height. He is pointing towards us, and talking to the others."

Eagerly did Jim and his followers watch the scene going on before them; and as they looked, first one, and then all, of the leafy screens which the tribesmen had carried before them with such craft and trouble were tossed aside with disgust, and those who were hiding behind them rose to their feet, giving vent to exclamations of annoyance and anger.

"Once more these dogs have made fools of us!" cried the sheik, shaking his fist towards the gorge. "First they poured their bullets into us from the farther end, and then, when we advanced for the second time, expecting to find them there, they lay hiding like foxes close in front of us. And now, when after infinite care and caution we have, as we thought, come within such easy reach of them that a few moments would have seen us triumphant, we discover that they are gone, that they have melted into the air. It is hard to fight with such men, and were it not for the losses we have suffered, I should counsel that we retire."

"And what then?" shouted one of his followers indignantly. "Do you ask us to return to our wives and children and admit defeat? We cannot do it. They would not receive us, but would drive us out with laughter and jeers. Think for a moment. Our trouble may not be thrown away, for seeing that victory was certain to fall to us, it may well be that these insolent people have fled for their lives. Even now they may be returning to the coast as quickly as their beasts will take them, leaving their camels and their baggage to us. Be not downhearted, for whether they have fled or remain to fight, our numbers are great, and make success certain in the end."

The man who had spoken strode some paces to the front, and turned as he harangued his brethren. Then he went to the sheik and spoke quietly in his ear.

"Abdullah Rishmar is right," cried the latter, after a few minutes. "Rather than despair we should be filled with exultation, for it is evident that the enemy has taken flight. We have discussed the matter, and are still of opinion that the best plan will be to move forward, and when we reach the farther end of the ravine, rush down upon the zareba. Then if we find, as seems probable, that the infidel has fled, we will return to our homes, and to-morrow, at the first streak of daylight, our fleetest camels shall convey a band of fighting men in pursuit. We know the lowlands well, and by nightfall should come up with those whom we seek. Then punishment shall be meted out for their insolence. As for those who are dead, does not Allah reward the true believer who falls in taking part in such a cause?"

At the old man's words the tribesmen gave vent to a loud shout, and, gathering together, ran swiftly towards the ravine.

"Another minute and we shall let them have it," said Jim quietly. "Call gently to all the men to make ready."

Raising his rifle to his shoulder, he aimed for the centre of the mass of struggling humanity, and pressed the trigger. An instant later a line of flame flashed from behind the barricade and from the ledges on either side. So rapidly did the men open and close the breeches of their weapons, that the volley seemed to be an endless one. Here and there it would stop for a few seconds, as the magazine was emptied, but within a very short while it broke out again, spurting into the darkness, till the opening of the ravine was almost as light as the plain outside. At the first discharge the tribesmen had stood aghast, thunderstruck at the audacity of their enemies. Then rage took hold of them, and they came on, this time in silence, their eyes blazing with hate, and their minds made up to kill their opponents, whatever happened. Surging forward, in spite of their losses, they reached the rocky entrance of the gorge, and became almost wedged. Then a few, breaking from their comrades, dashed at the barricade, and at once joined in a fierce hand-to-hand contest with Jim and the six men who stood beside him. To the last moment Jim kept on firing, and then, when there was no cartridge left in his weapon, he grasped it by the barrel, and leaping, in his excitement upon the wall of stones, dashed it down upon the heads of the attackers. Indeed, he seemed to be endowed with extraordinary strength, for he swung his rifle as if it had been a roll of paper, and brought it down with a force which could not be broken. Ali Kumar did his utmost to support his young leader, while the five remaining men, tossing their guns to one side, drew their swords and threw themselves upon the tribesmen with a fury equal to their own.

And all the while the men who were stationed on the ledges above kept up a terrible fire, sending their bullets swishing into the huddled masses of the enemy. But in spite of all the efforts of the garrison, it seemed at first as though the enemy would prove victorious, for nothing seemed able to check them. In another place, indeed, they would have been successful, without a doubt, but here their very numbers hampered them, and prevented more than a few from closing with the defenders at one moment. Had Jim and the natives who were with him given way, the tide of tribesmen would have surged over the barricade, and not a man would have lived to tell the tale. But they clung to their position with desperate bravery, and finally drove their assailants back.

"Now for the magazines!" shouted Jim. "Fill them up, and open again!"

Though they could not understand a word, his men saw his meaning at a glance, for he turned upon them, and flinging the lock of his rifle open, began to slip cartridges into it. Then, waiting until they, too, were ready, he brought his weapon to his shoulder, and once more the line of fire spurted from behind the barricade. A minute later Jim sprang over the breastwork, and rushed forward. But his intention was not to throw himself upon the assailants, but to commit an act of bravery; for suddenly one of the men posted upon the ledge upon his right had risen to aim at the enemy, and overbalancing himself, had come crashing to the ground, where he lay within a few paces of the wall of stones, at the mercy of the enemy. With an agile leap Jim was beside him almost as soon as he touched the ground, and catching him by the arm, dragged him towards his friends. Then, tossing his weapon to Ali, who looked on speechless with astonishment, he caught the native up in his arms, and scrambled back amongst his comrades with him. The whole had been the work of a few moments only, and was completed before the tribesmen could take advantage of the opportunity so suddenly presented to them. It proved, indeed, a turning-point in the conflict, for, filled with exultation at their young leader's bravery, the defenders set up a shout which set the rocks ringing, and then dashed forward to the attack, Jim joining them. Filled with consternation as these men, who seemed more than mortal, closed with them, the tribesmen turned about with one accord, and bolted into the plain, leaving their opponents proud masters of the scene.

"And now let us see who is hurt," said Jim breathlessly, sitting upon a boulder to rest for a few moments after the fray. "Line the men up, Ali, and tell me if any are killed."

"We have had great fortune," answered the native headman. "I have already been amongst the following, and I find that two only are killed, the one being Rigba Hamah, who fell from the cliff above, and the second Ali Tumbi, who fell at the last assault. As for wounds, we all have one or more to show, but they are nothing, and will be well in a week."

"Then I'll ask you to tie up my arm," said Jim quietly. "I fancy that a slug has ploughed a big hole through it."

Leading his master into the light, Ali at once examined his wound, and gave a cry of consternation when he saw the condition of the arm, for it was red with blood, while a stream was gushing from a ragged hole close above the elbow.

"How long is it since you received this?" he asked sharply. "It must have been some time ago, for you have lost much blood. Look at the condition of your clothing."

"A slug struck me as the tribesmen advanced for the last time," answered Jim faintly. "I scarcely felt it in the excitement of the moment, but it smarts now. Give me something to drink, for I feel dizzy."

Running across to the cliff, down the steep slope of which a tiny stream trickled, Ali quickly procured a handful of water, and at once poured it down Jim's throat.

"Ah, that's better; and now I feel less likely to make a fool of myself and faint," said the latter gratefully. "Now tie it up for me like a good fellow, and let us see what our next step is to be."

"We shall return to the zareba, master, and spend what is left of the night in peace," replied Ali with assurance. "The tribesmen are thoroughly beaten, and will not venture to advance again until we have withdrawn. Then they will collect their dead and wounded, and when the morning comes they will slink away into the plain and hide. This has been an evil time for them, and they will remember it for many a day to come."

"I think you are right," Jim agreed, "and I propose that you shout out to them that we will not interfere with them if they like to send in for the bodies. Tell them that we will retire to the pass below the ravine, and that they are on no account to attempt to approach us, or we will hunt them up to-morrow and burn their camp. When you have done that, we shall get back to the zareba, leaving three of our men as sentries until they can be relieved by those who have remained behind."

Accordingly, when Ali had seen to the comfort of his leader, he strode out into the plain, and shouted to the tribesmen, giving them Jim's message. Then the gallant band, who had fought so well in the gorge, retired, and within an hour were with their friends again.

CHAPTER XI

A MARCH INTO THE DESERT

"And so you have been behaving like a young hero?" said Tom Dixon, on the following morning, surveying Jim as he rose from his blanket. "You were tired out, so I allowed you to sleep on undisturbed while Ali and I had a long chat. Seriously, though, old chap, you have done nobly, and have again risen high in the estimation of our following. After this they will do anything for you, and will be just as keen as you are to bring the expedition to a successful issue. But tell me about the fight. I can only get a garbled account from Ali, who tells me that you defeated the whole tribe, and caused them enormous loss. But that cannot be the case. He must have been romancing, though I am bound to confess that we heard very heavy firing, which might easily have accounted for large numbers of killed and wounded."

"Ali Kumar was quite right," replied Jim quietly. "We did defeat the whole lot of the tribesmen, and I believe they will only be too glad to leave us alone in the future. You see, it was like this——"

Then Jim set to work to give his companion the details, leaving out his own share in the matter, for he was not a boastful lad.

"And now tell me how things went with you," he continued. "I was so done up when we got back to the zareba last night that I felt I could not listen. It was sufficient for me to find that you were safe, and that you had lost none of the beasts or baggage."

"We did not even see an enemy," said Tom with disgust. "Though we kept a very bright look-out, and even on one occasion blazed into the darkness, thinking that the sheik and his men were upon us, not a soul really came near the place. But we heard the firing from the gorge, and it made me feel so anxious that I very nearly came up to join you. If it hadn't been that our safety depends to such an extent upon our camels and food-supply, I should certainly have done so, and you would not have blamed me, for it is clear that you had a desperate time of it. However, all's well that ends well. And now for our next move. Will you go ahead, or will you retire for a time, till this fight has blown over?"

"I shall push on without a pause," answered Jim. "You see, news of this row is certain to fly to the Mullah's ears, and if we were to retire he would prevent any attempt in the future, by setting a watch at the ravine, and forbidding us to pass through. Then we should have to wait till the troops come this way, and by then anything may have happened to father. No, I mean to go right on, and my first act will be to ride to the camp from which these tribesmen came, and order them to give me any news they may have. Then I shall tell them that they are to keep quiet about their fight with us, or we will punish them on our return. Of course it will be a piece of bounce on my part, but now is the time to practise that sort of thing."

"You are right not to allow this quarrel to frighten you," answered Tom heartily, "and I think it quite likely that you may get important information from our enemies. Then, too, now is the time to take advantage of your victory. While the tribesmen are humbled, you will get more from them than at any other time, for they will hope to allay your anger by helping you. But we shall never be able to trust them, and from this moment our precautions against surprise at night must be doubled."

Long did Jim and his friend talk the matter over, and then Tom went to one of the bales which was carried upon the back of a camel, and, opening it, produced a bundle of surgical dressings and a few instruments. With these and a tin pannikin of cool water he proceeded to dress Jim's wound, and ended by placing the arm in a sling.

"There," he said, when he had finished, "you bore it like a Briton, and will soon be well. Luckily it is only a flesh-wound. Had the slug struck the bone on its way through, it might have been a case of amputation, and then where would have been your expedition? And now, if you feel capable of the exertion, we shall break up the camp and get through the pass. Best do it now, before the sheik and his following pluck up their courage again."

Accordingly, the zareba was soon astir, and the men bustling about their animals. Then, with a dozen of the best shots riding well in advance, and the remainder hovering in rear and on the flanks, the column set out for the pass, and went trailing up the steep slope of the hill. In due time they entered the ravine. Here they found but few traces of the conflict, for the tribesmen had taken advantage of the permission extended to them, and had removed their dead.

An hour later they were in the plain, and that night they halted at some wells distant about ten miles. Here Ali Kumar came to Jim to announce that a messenger wished to have speech with him.

"He comes from the tribe who suffered defeat at our hands," he said, "and has news of importance."

"Bring him along, then," said Jim, "and tell off a man to keep an eye upon him. He might become unpleasant."

A few moments later Ali ushered forward a native, whose head-gear proclaimed him to be one of the tribe who had received such a defeat on the previous evening. Coming up to Jim, he salaamed deeply and most humbly, and even trembled, so great was his fear.

"What do you want?" asked Jim sharply, Tom interpreting his words. "Have you been told to ask for mercy from us?"

"That is the case," answered the man. "The sheik bade me come hither and say that he regrets deeply that his men attacked you, and that they would never have done so had it not been for the words of one who was in your service, and who has now fled. He asks for forgiveness, and will promise never to molest you again."

"That is not enough," replied Jim sternly. "Why should we not march on his camp and loot it?"

"We are in your hands," the man said trembling; "but if you will overlook our fault, we shall give you news which will help you."

"What is it, then?"

"The man who betrayed you told us that you were in search of a white prisoner of the Mullah's. I am charged to tell you that he is now some thirty miles to the south of the Hoad, and that if you press through, you may rescue him, for many of the fighting men are away."

"Can we trust the fellow?" asked Jim doubtfully, turning to Tom. "Perhaps it is a trap, into which they hope we shall walk blindly."

"I hardly think so, old chap. You have given these beggars such a licking that they are in terror of their lives, and I believe they are telling you the truth. I should instruct him to say to the sheik that you will harm him no further at present, but that if you find he has been playing with you, you will punish him on your return."

"That is good advice, Tom, and I'll leave it to you to speak to him. Then let us talk over the preparations to be made before entering upon this desert march."

Accordingly, Tom repeated his words to the tribesman, warning him in stern tones that the slightest treachery would be severely punished.

"Now return to your sheik," he continued, "and be careful that in future you remain peaceful, for the British troops will be this way before very long, and will treat you far more severely than we have done, unless you can prove that you are friendly."

With many salaams and repeated thanks, the man withdrew; and then Tom and Jim called Ali Kumar to join them in consultation.

"The question of water seems to me to be the most important," said Jim, opening the conversation. "How are we to contrive to carry sufficient to last for one hundred and fifty miles?"

"We'll ask Ali," replied Tom. "You see, I've never been in this part before, and, though I have done a deal of spying in Aden, I've never joined in one of these expeditions. This is, in fact, all strange to me."

"I have crossed the Hoad on several occasions, master," interposed Ali, "and can give you my help. Once beyond the desert, I can do nothing, for I shall then be in strange country. Indeed, no caravan has ever penetrated so far, for the land beyond belongs to the Mullah. As to water, you have tanks with you, which should prove sufficient. But a guard must be set upon their contents, and the allowance for man and beast strictly dealt out. Again, five days is said to be the shortest time in which the march can be accomplished, but I think that we shall do well to press on more hastily. The camels are all in the best of condition, and can well stand the fatigue. Then again, the following and baggage are comparatively small, so that our movements should be correspondingly rapid. When we reach the other side, we can rest for a time, while we send out scouts to gather news."

"Excellent!" exclaimed Jim. "And now, when should we start?"

"I vote that we march on at once to the very edge of the desert," said Tom. "If we find wells there, we can fill our tanks, and get a good start."

"Bohotle is an advance post held by troops in the pay of the Sirkal," remarked Ali Kumar, "and it is situated on the fringe of the sandy waste which stretches into the interior up to the pasture country ruled over by the Mullah. There is water in plenty there, and also at a spot directly before us. I therefore counsel you to keep straight on. Seven hours' marching will bring you to the place of which I speak, and then all preparations can be made for the crossing."

Following the advice given by the native headman, Jim at once gave orders for the camp to be broken up, and by nightfall had the satisfaction of finding himself amidst a clump of palms and mimosa, which marked the position of the wells, and from which one looked out directly upon a wide-spreading sea of sand, a dreary waste, which went on and on to the horizon without a break, and without so much as a patch of green to relieve it. And here, as the caravan halted, and the men began to make a zareba, Jim had the pleasure of watching the most gorgeous sunset he had ever seen.

"It is a wonderful sight," said Tom, as he stood by his side. "It seems as if these parts, where nature appears to come to a sudden end, were given something out of the way to make up for their loss; for the sun rises and falls over the desert with such beautiful effect, that people who have travelled the world over declare it is the finest sight of all. Then, too, mirages are not infrequent, though what is their cause is more than I can say. But come along. Watching that beautiful sky does not relieve one's hunger, and I can tell you I am sharp set."

Returning to their camp, Jim and his friend were soon seated in front of a fire of thorn-wood, which blazed and crackled brightly, sending out a heat which was grateful, for the nights at this season of the year were decidedly cold. A native follower then appeared with a pan and some fat, and ten minutes later Jim was busily frying some juicy slices of meat cut from a deer which Tom had shot during the day. When they were finished to his satisfaction, Jim removed them to a plate by means of a fork, which, with a spoon and a knife, he carried in the form of an ordinary pocket-knife, as every sensible campaigner does. Meanwhile Tom had had the tea in hand, and before many minutes had passed both were seated at an excellent repast, which they enjoyed all the more for the fact that it was partaken of while squatting upon the bare earth, and from dishes and mugs of common enamelled tin.

"And now for bed," said Jim, two hours later, when Tom had finished his smoke and they had had a chat. "Let us hope for a fine day, and a good start."

"And luck on the other side, old chap. Good-night. It's my first watch. Turn in now, and I'll wake you in good time."

Soon the camp was hushed in sleep, save for the crisp, low sound of a sandalled foot plodding up and down upon the sand. A few hours later the sentries were relieved, and Jim took his turn, it having been arranged that he and Tom, together with Ali Kumar, should help one another to keep an eye upon their following during the hours of darkness.

Early on the following day the camp was astir, and an hour later they set out upon their long and hazardous march. Four days of hot and tiring work took them in safety to the farther side, where, worn out with their exertions, they formed a zareba, and called a long halt, to rest both animals and men. And now began the most difficult and dangerous part of Jim's undertaking.

"Thirty miles from here the Mullah and his men are said to be encamped," he remarked thoughtfully to Tom, as the two stood looking towards the interior of the fertile country which they had just reached. "I keep wondering whether we should push straight on, or remain where we are. I mean, whether we should post our men at this spot and go forward alone."

"But surely you will want every follower," cried Tom. "Careful as we have been to keep our movements a secret, it is almost impossible to expect that the Mullah will remain for long in ignorance. Then, as soon as he hears of us, out will come his cut-throats to visit us and eat up the whole convoy, if they are able."

"Exactly so, Tom, and it is because his men will come, and in large numbers, too, that I suggest that we should find a spot for our followers, and make a raid into the country alone. If we were discovered, we should make a bolt for it, and trust to rejoin our camp before we were caught. On the other hand, suppose we push on in a body. Unless we have the fortune to come upon another spot like the ravine, certain defeat will stare us in the face, for the Mullah has thousands of men."

"What a long-headed beggar you are to be sure!" exclaimed Tom, smacking him heartily upon the back. "You seem to get to the bottom of all these difficulties at once, and what you have said is, I feel sure, as wise a course as we could carry out. But what about a spot in which to make the camp? It must be a strong one, or it will be useless. Again, it must be within reasonable distance, for otherwise we should never reach it."

"The difficulty is great, but it is not beyond our powers," said a voice at his elbow, as Ali Kumar joined them. "I have already told you that I have once before crossed the Hoad, but that I have never penetrated the country beyond. I will now explain for what reason. It happened that I, with my father and my father's tribe, had suffered much at the hands of some neighbours of ours, who were far stronger than we were. For years they had harried our flocks, slain our men, and carried off the women and children. So that at last we decided to migrate and to place the desert between ourselves and our enemies. Carefully did we make our preparations, and then we set out upon the journey. Alas, master, it proved disastrous, for our beasts were in poor condition, and few in numbers. Then fortune was against us, for we stumbled into a storm of sand, which lasted for a day, and left us well-nigh dead. But we struggled on, hoping for the best. One by one our camels fell by the way, and soon men, too, joined them. At last, to make our troubles more than we could bear, the beasts, in their mad desire for water, tore open the sacks of goat-skin in which we carried our precious supply, and let the contents rush out upon the sand, where it disappeared at once, licked up by the parched land. From that moment all order was lost, and within a very few hours we had scattered, some in their madness returning, and all wandering from their path, their tongues lolling from their blackened lips, and their limbs staggering beneath them.

"With three of my comrades I struggled forward till I saw a patch of green before me. At first I thought that it was a mirage, risen to cheat me into hope. But it was real—a glorious sight!—and, together with those who were with me, I ran towards it. There was water there, master, and food, and when, after resting, we searched the place, we found that it bore no traces of a camp, and that in all probability none but wild beasts had ever visited it. Three days later we pushed on to the fertile land of the Mullah, but there my comrades were killed, I alone escaping. In fear and terror I returned to the oasis, and from there Allah helped me to trudge across the desert and reach that portion of the land which skirts the sea. My journeying may be of use to you now, master, for the green spot of which I speak lies some ten miles only within the Hoad, and it is wide enough to give grazing to all your beasts. Of food you have enough in store of the kind that is sealed in tins, and therefore cannot fear starvation, while of water there is abundance. Moreover, it occurs to me that a strong zareba might be made in the heart of the trees, for there is wood to be had, and do we not carry ample wire with hooks upon it to surround the whole place?"

"It sounds the very thing," cried Jim excitedly, having listened with great interest to all that Ali had to say. "If it is so close to the edge of the Mullah's country, it should prove an excellent base from which to set out on small spying expeditions. Then, if we do as you suggest, we ought to make it so strong that we could safely retreat to it when things become warm, and even defy the Mullah and his men. Yes, it is a good thing, I am sure, and I vote that we make for it at once."

Having discussed the matter with Tom—for, though nominally in charge of the expedition, he never neglected to call upon his friend for help—Jim decided to wait till the following morning, and then to raise the camp and search for the oasis of which Ali had spoken. Accordingly, at the first sign of dawn, all were afoot and marching to the west, in which direction the wells were situated. At length they sighted a grove of shady trees, and hailed it with a shout of joy. An hour later their zareba was formed, and Jim and his friend were closely inspecting the surroundings.

"It will be even more suitable than I had hoped," said Jim in delight. "Look at those trees, and see how they will help us."

"Yes—er—well, I confess that I cannot follow you," was the puzzled response. "We might hide in the trees—perhaps that's what you mean?"

"Partly, Tom; but I thought that they were placed in just the position to be of service to us. Look at the outside row. By cutting down a few we could have a square formed by the trunks, and giving a large clearing in the centre where the water is. Then we have only to connect the trees by means of barbed wire, and we have a fort into which the Mullah's men would find it a job to rush. Once our entanglement was completed, we could rig up some kind of a blockhouse inside, so that we should have plenty of cover, while as for the camels and horses, they of course must take their chance, though the long range of our rifles should make it possible to keep the enemy at a respectful distance, from which their old muzzle-loaders could not reach us."

"You're a wonder!" gasped Tom. "It seems to me that you are a born soldier."

"Not a bit of it," was the modest reply. "But, you see, my father was always telling me about the fights in which he had taken part. They were usually against natives, in some part of this continent, and there was always a ruse of this sort, some dodge by which he and his men held the larger numbers of the enemy at bay. That's how it is that I have an eye which seems to take in the possibilities of a place, and I put it down to my father and his yarns that I was able to make defence practicable away back at the ravine. But, seriously, what do you think of the dodge?"

"It is the best thing you have yet thought out, Jim, and should prove of enormous advantage to us; for, knowing that we have a haven to retreat to, we shall go about our work of tracking the Mullah far more fearlessly, though I tell you that, in any case, it is going to be a risky game."

Pacing backwards and forwards amongst the trees, Jim and his companion soon marked out the site of their fort. Then they called for an axe, and cut a wide slit at the base of each trunk which they had decided was to be removed, giving orders that the men were to set to at the work on the following morning. That done, they went well beyond the trees, but finding nothing but a weary sandy waste, and no cover that could be of the slightest use to an enemy, they returned to the zareba, and selected a site close beside the well, and almost in the centre of the square which they had marked off for the fort. On this a rough circle was drawn, and calling Ali to his side, Jim gave directions that the trees, when felled on the morrow, were to be dragged there, and arranged to as to form a blockhouse.

"We want a raised platform," he said, as he walked over the spot once more, and deepened the line in the earth by means of his toe. "If we set our fellows to throw up a mound round the edge of this circle, and then pile the logs there, morticing them roughly together, we shall have a fine blockhouse, from which we shall be able to command the surrounding desert for many yards. I reckon that our rifles carry a good mile, and very likely even more than that; so that in the daytime we can make it impossible for the enemy to approach, unless in overwhelming numbers. If they come in a huge army, we shall lie behind our cover and blaze at them from a position of safety, and as we have been careful to bring a large store of ammunition, we need have no fears that it will become suddenly expended. I should think, too, that a watch-tower of some sort would be useful."

"Then why not make one of these trees serve the purpose?" asked Tom, staring aloft at the green top of a palm which overhung the party. "It happens to occupy the very centre of your circle, and can easily be pegged so as to make ascent possible."

"A grand idea!" exclaimed Jim, "and that, too, shall be carried out. But now about the camels and ponies. We want a zareba into which we can drive them at night, and in case of attack."

"Then do the same for them as for ourselves," said Tom. "Look here, old boy, you ought to take particular pains to keep them well away from the water, or our supply may be fouled and rendered unfit for our consumption. Why not dig out a place for them, throwing the earth removed into a wall, which will protect them? Then, if you place the zareba over there, a trench from the wells will carry the water to them, so that their wants can be supplied."

Tom pointed to a spot within thirty yards, where the ground fell slightly, and where numerous big palms grew, offering shade for the animals.

"It would be an easy matter to do as suggested," interposed Ali Kumar, interrupting his masters. "I have seen such an arrangement before, and will see that the trench is dug, and a small wooden gate put at the head, so that a certain quantity can be allowed to run through at any time. Otherwise you would have the zareba filled with water, and the animals would quickly die. As to our being able to do all this, I can promise that the end of the week shall see the work completed, for the men will have little to do now that we are in camp, and when the beasts are driven out to graze, and sentries posted, the others will have their hours free, and will devote them to getting the camp into a state of defence."

"And while they are at work we shall make excursions into the Mullah's country," remarked Jim. "We'll just wait until the wire is stretched and the blockhouse begun, for it would not do to have the enemy coming down upon us before we were ready. Then we'll take the best camels and set out. Who knows but that we may have the luck to rescue my father without much trouble, and in a week we may even be marching for the coast once more?"

He spoke in the most hopeful manner, for the good fortune with which they had hitherto met had raised his spirits to the highest, so much so that complete success seemed even now in sight. But Jim had not yet encountered the terrible Mullah, he whose name was a byword in Northern Africa, and whose cruelties and whose cunning were talked about in every part of the civilized world. Had he had personal experience of him, his ideas would have undergone a change, for this leader of the Somali fanatics was not likely to sit down tamely and submit to the theft of a slave. Why should he indeed, when he openly boasted that he was ready to meet all the troops which the British Government could bring against him? It was out of the question to imagine for a moment that he who had so recently defeated a British column would dream of allowing this small expedition to escape his clutches, if he obtained news of its coming. Why, the guns and ammunition Jim and his following possessed would alone have been a prize, while the death of all who took part in this audacious enterprise would elevate the Mullah still higher in the estimation of the savage tribesmen who lived in these parts. Yes, had Jim been able to see into this matter as clearly as he was able to observe the strongest position for defence, he might have been less sanguine, indeed he might have trembled at the thought of all the danger before him. But he was blissfully ignorant, and went on with his plans of rescue, without allowing his mind to dwell unduly upon the prospect of difficulties which might yet have to be encountered. Would his determination have been altered had he known that at that very moment the Mullah was listening to the tale of a scout who had witnessed the march of the column on the previous day? We doubt it, for Jim was not the lad to give in till convinced that he was beaten. But, as it was, he knew nothing, and went on with his preparations with a mind which was free from uneasiness.

"We have all had a hard day," he said, "so I propose we turn in early to-night. Then we can be up with the lark, and set to at the work we have before us."

Scarcely had day dawned when all were awake, and guards having been posted to watch the grazing beasts, the remainder took spades and axes, which had been included in the baggage of the column, and, stripping to the waist, began to cut down the trees which Jim and Tom had marked on the previous day. Then, while some dragged the logs to the centre, others unrolled the barbed wire, and began to form an entanglement. A tiny doorway was left, so that the garrison could enter at will, but it was protected inside by a semicircle of the wire, so that should one of the enemy happen to rush in, he would still have an impenetrable barrier before him.

When the entanglement was completed to his satisfaction, Jim set the men to work to throw up the platform for the blockhouse, and, before darkness fell, saw it completed.

"And now for a zareba for the animals," he cried gaily, on the following morning. "Not till that is done can I leave the camp."

With Tom beside him to aid him with his advice, he directed the men how to proceed with the work, and, by way of encouraging them, seized a spade himself, and began to delve with all his might. For hours together all laboured, but, thanks to the fact that the soil was light and easily turned, the task proved easier than it might have been. Indeed, by nightfall the animals were safely enclosed, and an entanglement of wire surrounded them, so that even if the enemy managed to rush up to them, they could not cause them to stampede. A trench had been cut from the wells to this zareba, within which a long trough had been constructed of mud, so arranged that it could be filled to the brim at the will of those who lived in the blockhouse, while the contents would drain slowly away and soak into the soil outside. Standing in the centre of the miniature fort which he had caused to be erected, Jim looked about him on that evening with feelings of pride and satisfaction.

"I never could have thought it possible," he murmured to himself. "When we started from the farther side of the Hoad, it often troubled me to think what we should do to protect ourselves once we reached the Mullah's country, but I never dreamt that we should have the luck to fall in with this oasis. Why, we could live here for a month, or longer, and stand a siege without much fear; for, with these logs to protect us, we ought to be able to keep the plain outside clear of the enemy during the daytime, while our animals could graze in the large square of barbed wire which we have made. Then, as soon as they had eaten the grass there, we could send our fellows out to cut more during the night. Yes, we are in clover here, and can now take measures to rescue father. Tom, I want to ask you a question," he continued to his friend.

"Well, what is it, old boy?"

"How about leaving the camp? Will it be sufficient if Ali remains in charge?"

"I think not," Tom answered with decision. "Now that we are so close to the Mullah, we must take it for granted that an attack, sooner or later, is inevitable. That being the case, it would be fatal to leave our natives to themselves, for, if deprived of a leader, they would be like sheep, and would quickly be overcome. I know what you are worrying about. You want to know who is to stay behind?"

"That is it," responded Jim. "You see, I have had the best of it up to this, and it seems unfair to ask you to sit down here while I have all the excitement and adventure."

"Not a bit of it!" exclaimed Tom eagerly. "You must remember that this is your expedition, and that the rescue of your father is of the utmost importance. If we are successful in that, we shall have obtained plenty of information concerning the Mullah, so that we shall both be satisfied. There! Don't consider me any more, but just act as you think best."

"I'm glad to know that you think in that way, Tom," answered Jim. "And now, as you are agreeable to the arrangement, I will ask you to take charge of the camp while I go off on a scouting expedition. I propose to take Ali Kumar alone, and to strike at once for the enemy's country."

CHAPTER XII

IN TOUCH WITH THE MULLAH

Scarcely had the sun risen above the sandy horizon when Jim and Ali Kumar rode from the oasis mounted upon two of the fleetest camels which the expedition possessed. They carried upon their saddles sufficient food and water to last them for a week, while each had a rifle and abundance of ammunition. Turning their faces toward the south, they urged their beasts into a long swinging trot, and sailed away over the desert with the cheers of their comrades ringing in their ears.

"Before we return I hope to have obtained full news of my father," said Jim, as they swept along. "If I find that he is only slightly guarded, I shall take advantage of some dark night and try to reach him, and if we get him to the camp, the Mullah may do as he likes, but I defy him to capture us, for our position there is remarkably strong."

"During the daytime the attempt will be hopeless," answered Ali Kumar thoughtfully. "But, master, I tremble to think of the consequences during the night, for we are few, and they would be many. Creeping up to us, they would rush upon us before we were prepared, and then nothing could save the expedition."

"We shall see about that," exclaimed Jim doggedly. "It seems to me that if we were to light big fires round our square, we ought to be able to keep the enemy out. But I agree with you, it would be a hard matter, and could not be accomplished without fighting. And now for ourselves. Are we likely to strike the Mullah's camp if we push on in this direction?"

"I cannot say for certain," responded Ali. "But you will remember that the tribesmen informed us that the white prisoner was some thirty miles south of the Hoad. If that is the case, we should be nearer the Mullah by nightfall. By that time it will be advisable to find some spot in which we can safely hide. Then, on the following day, we can sally out, and, pretending to be peaceful peasants, try to ascertain news of your father."

"It sounds a good plan, Ali, but you must recollect that I am ignorant of the language. That being the case, it may be necessary for me to remain hidden while you go out, though when the time for rescue comes, I insist upon taking a full share in the matter."

An hour after they had set out from the oasis the two riders entered upon a stretch of country which differed vastly from that which they had just left, for it was thickly clad with a carpet of fresh green, and was dotted everywhere with bushes and trees, and in parts with huge masses of foliage which showed the position of a forest. But nowhere was there a habitation visible, and not a native was to be seen. Half a mile farther on, however, was a large pool of water, from which the rays of the sun were reflected with dazzling brilliancy; and to this they at once rode, following one of the many paths that had been worn through the bush in all directions by wild animals.

"Half an hour's halt here, and then on we go," said Jim. "How thankful I am that this is the cool season, and that the heat of the sun is not too great to prevent our marching during the day."

"It is fortunate, master," answered Ali, "for less than three months hence the journey which we have already accomplished would have had to satisfy us until nightfall. Then only could we have ventured to start forward again, for at the time of noon the glare and strength of the sun are so great that even a native prefers the shade, and loves to lie there and sleep. But now we need have no fears of sunstroke, and can ride on. Our beasts are in the finest condition, and we can rely upon them to carry us the remaining thirty miles with the utmost ease. To-morrow, if necessary, they will bear us back again with the same certainty, for these are picked animals, and are worth some thirty of the common kind. But I shall prepare food, so that we may eat now and then pass on without halting."

Taking the rough bits from the mouths of the camels, Ali led them to the water and allowed them to drink. Then he picketed them in the centre of a patch of luxuriant grass, and left them there to graze to their hearts' content, while he returned to help Jim with the meal. Already the latter had a cheery fire burning, and was toasting two large juicy steaks of deer-flesh over it. When they were ready, and the water boiling, both sat down beside the embers, there being no ceremony between master and man. Indeed, looking at them there, a stranger would have been troubled to tell the difference between these two Somali natives, for both had dusky features and dark hair, while their gestures were apparently the same. A closer inspection, however, would have shown him that the younger of the two could find no comfort in the squatting attitude of which the natives are fond, and preferred to lie upon the ground reclining upon his elbow. Then, again, he ate more daintily, and drank from his tin mug as if he had been accustomed to better things. But what was remarkable about the two was the fact that each possessed a rifle of modern workmanship, while Jim had a pair of revolvers, the butt of one of which peeped from beneath his clothing.

Their meal finished, Ali took from a pouch which dangled about his neck a pinch of tobacco, and securing it in the hollow of his hand, proceeded to roll a cigarette. Surely this was a strange thing for a native in this wild part of the country to do! True, many followers of the Mullah indulged in the smoking habit, but none knew of the cigarette. Ali, however, had learnt the art at Berbera, and, indeed, behaved more like a civilized individual than any native that Jim had as yet seen.

"I am a Christian and can sit at meat with my master, when he wills," he had said some days before. "Therefore, should it fall out that you and I ride away together, there will be no trouble on that score, though with any other of your followers difficulties would arise, for they could not eat with you, while to drink from the same vessel would be an insult to their religion."

Having finished his cigarette, Ali sprang to his feet, and soon they were on their way again. Riding across an undulating country, they at length reached a part which was studded with hills, and upon ascending to the summit of one of these, both came suddenly to a halt, and uttered a cry of satisfaction.

"Back, master!" cried Ali in alarm, a second later. "Dismount from your camel, and cause him to kneel, then creep forward with me, and lie full length among the bushes, for, were we to ascend to the sky-line, our figures would be seen at once. There, look!" he continued a moment later, as they threw themselves upon the grass and stared into the valley beyond. "You can see the mud huts which the Mullah's followers occupy, and there are his herds."

Stretching his arm before him, Ali pointed down the farther slope of the hill into a long winding depression, down the centre of which ran a broad stream of water. Following his finger, Jim saw some hundreds of low mud hovels, nestling close to the bank of the river, and so clear was the atmosphere that he was able to distinguish numerous figures moving about, while herds of camels, sheep, and horses were visible everywhere.

"What is that?" he suddenly asked, pointing in his turn to a dark mass in the centre of the valley. "It looks to me as though there were horsemen there, but I shall soon tell you, for I have brought my glasses with me."

Hastily withdrawing his field-glasses from the case, he raised them to his eyes and looked long and carefully towards the object which he had discovered.

"It is the Mullah's army," he said in an excited whisper, as if he feared that the ordinary tones of his voice would be overheard at that distance, and so alarm the enemy. "I can see a host of horsemen, and more than three times as many men on foot. And—yes, there is someone riding in front of them, who must be the Mullah."

The sight at which he gazed filled Jim with a feeling of excitement, for now, at last, he was within touch of his goal. There, below him, was the man to whom his father was a slave, and there, careering up the valley, were a portion of the following who might even then be on their way to attack the foolhardy Englishman who had come in quest of the prisoner. Could Jim have read the thoughts of that tall man who so proudly rode his charger in front of the gathering of warriors below, he would have learned something that intimately concerned himself. As he sat his horse there before his following, his face was turned in the direction from which Jim and Ali had come, and his mind was engaged with the news which had come to his ears two or three days before.

"An insolent Englishman has dared to cross the Hoad," he was murmuring to himself. "His purpose, as told me by the spy, is to rescue one of my beggarly prisoners. Let him beware. Before many hours have passed I will slay his whole following, and he, too, shall find himself a slave."

Turning his horse with a touch of his heel, the Mullah held his hand above his head and arrested the progress of his following. Then spurring close up to them, he gave them their orders, and stood by as they marched away.

"I wonder where they are bound for?" said Jim, as he watched the movement through his glasses. "Their heads were turned towards the north, and it looks as though they were bent upon a journey which would take some time, for camels laden with baggage are accompanying them, while some followers are driving a small herd of sheep and cattle. I hope it does not mean that they have discovered our camp, and are marching to attack it."

"I cannot say, master," answered Ali thoughtfully. "But their movement looks suspicious. However, should they have gained news of our coming, it will be only as I have expected all along, for how could we hope to enter the country of this man without being discovered, when spies abound, and when news may even have been sent from Berbera? Besides, what of the traitor who induced the tribesmen to attack us? He had fled, so said their messenger, but where or how he did not mention. Perhaps he took advantage of the confusion to steal a camel, and with that to help him, crossed the Hoad, knowing that he would be welcome to the Mullah. If that is the case, we have trouble before us, and perhaps it would be better for us to retire at once, so as to rejoin our companions."

"I think not," answered Jim promptly. "If those fellows down there are bound for our camp, we can do no possible good by returning to our friends, for we should only make a small addition to their numbers. No, when we set out for this part, we did so with the full knowledge that the camp in the oasis might have to defend itself at any moment. We placed my comrade in charge, trusting to him to keep the enemy out, and we must not allow this to break our faith in him and our followers. Let us leave them to do their work while we complete ours. When you come to think of it, the movement of those men below is probably the best thing that could have happened, that is, supposing they are not successful in their attack, as I firmly believe will be the case; for, knowing that his followers have gone to intercept us, the Mullah will never suspect that two of our expedition have detached themselves from the main body, and are already in touch with his camp. He and those of his men who remain with him will have no fear of a surprise of any sort, and will therefore neglect all precautions. What could be more advantageous to our cause?"

"It is a fine argument," replied Ali Kumar, after a long pause, "and I believe you have seen this matter in the right light. As you say, to lose faith now in our friends would be foolish. If they are attacked, as I think is more than probable, they must trust to themselves, and live or fall according to their ability. Meanwhile we have a chance which may never occur again. Therefore, master, while you keep your glasses fixed upon the Mullah's following, I shall leave you for a time and search for a hiding-place. When I have found it I shall return, and then we shall make our way down to the camels."

Accordingly Ali turned and descended the hill, leaving Jim stretched out upon the summit, with his eyes fixed upon the distant warriors. In half an hour the Mullah's expedition had disappeared behind an elevation, and Jim at once turned his glasses upon the solitary horseman who had watched them depart. He saw him put his horse into a furious gallop, and head him towards the collection of mud hovels. Then he watched as the rider pulled in his animal, and threw himself from the saddle. At this moment a native ran out and took the reins from him, while the Mullah strode into the midst of the camp. Though he was often hidden for a considerable time by some clump of huts, Jim was able to follow him as he advanced by watching for him as he crossed the open spaces. At last he reached a house of considerable proportions, above the flat roof of which a tattered banner blew out in the tropical breeze, showing a groundwork of brilliant red, with figures worked upon it in darker colours. A spear seemed to form the supporting post.

"He's gone in," said Jim, watching the figure of the Mullah with the utmost eagerness. "I must make a careful note of the position of his house, for I might have to find my way there some day. Indeed, if father is there—and I see no other way of rescuing him—I shall choose a dark night, and creep into the mud hut into which the Mullah has disappeared. Then I'll put a pistol to his head, and give him the choice of death or the loss of his slave. But I should have to be very careful of treachery, and in any case it would be a desperate game to play. However, we shall see. Having come so far, I do not mean to turn back before I have made every effort, and if I fail after all, why, I'll return to Berbera, join the British troops, and march in this direction again in their company."

For long Jim lay full-length among the grass with which this hill was thickly clad, and gazed down into the valley which formed the home and hiding-place of the Mullah and his adherents. Every now and again he would catch sight of some figure moving along the bank of the river, or passing down the only street of which the village boasted. Instantly, up would go his glasses to his eyes, and he would focus them upon the object, hoping that this might prove to be the white prisoner, his father. But in every case the figure proved to be some dusky warrior, trudging along with his spear over one shoulder, and his hide-shield dangling on his other arm, or one of the many wives with which these Somali fighting men were blessed, walking down to the water to replenish her household stock. Full as Jim's thoughts were of other things, he could not help remarking the graceful carriage of these people. With erect figures, and arms swinging easily at their sides, these women bore upon their heads a tall earthen jar, which they balanced there with as much ease as the average individual contrives to retain his hat.

Later, a movement about the central dwelling from which the flag flew attracted his attention, and looking closely in that direction, he saw four armed men suddenly emerge from the shadow of the walls into the road in front, where they formed up in line. Four others at once placed themselves in front of their comrades, and having saluted one another in ceremonious fashion, as people of the East are accustomed to do, they separated, the first party disappearing down the street, while the second filed into their positions about the Mullah's residence. But of the latter there was never a sign; he remained in the seclusion of his mud hut, his thoughts, no doubt, fixed upon that tiny camp belonging to the insolent Englishman, which he hoped to hear, in the course of a few hours, had fallen a prey to his followers.

"I must be careful to remember about those guards," murmured Jim thoughtfully, "for should it become necessary for me to visit the house, they might interrupt our interview and spoil my chances. But we shall see; perhaps Ali will have good news for me."

For three hours he lay on the summit of the hill, keeping a careful watch on the Mullah's camp, and wondering all the while what had happened to his native headman, and why his return was so long delayed.

"I hope nothing has happened to him," he said at last, in anxious tones. "It would be a serious matter if he were captured, for it would let the Mullah know that there were spies close at hand. But I can't think what has happened to him, for amongst the following below there must be a huge number of strange men collected together, and Ali's clever enough to pass himself as one of these. Besides——Hallo! Who's that?"

Happening to turn his head to look at the two camels which were grazing some two hundred yards in the rear, Jim suddenly caught sight of a figure running towards him, and waving an arm to attract his attention. Grasping his rifle, and shooting a cartridge into the breech, he at once retired from the summit of the hill, taking care to creep on all-fours through the grass until well away from the sky-line. Then he started to his feet, and running forward until close to a large mass of rock, he knelt behind it, and, raising his weapon to his shoulder, covered the man who was approaching.

"Very likely it is Ali," he said to himself; "but should it happen to be anyone else, I shall be quite ready for him."

A minute later any doubts which he might have had were dispelled, for, topping a rise which intervened between himself and Jim, the stranger showed clearly against the distant horizon.

"Ali!" cried Jim, in tones of relief; and at once rising from his seat, he hastened towards him with his rifle over his shoulder, and his mind filled with alarm at the evident excitement under which his follower laboured.

"What is it? What has happened, Ali?" he demanded. "Have you been discovered? And if so, are you being followed? In that case we had better get the camels ready at once, so that we may ride for our lives, for to attempt to remain here would be madness."

"No, do not touch our animals, but sit down and listen," answered Ali breathlessly, throwing himself upon the ground, as if he were exhausted, and lying there panting so hard that he seemed unable to speak. At length, however, he took a sip of water from the gourd which dangled at his waist, and seeming to revive at once, sat up and gazed at his master.

"All is well," he said, "and I have not been discovered. But I have seen things which have caused me to tremble with alarm, and which sent me back to you at my fastest pace to warn you."

"What is it, then," asked Jim anxiously, unable to guess what could have happened to his follower. "Come, tell me at once, Ali."

Leaning forward, he placed his hand upon the native's shoulder and shook him gently so as to hasten him, for the sight of Ali's excitement had filled him with a vague feeling of alarm.

"Listen, then, master, and I shall tell you what happened to me after I left you upon the summit of the hill. But first let us climb to our position again, and take our posts there, for I warn you that if we are to escape from this place alive, we must be ever watchful, and keep our eyes constantly fixed upon the valley below."

This wise precaution was immediately carried out. Then Ali turned towards Jim and continued his story.

"When I left you," he said, "I placed my rifle beside a boulder, for I knew that it would at once arouse the cupidity and suspicion of any whom I might meet. Then I descended the hill, and taking advantage of a long stretch of thick undergrowth which ran towards the village, I reached its outskirts without having seen a single stranger. Then I watched for an hour as the people walked to and fro, and happening to see two women who were busily engaged in crushing corn for their bread, I crept into the house behind them, and sat in the doorway listening to their conversation. From what they said I gathered that the Mullah can collect as many as sixty thousand men to march behind his banner, but that the greater portion are at present living peaceful lives in their own particular portion of the country. However, as soon as the British troops advance, the call to arms will be sounded, and all will hasten to join the Mullah. A little while later, one of the women began to speak of the expedition which started out this morning, and from her I learned that it has undoubtedly gone in search of our camp. But guns are scarce, and it seems that the band only has about fifty with it. That the Mullah had warning of our approach was evident, for one of the women stated that her husband was the scout who had observed our arrival on this side of the Hoad.

"Though I listened to their chatter for long, I learned nothing more of importance, for they conversed about their children and their homes. And so, carefully looking down the street, and observing that large numbers were about, I slipped in amongst them, feeling confident that my presence would not be noticed. Soon I was in their market, and following the lead of others of the men who were about, I purchased some fruit, haggling over the price, as is customary. Then, as I wandered from the stalls into the street again, I saw the white prisoner coming towards me."

"The white prisoner! My father!" almost shouted Jim, his pulses throbbing with the news. "Are you sure that it was he? What did he look like? Was he ill, and overcome by his miserable condition?"

He clutched Ali eagerly by the arm and poured the questions upon him so rapidly that the latter could not answer, but lay there gazing at him stolidly, as if astounded at his excitement.

"Gently! Speak quietly, master," he replied. "The questions which you ask are unnecessary, for there is but one prisoner, one white slave owned by the Mullah; assuredly, this one whom I saw is your father, and that he is ill and downcast is only to be expected. Indeed, so heavy are his cares, and so great the labour demanded of him, that already he has aged. Though but a few weeks have passed since he was cast upon this coast, and fell into the hands of these, our enemies, yet the time has been sufficient to make great changes in him. He is a tall man, but no longer does he bear himself proudly, for this drudgery and the hopelessness of life have overcome his spirit. He lacks energy, and walks along with eyes cast down and with never a thought of his surroundings. Indeed, it is clear that his mind is forever bent upon escape, and that when he chances to look to right or left he does so with the hope that something shall be there to help him—some friend who, pitying his condition, has come prepared to stretch out a hand, and aid him to reach his countrymen once more. As he passed me by, and looked at me vacantly, ignorant of the fact that I was in reality a comrade of his son who had marched all this way and had encountered so many dangers in the hope of rescuing him, it went to my heart to notice the deep lines that care had set upon his face, and the whiteness of his hair. Yes, master, no longer is it grey at the temples alone."

"Poor father!" murmured Jim sorrowfully, his pity raised to the highest at Ali's words. "Poor dad! What a change in his condition!"

For more than a minute there was silence.

"Go on!" at last said Jim, in more resolute tones. "It was a blow to hear that there is such a change in my father, and that he was so downcast. But after considering the matter, I am bound to confess that it is only to be expected. I must congratulate myself upon the fact that you have seen him alive, for we might have arrived at the Mullah's camp to find him dead, worn out by his sufferings. What if his hair is grey? Other men have lost their colour in a night under some great strain, but they have recovered it to some extent later on. Father will do the same. Once free, he will become the same jolly fellow I have always known him."

Tears stood in Jim's eyes as he spoke, for he was deeply moved at the thought of his father's condition, but with an effort he steadied himself, and signalled to Ali to proceed by raising his hand, for he could not trust himself to speak.

"Be happy, master. It matters nothing, whatever the colour of the hair, so long as life is there," answered Ali, in reassuring tones. "But let me proceed. Had I dared to do so, I would have signed to the prisoner and endeavoured to meet him in some out-of-the-way spot, but I saw that such an act would have been madness, for as he approached, I noticed first one, and then a second, armed warrior lounging amidst the throng, but keeping a careful eye all the while upon their charge. Even when my eyes and the prisoner's met, I could do nothing but turn hastily away and gaze at the passers-by on the opposite side. Then, little by little, I moved in the direction taken by your father, hoping to discover the house in which he dwelt, and have speech with him. But the attempt was doomed to disappointment in the last respect, for his guards kept ever at his side. However, I had the good fortune to find where he slept. It is that tumble-down dwelling which stands behind the central one from which the flag hangs, and some few paces away from it. See! There it is! And before the door is an armed Somali warrior keeping watch upon the prisoner."

Rising to his knees, Ali leant one hand upon the ground and with the other directed Jim's eyes to the house of which he had spoken.

"Behind the big one, and with a man in front of the door," remarked the latter, with his eyes glued to the glasses. "Yes, I can see it, Ali, and feel sure that I can make my way to it in the dark. But go on with your story."

"Half an hour passed without my seeing the prisoner again," said Ali, sinking into the grass once more, "so I crept away, and rejoined the people. Then, just as I was about to make my way back to you, I suddenly caught sight of a face which set me trembling. My knees knocked together in my terror, and had I not clung to the post of a doorway which stood near at hand, I should have fallen, for never before has death been so near to me."

He turned to Jim with flashing eyes, and with cheeks which looked pale in spite of his dusky complexion. Indeed, glancing at his features, it was easy to see that his fear was great, and that the face which he had caught sight of had caused him no little uneasiness.

"I should have fallen," he repeated, "but the doorpost held me up while this man passed. Then I turned upon my heel, and slipping from the village, fled hither for my life."

"Who can it have been? Speak, man!" demanded Jim impatiently, bewildered at his follower's words. "A strange face? Why! It cannot have been——"

"Yes, master, it was the traitor who led the tribesmen against us," gasped Ali. "Of a sudden I saw him coming towards me, and I trembled lest he should recognize me; for, had he done so, that instant would have been the signal for my death, and with my life would have gone all your hopes, too. Our danger is now greater than ever before, and it seems to me that we should be foolish to remain any longer."

"And why?" demanded Jim curtly, a look of determination coming over his face. "You are unmanned by this incident and your imagination. What if the traitor is in the Mullah's village? Is it likely that he suspects that we are close at hand? No! I tell you he is chuckling at the thought that we are with our friends, and that the followers of the Mullah are about to attack us. Pull yourself together, Ali, and be a man! Or, if you cannot, leave me to carry out the rescue alone, for I declare that I will not retire. To-night I shall go down to that hut and endeavour to rescue the prisoner. If it is impossible, I shall wait for another opportunity; but turn my face the other way and leave father to his fate I will not, not even if our presence here is discovered."

He spoke the words almost fiercely, and turned upon his follower with flushed features and angry eye.

"Well, what is it to be?" he demanded curtly. "There are the camels below. Take one, and fly at once, if you will, for I had rather that you did not stay if you are not ready to stand by me."

"Master, I was a coward for the moment," answered Ali humbly. "The sight of that traitor and my narrow escape filled me with fear, and I returned to you feeling as though the Somali warriors were following closely upon me, shouting for my life. But you are brave, and help me to act rightly in this matter. Forgive me. I will stand by you, whatever the danger, and if you persist in going into the Mullah's village to-night in the hope of releasing the captive, I will follow you at a distance and await you with the camels. If, by chance, you are unsuccessful, and fall into the hands of these people, I swear that I will not leave this part till I have done my utmost to help you. Go, then, and may God aid you in your undertaking!"

There was no doubt of his earnestness, for, rising to his knees once more, he extended his hand and grasped Jim's firmly, looking steadily into his eyes.

"You are a man again, and will be true to your word," said Jim simply. "Now bring up the food and water, for at sundown I shall leave for the Mullah's camp."

CHAPTER XIII

THE WHITE PRISONER

Wearily did the hours pass as Jim and his companion lay upon the summit of the hill, gazing down into the valley below. Indeed, it seemed as though the sun would never sink, and as though its course from east to west was slower upon this eventful day than upon any other. At length, however, when they were almost worn out with impatience and anxiety, the huge golden orb sank out of their sight below a distant line of blue hills, setting the sky aglow with every shade of the spectrum, blended together to form one magnificent whole. Soon, too, sunset hues faded into mist, and with a suddenness which is peculiar to these latitudes, a pall of darkness covered the earth. Then out came the stars, twinkling above like so many diamonds, while down below a point of fire here and there showed where the camp was situated.

For an hour Jim lay there busy with his thoughts, and listening to the sounds which were distinctly borne upon his ear, in spite of the distance which intervened between himself and the village.

"It will take me the better part of an hour to get from here to the neighbourhood of the hut in which father sleeps," he said, "so I shall start now. I have thought the whole matter carefully over, and it seems to me that I cannot do better than leave my rifle and cartridges behind as Ali did. But I shall take a dagger with me—my hunting-knife will answer the purpose admirably. Then if I knock up against anyone and he proves disagreeable, I shall have a weapon at hand with which to overcome him silently. If more than one should attack me, I shall have to fall upon my revolvers, which I shall, of course, carry with me. Ali! I want you."

He called softly to his companion, who crept to his side immediately.

"What can I do, master?" he asked.

"I am going to start now," said Jim quietly, "and want you to accompany me half-way. I shall then leave you with the camels and go on alone. But it is important that we should arrange a meeting-place to which I shall be able to find my way without fail. You have already made a trip to the Mullah's stronghold, and may have fixed upon a likely spot."

"That is the case," answered the native follower. "I shall come with you now, and when within half a mile of the huts, I shall halt in a tiny ravine. You will have no difficulty in finding your way to it on your return, for a path leads to the entrance, where there is a well, and then branches off to the right. Though the place is close to the enemy's sleeping quarters, it is secluded, and will form good cover for myself and the camels. There I shall await your coming, and that you may be accompanied by your father is the sincere wish of your servant."

"I trust that it will turn out like that, Ali; and if hard work and a little boldness on my part will help towards it, why, success ought to follow. But we shall see. Now let us be going."

A few minutes later both were silently descending the hill, taking the greatest pains to refrain from stumbling over boulders, or setting smaller stones rolling down to the plain below; for there was never any knowing when and where an enemy might be lurking, though the fact that it was a cold night made it probable that all the Somali warriors would be comfortably ensconced in their mud huts, enjoying the warmth to be obtained there. Indeed, there seemed to be none but themselves abroad that night, for they caught sight of none, and, but for the yapping of a native cur, heard not a single sound. But that someone was awake and alert in the Mullah's stronghold was certain, for the reflection of a big wood-fire which burnt in front of the central building could be seen in the sky, while the peculiar smell came pungently to their nostrils.

"Here is the ravine," said Ali at last, when they had descended to the plain, and had traversed a mile of the level country. "Look at the spot closely, master. There is the well. You cannot mistake it, for the light of the stars is reflected from the water, while here is the entrance to the ravine of which I spoke. I shall await your coming some yards further in, and should it fall out that you do not return, I shall make my way back to the hill-top an hour before the day dawns. To-morrow night I shall be here again, and if it should happen that you, too, are made a captive, then I will find my way into the village, and seek to help you. Ali Kumar has sworn to stand by his brave master, and he shall do so, even though he comes by his death in keeping to his word. And now good-bye. I wish you all success."

"Good-bye," repeated Jim heartily, gripping his dusky comrade by the hand.

"I have little fear of failure, though I shall not allow that to prevent my taking every precaution. If I should have bad luck, I know that I can trust you to keep your promise, and I shall expect to hear from you. But let us hope that it will not come to that. Stay quietly where you are, and when you hear a low cough, step forward and declare yourself, for we shall have arrived. Good-bye."

Releasing the native's hand, Jim at once strode off into the darkness, and in another moment was lost to view. But as he stood there at the mouth of the ravine, listening with all his ears, the faithful Ali could hear the sound of his muffled footsteps shuffling along over the loose soil of which the path was composed.

"Farewell," whispered Ali, as the sound died away. "May fortune smile upon you, for you are a brave and loyal son, and are deserving of much reward."

Turning his face towards the glare of the distant camp-fire, Jim struck off into the darkness, and was soon close to the huts which stood on the fringe of the village. By now the moon had risen higher, and enabled him to see his way more clearly, though, being only a small crescent, it did not give sufficient light to show his figure at more than a few paces. Taking advantage of this fact, he pressed on without hesitation, and, before he had expected it, was close to the dwelling which stood in the centre. Yes, there it was without doubt, for he could see the folds of the red flag floating lazily in the still night breeze, beating ever and anon against the spear-shaft which supported it, and giving rise to a flapping sound, which, until the cause of it was clear, was decidedly disconcerting.

"At last!" murmured Jim. "Over there is the hut which shelters the Mullah, while in the other sleeps his slave, my dear father. Whatever happens, I must and will reach him and rescue him. But how?"

The question was one which could not be answered easily, and which set him puzzling his brains. Half an hour before it had seemed to him more or less a simple matter to creep close to the mud dwelling beneath which his father slept and to gain access to him by means of a doorway, or perhaps by cutting a hole through the wall. Now, however, when the reality was before him, and he was actually brought face to face with the difficulty, he could not but admit that the danger and magnitude of the task were far greater than he had ever imagined.

But he was not the lad to give way, or to be easily discouraged, particularly where his father's life was concerned.

"It looks rather difficult, I must admit," said Jim to himself, going on all-fours at the same moment, and then lying flat upon his face. "It seems to me that I cannot do better than wait here, hidden in this long grass, until I am certain of the whereabouts of the sentries. During the daytime I know that four keep watch over the Mullah, while one sits before the door of the prisoner. But do they still act as sentries when night has fallen? I should think that their number is reduced, particularly now, when all seems at peace, and the British have not yet entered the country. Still, it will be well to make certain of the fact, for it would be fatal to walk into the arms of one of these Somali warriors just as I was about to communicate with the prisoner."

Many minutes passed as he reclined full-length in the grass, and it was only when his stock of patience was well-nigh exhausted that he observed a movement close to the door of the hut in which the prisoner lived.

"A sentry," he said to himself, as a figure suddenly rose from the ground and stood erect, with arms wide outstretched. "And evidently sleepy, too," he added, as the native again raised his limbs and yawned deeply, showing a profile which was clear and distinct against the watch-fire which burnt some paces beyond. "I must keep my eyes upon him, and see where he rests, for that is what the fellow will do, I should fancy. He knows, or rather thinks, that there is nothing to fear, and being tired, he will indulge in a snooze. Well, if he does so, all the better for my hopes."

A few moments later the native slouched across to the opposite dwelling, the one in which the Mullah lived, and after looking about him and conversing for a short while with a second sentry who marched at the front, sat down deliberately against the wall, and folding his arms, gave himself up unrestrainedly to sleep.

"They have most likely arranged to keep watch for one another," thought Jim. "This fellow will have a couple or more hours' rest, and then will have to relieve his comrade. If that is the arrangement, it will suit me very well, for the man who is on duty now will devote himself to the Mullah, and will pay only casual attention to the prisoner's hut. I shall wait till he has strolled round this way, and then I shall make a dash for the door, and trust to getting in before he takes it into his head to have a second look. Ah, here he comes!"

The guard came sauntering round the larger of the two huts, and allowed Jim to obtain a good view of his features, for he, too, as if he had caught the infection from his comrade, stopped in the glare of the firelight and yawned loudly, throwing his head back and stretching in a manner which showed how drowsy he was. Then he went to the mud hut, and fumbled at the door. To Jim's delight, it opened, showing that it was not secured in any way. But the sentry had another object in view than to test the fastenings, for, drawing it back as far as it would go, he stepped on one side so as not to obstruct the rays of the moon, and then peered in. Evidently he caught sight of the prisoner, for he gave vent to a guttural murmur of approval, and then closed the door to with a jar. Then he slouched away, carrying his spear over his shoulder, with his shield dangling to it by a length of twisted leather.

"Now is my chance," murmured Jim. "I'll give him a moment to get round the corner, and then I'll make a dart for the hut. Here goes!"

Turning his eyes for one second to the figure of the sleeping man, he sprang to his feet, and crept softly across the ground. An open space was before him, but he did not hesitate, and, pressing on, was before the door of the prison in half a dozen strides. A moment sufficed to unlatch it, and swinging it back, he crawled in on all-fours, closing it after him with the greatest caution.

"And now for the prisoner," he said. "I must be careful how I awake him, for in his astonishment he might unwittingly give the alarm and ruin all my plans. But first, where is he?"

Kneeling upon the floor of hard-beaten clay, he stared into the darkness in which the interior of the dwelling was buried, endeavouring to make out the figure of the prisoner. And all the while, though he fought to steady himself, and struggled to keep his limbs from trembling, his heart would beat against his ribs with such force, and with such a resounding noise, that it threatened to betray him. And who could blame him for being so excited, for being so unnerved that he was almost incapable of any movement, and knelt there as if carved in stone? Who, indeed, with such interests at stake? Had he not toiled over miles and miles of sandy desert and sun-baked ground to reach this spot? Was not this almost the summit of his hopes and his ambitions? Here he was, after long marching and infinite toil, in reach of his prize at last, within sight of the end of his arduous task, and, wonder of wonders, the thought of it all had so excited him, so unmanned him, indeed, that for more than a minute he was helpless, a mere child in the heart of the enemy's camp. But the change did not last for long; for of a sudden his eyes fell upon a huddled figure lying in the corner, and with a thrill he realized that it was the white prisoner.

"Father! father!" he murmured, with lips which would tremble in spite of himself. "I am here—Jim! Your son—come to rescue you! Wake up, and talk to me."

But there was no answer to his words save a deep snore, and the sound of heavy breathing, which showed that the white prisoner was still fast asleep. A moment later, however, Jim had crawled to his side, and taking the very necessary precaution to place a finger upon the sleeper's lips, shook him gently with his other hand.

"Wake up, father," he whispered, placing his lips close to his ear. "It is Jim. Don't you know me?"

"Who's that? What's the matter?" asked the prisoner, suddenly sitting up and speaking as if bewildered. "I swear that I heard someone talking in English. But no, it cannot be the case. I've dreamt the same thing time and again, until my heart is sick at the thought. No, I am a slave to these brutes, and shall remain so till the end of my days."

Strange! The voice seemed harsher than that to which Jim was accustomed. But, no doubt, hardship had altered it.

"Don't try to sleep any more," he whispered eagerly. "The voice is real. I am here—Jim! Can't you tell?"

The prisoner, who had again thrown himself upon the floor, shot up into a sitting position as if he had been struck, and sat there staring at the figure beside him, as if unable to believe his ears.

"It's true, then?" he said huskily. "But who are you? Jim? Who's Jim? I know of none of that name, save an old shipmate who sailed a trip or two to the 'shiny' with me. Who is it, then? But anyway I reckon that it is a friend."

At the words a dreadful fear fell upon Jim, and crawling closer to the prisoner, he stared eagerly into his face, endeavouring to make out in the obscurity of the hut what were the features. As if to help him in his trouble, a few stray rays of the moon managed at that moment to penetrate a chink between the door and its post, and, falling upon the white stranger, allowed a closer scrutiny than would otherwise have been possible. To describe the disappointment, the dismay, which Jim felt would be impossible; for, after all his care, after all his labours and trials, he saw that a hideous error had been made, and that the white prisoner was not the Colonel Hubbard who was reported to have escaped the wreck in the Gulf of Aden.

"Not my father?" murmured Jim brokenly, feeling crushed by the weight of the blow. "I have marched miles to win this meeting, and came here this night in the hope that I was about to release my father from prison. And now I find that you are a stranger. The disappointment is almost too hard to bear."

"And where have you come from, may I ask?" whispered the stranger. "As yet I, too, am bewildered, and it is as much as I can do to understand that at last I am listening to another Englishman. Why, man, it seems years since I heard the language, though in reality it's a matter of a week or so only. But you say you have come here to rescue. Where from, then? I cannot make head or tail of this affair. But steady! As you value your life, keep your words low, for our guards have sharp ears, and sharper and more ready spears."

For some minutes Jim could make no reply to the man's questions, for he felt stunned with the blow, indeed, so dazed and bewildered that he might have been totally unconscious, so still did he lie. His breath came in gasps and catches, and it was with difficulty that he could repress the tears which welled to his eyes, and made frantic efforts to overflow.

"Not my father?" he repeated at length. "But who are you?"

"An unlucky dog who happened to be thrown ashore after a wreck in the Gulf of Aden," was the answer. "For three years have I been a prisoner to this fiend who goes by the name of the 'Mad' Mullah."

"Then, do you know of another?" asked Jim eagerly, seizing the stranger by the arm, and bringing his face so close to his that they almost touched. "Tell me at once! Quick, I cannot wait!"

In his anxiety to hear the news, Jim shook the stranger and whispered the question fiercely in his ear, feeling as though his own life and happiness depended upon the answer.

"Hush! Steady, man! You will have our guard rushing upon us if you are not careful. There! What is that? I can hear the man outside coming to make his usual inspection. We are discovered, and shall be killed."

For the space of a few seconds both sat upon the mud floor, staring at the wicket and listening attentively. As they did so, the shuffling sound made by a man walking with sandals upon his feet could be heard approaching, and instantly Jim realized that this must be the sentry who was doing duty for himself and for his comrades.

"Lie down just here, and pretend to be asleep," he whispered quickly. "He will do as he did before, and will throw open the door so as to obtain a clear view of the interior. But the light of the moon will only fall just where you are, while the remainder of the hut will be in darkness. I'll get over into the corner, and level my revolver at his head. If he discovers me, I shall shoot, and you had better be ready to join me at once. In the confusion we shall make a bolt for the hiding-place in which I have a follower and two camels. Do you understand? Quick with your answer!"

The white prisoner gave a rapid response in the affirmative, and at once lay down in the attitude of sleep, whilst Jim leaped across the hut into the darkest corner. Then gently drawing a revolver from beneath his waistcloth, he shuffled a few inches to the left until he could get a partial view of the doorway, at which he at once presented his weapon.

Almost immediately the sound of the latch was heard, seeming to break upon the stillness with startling loudness. Then the twisted leather hinges creaked, while the foot of the door scraped over the ground, allowing a flood of moonlight to pour into the room. In the centre of the brilliant patch could be seen the dark shadow of the sentry, slanting across the floor until it fell upon the sleeper, and hung over him. But a moment later the man stepped on one side, and then there was silence once more as he peered in. Sitting there, in his dark corner, Jim could hear the man's heavy breathing, and kept his revolver steadily levelled, knowing that if he were to be discovered it would be during the next few seconds. Breathlessly he waited, not daring to move a finger, but feeling all the while as though the man's eyes were searching every nook and cranny of the hut, and had fixed themselves upon him. Indeed, so firmly was he convinced of this that he began to stretch a little farther to one side till the head of the sentry came into view. And there he remained in his strained position, the muzzle of his weapon covering the intruder, and his finger on the trigger, ready to press it and send the death-dealing bullet home. An age seemed to pass before the Somali warrior ended his scrutiny of the hut, and it was with a feeling of indescribable relief that Jim saw his head withdrawn, and heard the rasping of the wicket again as it closed. As if fascinated, he watched the patch of moonlight diminish, and then sat there with the moisture pouring from his forehead, listening to the sounds outside.

JIM KEPT HIS REVOLVER STEADILY LEVELLED.

"A narrow squeak, I think," said a voice from the farther end. "That beggar seemed to be suspicious, and as I lay there watching him through a half-closed eye, I felt sure that he was about to enter. Had he done so, and you had not fired, I should have been upon his back in a moment, and you could have trusted me to bring him to the ground with a broken neck, for that is a trick of which these Somali people are very fond. Come over and join me, and I will go on with my tale."

Creeping across the floor, Jim took the precaution first of replacing his revolver, for in the darkness there was the danger always of an accidental explosion, which would have been a very serious matter. Then he seated himself close beside the stranger, and together they conversed in whispers.

"Answer my questions," said Jim eagerly, "then you can tell all about yourself."

"Make your mind easy," was the answer, "for I have good news for you. But first, say who you are."

"Jim Hubbard, son of Colonel Hubbard, wrecked on the Somali coast a matter of six weeks ago."

"And a gallant young fellow!" was the energetic response.

"Your father, I am glad to say, is alive, and at this moment within three hundred paces of you. Like myself, he is a slave to the Mullah, but being new to the work, he has not yet lost his independence and spirit, and a week ago, hearing news the facts of which never reached my ears, he made a desperate attempt at escape, but was discovered and recaptured. I have been a prisoner so long that I can speak the language perfectly, and have many friends amongst the natives, and from them I learnt that the colonel had made a desperate resistance, and had been wounded. But the injury is not severe, though it prevents him from walking, and has given him a blessed release from slavery, for the time being at least."

Jim listened to the news with feelings of the deepest gratitude, and when the stranger had finished, sat there without answering a word, thinking the whole matter out.

"A few minutes ago I felt like a baby," he said. "The disappointment was so great that, if I had been a girl, I should have cried. But the information which you have just given me raises my spirits again, and I feel that, after all, things are about to turn out as I wished. Can you lead me to my father? If you can, we must go at once and rescue him. Then we shall rejoin my follower, and when the morning dawns we shall be miles away amongst our friends, ready and willing to make a fight for it, should we be followed."

"And you'll take me with you?" asked the prisoner. "Just think of it for a moment! I'm John Margetson, third mate aboard an ocean-going steamer, and no great person at any time. In the search for your father chance has brought you to my side, and I tell you candidly to leave me where I am, and go on with the business you have in hand, for if you include me in your party your risks will be doubled. For think, in another quarter of an hour that sentry outside will poke his ugly head into the hut again, and then the cat will be out of the bag. On the other hand, I can tell you where your father lies, and can describe the position so accurately that you will be able to find him without further help."

The stranger caught Jim by the hand, and whispered the words eagerly into his ear, repeating them in his unselfish attempt to persuade this lad to leave him to his fate.

"Do you think I am a coward?" asked Jim quietly. "Should I be worthy to be called the son of my father if I left you in the lurch? Ask yourself that question, and then give me the answer, though, whatever it is, I tell you that if you will come I will gladly take you with me, and should never forgive myself if I were to leave you behind."

"Spoken like a man!" exclaimed John Margetson. "I wanted to put the case before you clearly, but you cannot tell what your answer meant to me, for I have endured three years of hopeless slavery. For all that time I have been the butt of every man, woman, and child who owed allegiance to the Mullah, and whenever his adherents met with a reverse, I have gone in terror of my life. I have been threatened, beaten, starved, until life has become at times such a misery that, but for the fact that at the worst it is dear to every man, and that our religion forbids it, I would have thrown myself into the river yonder and ended my wretched existence. Rescue me from my captors. Take me back to my old life, to my old friends and associates, and I shall be your debtor till the end of my days. I shall, indeed."

There was no doubt of John Margetson's earnestness, for his voice trembled as he spoke, and his lips twitched so violently that he could scarcely form the words.

"I know what you feel," responded Jim soothingly. "Help me to find my father, and then all that I may have done for you will have been amply repaid. And now let us discuss our plans."

For some twenty minutes the two sat side by side with their heads close together, whispering in the darkness, and then separated, for the shuffling step of the sentry was again heard. But on this occasion he seemed to be satisfied with a casual inspection, and barely troubled to do more than place the wicket ajar and peep in. The sight of the prisoner's legs, upon which a patch of light fell, made his mind easy, and he at once retired, and, striding to the front of the larger building, walked to and fro within a few paces of the log-fire which blazed there. Then he shivered, and, drawing his blanket closer about him, thrust the haft of his spear into the blaze and stirred the embers till the flames leapt high into the air. And all the while the second warrior sat propped against the opposite hut, a blanket drawn tightly about him, and his chin resting upon his breast. There was no doubt that he was fast asleep, for his snores proclaimed the fact, while he made no movement, though Jim and his companion stared at him through the open door for the space of five minutes. As soon as they were satisfied of this, they went out and pushed the wicket to. Then John Margetson stepped to the front to lead the way, and at once began to cross the open space which surrounded the dwellings, Jim falling silently behind him. Like ghosts they flitted across the ground, and, hastening from the moonlit area, dived into the deepest shadows that could be found. A hundred yards farther on both came to a sudden halt, and crouched in the darkness, listening apprehensively.

What was that? A shrill cry of alarm suddenly rent the air, and was followed by another. Then there was a loud report of a gun, and instantly, it seemed, the village hummed and buzzed with life. Doors flew open, and men came rushing out with arms in their hands, each one shouting to the other to ask what the trouble was, till the air was alive with their voices. Then, as a sudden silence settled over the Mullah's camp, for the space of a few seconds, a tall man was seen to be standing beside the flagstaff upon the roof of the central house. His hand was uplifted as if he were about to speak, and instantly all turned their heads in his direction and ceased their clamour.

"Awake!" shouted the man. "The prisoner has escaped, and is even now within our reach. I, the Mullah, order you to arm and separate in parties. To the one who returns with the infidel I will give a great reward."

At once all the men of the village ran back to their houses, and within five minutes there was silence once more, save for the pattering of many feet, as the warriors left the camp in search of their prisoner.

CHAPTER XIV

HEMMED IN BY THE ENEMY

Nothing but misfortune seemed to be in store for Jim Hubbard upon this eventful evening. First, he had experienced the bitter disappointment of learning that the white prisoner at whose rescue he had aimed, and for whose sake he had marched so many miles, was, after all, not the one whom he had hoped to find. But the news that his father was actually alive and within a few yards of him had revived his flagging energy, and with his new-found friend, John Margetson, he had set out for the purpose of reaching him, only to hear suddenly that wild shout, to crouch there in the shadow cast by a large square hut and watch that tall uncouth figure standing on the roof beside the flag in the light of the flames from the watch-fire below. It was a bitter blow, and in his anger and desperation Jim even levelled his revolver at the Mullah, and would have fired in the hope of slaying him. But he had beside him a man whom long-suffering had taught to be cautious, and instantly a gentle but firm grasp was laid upon his arm, and his companion whispered in his ear.

"You are mad!" he said fiercely. "Drop your weapon, and lie down close against the foot of this wall. We are not discovered yet, and may even escape if we make use of our wits."

"But how?" asked Jim. "Already the place is alive with search parties, who will run over every inch of the ground, and are certain to fall upon us. I tell you that our chances are ended, and that we shall never get away from here. But I admit that it would have been a foolish act to fire at the Mullah. I was in a temper, and felt that if I could only kill him I should be satisfied. However, we shall do as you say, and wait to see how things turn out."

Throwing themselves upon the ground, with their heads close together, they lay so still that they might have been logs of wood. Around them, and stretching away from the wall for the space of some five feet, was a dense shadow cast by the roof. But there it ended abruptly in a sharp clear line, from which point the ground was lit by the rays of the moon. And across this, hurrying hither and thither, and searching every corner, went parties of fully armed Somali warriors, each numbering from six to a dozen. Like hounds in search of a fox, they thrust their bodies into every crevice, prodding walls and ground with their spears, and drawing the covers blank, turned away with a snarl of rage, to proceed with the hunt elsewhere.

"If we can only manage to give them the slip here, there will be still some chance of safety," whispered Jim, with his eyes fixed upon the search-parties. "Put yourself into their position, and ask yourself what would be the natural act of any prisoner who was attempting to escape."

"He would be a fool to stay here," was the emphatic answer. "It would be sheer suicide to remain in the Mullah's village, and, were I flying for my life alone, I should have turned away to the open country, and endeavoured to place miles of plain between myself and my enemies."

"Just so," replied Jim coolly, seeming to become more collected as the danger increased, "and, as one of the Mullah's followers, I should leave the search of the village to the women and children and the stray curs with which it is infested, and, mounting my fastest horse, should gallop so as to get beyond the prisoner and head him. That is what these fellows will do, and we must consider ourselves fortunate in that we are where we are. Let us move along to the corner, and then, if a party approaches, we can slip round to the other side."

"Why not try the roof?" suggested his companion eagerly. "It's as flat as a pancake, and has a ridge all round it, which will effectually hide us. I quite agree with you that, desperate though our position seems, we are far safer here than we should have been had we ventured beyond the village. Come, let us get up on the top, for I can see a group of Somalis coming this way."

In a moment both were on their feet and endeavouring to get a grip of the coping of the roof. But, though they stood upon their toes, and even leapt into the air, they found, to their disappointment, that it was still well beyond their reach.

"Then we must try another way," whispered Jim. "Are you fairly strong in the arms?"

"I ought to be," was the answer, "for I have had three years of slavery. What do you propose?"

"Up on to my back! Quick! That's it. Now lean against the wall, and steady yourself while I straighten to my full height. Can you reach now?"

Without wasting a moment, for time was of the utmost value to them, Jim placed his hand against the side of the dwelling and rounded his shoulders. Grasping his meaning, his companion leapt upon him with one agile spring, having the fortune to alight on the very centre of his back. Then, gingerly advancing his sandalled feet, he placed them on either side of Jim's head, and leant forward till his hands came in contact with the wall. He was a big man, and weighed some twelve stone or more, but though Jim groaned under the burden, and at any other time would have found it a difficult matter to raise himself to the erect position, he now stood upright with scarcely an effort, fear lending strength to his muscles.

"Got it! I've a grip of the coping, and can hang on here until you are up," whispered John Margetson. "But hurry up!"

Stepping back from the wall so as to obtain a little run, and yet carefully keeping within the shadow, Jim leapt forward, and then sprang high in the air, grasping at the dim figure of his companion with both hands. As he dangled there, with fingers clasping his comrade's limbs, he could almost feel the man's sinews crack with the strain, and wondered whether the weight would be too much for him, whether his grasp would be torn from the coping above, and with what sort of crash they would tumble to the ground. Then, as nothing happened, he drew his legs up, and obtained a grip of his living rope. Another hoist, and his hand closed upon his comrade's hair; but, unheeding the pain it must have given, his fingers gripped it, and he pulled without remorse, and tugged, till, little by little, he won his way upwards. Another moment, and the arm was within his reach, then the wrist, and with one last, almost superhuman effort, he found himself clambering over the low parapet. To turn and help his comrade was his next duty, and then both threw themselves upon the hard-beaten mud, breathless with their struggles, but glowing with excitement and the feeling of success.

"Look out! Here they come!" whispered Margetson at this moment.

Taking a hasty look over the parapet, Jim saw some ten men hurrying towards the building, and at once flattened himself upon the roof, squeezing as close to it as he could. Then his hand stole down to his revolver, and he drew it silently.

Scarcely had he done so when footsteps and voices were heard below, and, though he dared not look, he was well aware that the very shadow which had proved their hiding-place but a few seconds before was now undergoing a thorough search, from which they could not have hoped to escape had they not climbed to the roof.

"Ah, what is this?" asked one of the Somali warriors, suddenly stooping and picking something up. "I have found a knife, which I am sure did not belong to our prisoner. Here, let me get into the light and look at it."

Following their comrade, the others at once left the shadow and went into the open, where they pressed about him, and gave vent to exclamations of anger and astonishment, for the prize which had been found was Jim's hunting-knife, which must have slipped from his belt during his efforts to reach his position above. Fortunately for him, however, he did not know more than a word of what was being said, and certainly did not grasp the meaning. But his friend did, and trembled as he lay.

"I tell you that someone else has had a hand in his escape," cried the first speaker again. "I have been to the coast, and I say that this is a knife which has but lately come from the country of the infidel. Have we not heard already that one of them is bound hither for the rescue of one of our slaves?"

"That is the case," was the excited answer.

"Then this man has arrived, and released the prisoner to-night. They fled here in the darkness, and then, at the alarm, hastened off into the country, where they will be captured to a certainty by our brothers."

"And what if they have not done as you so wisely guess?" sneered one of the group. "Look at the question for yourself, and remember the short time which elapsed between their leaving the hut and the raising of the alarm. This dagger tells us that another has been here to lend a hand, but it does not state that the men are fled to the hills. More likely they are within hearing at this moment. Perhaps even lying upon the top of the house against the wall of which the find was made. Let us search there."

He started towards the dwelling, intent on carrying out his purpose, but at that moment the arrival of another dusky warrior arrested him, while a harsh voice took up the question.

"You are too clever for this tribe," said the new-comer, in tones which Jim at once recognized as belonging to the man who had shouted from the roof of the central building—in fact, no other person than the Mullah. "In your foolishness you would send my followers climbing like cats to the roofs, when, had you any sense, you would know at a glance that desperate men would scoff at such shelter. Hiding up there, forsooth! Why, you will tell us soon that they are in my house!"

At this sally all laughed merrily at the expense of the man who had suggested that the roof should be searched, and he at once slunk away to the back of his comrades, where he stood biting his lips with anger and annoyance.

"But show me this weapon," continued the Mullah haughtily. "Ah, it is English made, and shows without a doubt that there is a spy in our camp, or, rather, that there was but a few minutes ago. The impudent infidel must be captured, but take care of him, as you value my good will and your lives, for I have need of prisoners. One day they will prove useful, for when these dogs advance against us, we will show them their brothers, and then slay them before their eyes, just to let them see that we have power to do as we will, and have no fear of them. Then, with Allah to aid us, we will scatter the enemy. But we are wasting time. Off, all of you, and search farther afield for your man."

He stood there in the moonlight watching as they departed, and shouted out to them a second warning to protect the captives from harm.

"Yes," he murmured to himself, as the last of the warriors departed, "keep them alive, and I shall make use of them. If we conquer the British forces, I can keep or slay them at my will. If otherwise, and we fall into their hands, I can still treat for my own life by using these white slaves as hostages, and giving them up to their fellows in exchange for my own liberty. It is in such ways that I show my power to lead these ignorant men. For I think of more than the needs of the passing hour, and, knowing that the time for action arrives, I prepare a loophole of escape for myself, which I shall use when all my followers are slain. And then——"

Deep in thought, the Mullah walked away to his own hut, and disappeared into the interior. Not till then did John Margetson allow himself to break the silence, for all this while he had been flattened upon the roof, scarcely daring to move, and yet drinking in the words of his pursuers. Now, however, there was little fear of being overheard, and at once shifting his position, he crept close to Jim's side, and narrated all that had passed.

"Jove! What a narrow squeak!" exclaimed the latter. "Of course, I could not make head or tail of their jabber, but I knew that it referred to us, and I can tell you that my heart went into my mouth, for at any moment I expected to have them up here. But all's well that ends well,—only this matter hasn't finished yet. What are we to do now? It seems to me that we have a little breathing-space, and that we had better make the best of it to hunt about and ascertain what our surroundings are like, for this may not prove a very good hiding-place once the day dawns."

"We shall certainly be seen if we remain," answered his comrade, with conviction. "I know every inch of the spot, and to-morrow, when the Mullah goes upon the roof of his dwelling to pray before the eyes of all his followers, he will catch sight of us, and capture will be our reward. But I can see no other way out of the difficulty."

"Who lives below us?" asked Jim suddenly.

"Not a soul. The hut, as you can see, is a very large one, and in it are stored bags of dates and native wine for the use of the Mullah and his special favourites when on the march. There are a few weapons also, of the usual muzzle-loading variety, and occasionally powder and shot, too. This I know, for I have been working here as a slave, and have carried the things to their places."

"How does one enter?" asked Jim again.

"There is a door, such as the other huts have, and on the farther side a roughly constructed hole in the roof, through which the smoke from the fire below passed. I suppose it was the residence of a native chief before the Mullah came this way, and that he liked a little comfort. Now, of course, no wood is burnt, and the aperture is covered with a strip of hide. But why do you ask these questions? It would be madness to go into the place."

"Then what are we to do? Suggest some better plan which gives a reasonable hope of escape."

Jim turned upon his companion curtly, and demanded an answer with no little impatience, for now was the time for action. To hesitate was to become a prisoner.

"Well, what have you to propose? Shall we leave this place, and make a dash for the open?"

"It would be useless," was the emphatic answer, given with a vigorous shake of the head. "I know the ways of these Somali warriors too well, and I am as certain that we should fall into their hands as I am that we are here. Why, a hare could not hope to get through their lines, for now they are arranged three or four deep, and if we crept past the first and went on our way, the second, or a later one, would spy us out, and come galloping after us. No, the attempt would be hopeless, for the country is alive with their horse and foot."

"Then is there any other way? Would the river help us?"

"Had we a boat it might, but without that we should soon fall victims to the alligators which abound."

"How often is this hut visited?" asked Jim quietly.

"Perhaps once a week, and then not for a month. This is a reserve store, and it is only when the Mullah is about to give a feast to his followers that there is need to draw upon the contents."

"Then let us take our place amongst the stores," said Jim coolly. "There we shall find food and drink sufficient to keep life in us, and there, it seems to me, we can repose with some amount of safety. After all, the idea is a good one, for it offers some chance of a hiding-place."

For long John Margetson lay at his side, considering the question ere he ventured a reply. Then he turned slowly to Jim, and stretching out his hand in the darkness, pinched the latter sharply upon the arm.

"George!" he whispered, in tones of mingled delight and amazement. "You are a regular general. You ought to have been a scout, or something of that sort, for you are as cute and as slim as they make 'em. At any rate, you have spied out the only path for us. I've looked at the matter from every point of view. I admit that I've said to myself that you are evidently a youngster with the usual impetuosity of your age, and that your schemes were not to be listened to with much attention. Then I've tried to find a better plan, and have failed miserably. At last I have come back to this dodge of yours, and, hang me, it's just the thing. It's the cheek of it, the impudence, if I may call it so, which will help towards its success, for who amongst these Somalis would dream that we had elected to remain in hiding amongst them? Yes, it's the very boldness of it all that will make us safe, and—look here, I haven't a ghost of an idea what your age is, or what you're like, for I've only seen you in this moonlight, but after this you must take the helm. You'll act as skipper, while I take my old place as mate. Tell me, what are you? A young chap with a budding moustache, and heaps of go; or a lad with scarcely a hair on his face?"

"The second," answered Jim, blushing at his youthful looks, even though there was no fear of observation. "A few weeks ago I was one of the senior fellows at a public school, but now—well, I feel years older. But what about this hut? If we're going to retire to the interior, the sooner we do so the better."

"Then we'll disappear at once. Come along, but be very careful to keep below the level of the parapet, for here we are in shadow, while if we stood above the edge, our figures would at once be outlined by the moon."

Bearing this warning in mind, the two slowly crept round the edge of the roof, not daring to take the shorter cut and cross directly to the other side, for to have done so would have been fatal, the centre of the enclosing parapet being brightly illuminated. Arrived at the farther corner, Margetson halted for a few seconds, while he removed the skin covering. Then he began to wriggle his way through the hole, and in due time disappeared in the dark depths below.

"Hold on," whispered Jim, who was on the point of following, and, indeed, had already allowed his legs to dangle through the opening. "What if someone happens to notice that the covering has been removed?"

"Ah, that would be awkward, lad. It's fixed by pegs, and we cannot very well fasten them from the inside, though we could easily burst them open if we wished to do so."

"Then how's the door held?" asked Jim, lying down full length, and thrusting his head through the aperture.

"Just latched, that's all. No one would dare to meddle with the Mullah's goods, you see. It would mean certain death."

"Very well," responded Jim. "I'll fix this thing up here, and then slip over the wall. The drop's nothing, and I shall not be seen if I choose a moment when a cloud is passing over the moon. Hurry up, for there's one about to cross it now, and it won't do to be kept waiting."

Fumbling about in the darkness, it was not long before he had contrived to cover the opening in the roof, and to peg the skin down securely. Then he waited, with his eyes upon the disc above, and when it was clouded by a dense mass of vapour, he looked to see that no one was near at hand, and then clambered over the parapet and dropped noiselessly upon the soil below. The door was standing open, and as he entered Margetson closed it carefully behind him. Then they buried themselves in the darkness of the interior, carefully picking their way amidst the bundles and bales which were stored there.

"We shall be as cosy as possible," remarked John Margetson, indulging for the first time in a laugh. "Take care where you tread, for otherwise you will be tumbling into one of these bags of dates, or kicking against a skin of wine. Why, man, this is just the place for us, for we have food at hand, and can dine like gentlemen, with wine to wash the stuff down. An alderman could not hope for more. But supposing these ruffians find us out!"

"You said that we were not to be injured," answered Jim, "and therefore we have very little to fear. Let us make the most of our good fortune, and be content. What we have now to think about is not the possibility of capture, though we should do well to bear that in mind and take all due precautions, but our action in the future. How are we to get away from here when the scent and search are less keen, and how can we manage to take my father with us? There, you have enough to keep you awake all night."

"It's likely to prove a puzzling question, my lad, and at present I can see no more daylight through it than I can—well, through these walls. And talking of light, how are we to keep in touch with the outside world, and learn what is happening? To attempt to leave these snug quarters and slip out into the village would be suicidal policy. It would not help us in the slightest, and would lead to certain discovery."

"Then we must have a peephole," responded Jim promptly. "Perhaps there is one already in this hut. Let us look round, and watch for a ray of moonlight. It is more than likely that we shall find something to suit our purpose between the roof and the walls."

Accordingly, both crept round the confines of the building in search of a chink, and very soon came to the conclusion that there would be little difficulty in overhearing any conversation that might take place in the immediate neighbourhood. Then they made a tour of the place, and satisfied themselves of the position of the various bales and bags.

"We'll set to work as soon as there is a ray of light," said Jim's companion, "and rig up a kind of cabin amongst all this stuff. If we're careful to move only those which lie out of sight of the door, we are not likely to be discovered. Then, too, it ought to be possible to leave a hole here and there through which we could fire at the beggars. But I am forgetting. You are the only one in possession of a weapon."

"I've two, and you are welcome to one of them. But what of the muzzle-loaders which you stated were kept here? If they have not been removed, we might press them into our service, and rig up a regular battery."

"It's the very thing I meant," was the answer. "With half a dozen we could make these beggars sit up, and unless they managed to rush us, or bring the hut about our ears, we could keep them at their distance. But what do you say to a bite at something? I own that I am precious hungry, for this excitement has given me an appetite; and then you must recollect that the diet of a slave is never noted for its liberality."

"I'll join you willingly," answered Jim with promptness. "Let us borrow a few of the Mullah's dates."

"Yes, and wash them down with some of his best wine," laughed his comrade.

Nothing loth, and, indeed, in the highest spirits at their unexpected good fortune, both at once went in search of a bag, and quickly secured a handful of dates apiece. Then they retired to a point as far from the door as possible, and sat down in comfort, John Margetson dragging a skin of wine to their feet.

Their meal finished, each indulged in a draught of the fluid, and found that it braced them up in a marvellous manner.

"You need not fear the consequences," said Jim's companion. "This wine is made from the fat removed from sheeps' tails, and is notorious for nothing more than for its taste. To the natives it is a great luxury, though to a stranger, I fancy, it is anything but appetizing."

"It has a most horrid flavour," answered Jim, "but beggars must not be choosers. We have much to be thankful for, and particularly for these skins of wine, for they will keep us from thirst. And now tell me more about yourself, and of your life with these followers of the Mullah."

Making themselves comfortable upon the floor of the hut, the two sat close together and passed the remaining hours of the night in conversation, taking the precaution, however, to lower their tones till they were little above a whisper. Then, as the interior of the dwelling became lighter, and they could see their surroundings, they set to work in earnest to build a hiding-place. Fortunately there was ample material at hand, and as it lay at their feet, the task was soon completed. A search also quickly brought to light a dozen old guns, which had probably been made by some dishonest European for the special purpose of being sold to the Mullah. But, bad as they were, they were too valuable to be tossed aside with contempt. Therefore, having discovered a small store of powder and shot, the fugitives loaded them at once, cramming the weapons to the muzzle with slugs.

"That will do capitally," said Jim, surveying the work when it was finished. "These beggars can come right into the hut without suspecting that we are here, for this place shelters us. If they happen to find us, we shall give them a warm reception with the guns, though at any other time I should be sorry to be called upon to fire them, for they look as though they would burst at the slightest provocation."

"Beggars cannot be choosers," replied his comrade, with a laugh, repeating the words which Jim had used but a short while before. "If the enemy comes here with the intention of molesting us, I should fire fifty of the muzzle-loaders, and chance a burst with the greatest calmness. But we're ready for them now; and as we have a moment to look round, permit me to see what my young comrade is like. Up to this you have been more or less of a mystery, for since the morning dawned I have been too occupied to take stock of you."

Catching Jim by the arms, John Margetson turned him round till the two stood face to face, and then treated him to a long and curious stare.

"Yes," he said at last, finding that Jim returned his gaze without a sign of flinching, "a bold, high-mettled lad, filled with a feeling of duty. Shake hands!"

The request came so suddenly that Jim started, but the next second he clasped his companion warmly by the fingers, showing equal eagerness to return his good feeling.

"Straight and true, and sturdy to the backbone," continued Margetson. "I admire you, and I thank you for what you have done for me. Had it not been for you, I should still have been in my prison, a spiritless slave, doomed to lifelong serfdom. But now I am free—free, I tell you; and now that my liberty is regained, no one shall wrest it from me. I live to escape with you, to reach friends and old England again; or I die fighting for my life, my own master at the end."

He ended his impassioned words with another squeeze of Jim's hand, and then, as if to hide the evident excitement under which he laboured, turned towards the door, and, applying his eye to a crevice, stared out into the open. As for Jim, he was deeply impressed by his friend's speech, and followed him thoughtfully with his gaze. Then he, too, took post at an aperture, and sought to discover what was going on outside.

And meanwhile, what of Ali Kumar, and what of the numerous search-parties which had raced into the plain? Then, too, what fortune had befallen the troop of horsemen which had ridden from the village in search of Jim's camp?

CHAPTER XV

A CLEVER RUSE

While Jim Hubbard and his friend John Margetson are hiding in the store-hut, let us return for a few moments to the coast-line.

The reader will remember that a Somali levy had been raised and officered by Englishmen drawn from the various line regiments, and that this force had many months before marched into the interior by way of Bohotle, and, dividing into two portions, had left its baggage, its reserve ammunition and its camels, in charge of the smaller half. He will recollect also that the cunning Mullah, aided by information given by his spies, contrived to elude the larger force, and gloating over a victory which he already counted as his, had thrown himself upon Captain McNeill's zareba. Not once, but on three successive occasions was his frantic onslaught stemmed by the few men gathered in the zareba. So heavy, indeed, were the losses amongst the Mullah's following, that their enthusiasm and fanatical hate had changed to dismay and secret admiration for these men whose officers were spoken of as "infidel dogs."

Following upon their defeat at the hands of Captain McNeill and his tiny garrison, the Mullah's horde was split into pieces and scattered in all directions by the larger half.

But in Somaliland a holy man has enormous powers of persuasion, and the reader has already learned that the Mullah rapidly gathered his following together again. Then came the action with Colonel Swayne at Erego, where the Somali soldiers, who were enlisted by the "Sirkal," turned tail and bolted, leaving their comrades to their fate. From that moment adherents had flocked to the Mullah's banner, and their depredations becoming serious, an expedition was decided upon. Of this General Manning was given the command, while the force itself was to consist of Indian troops and of men from the West Coast of Africa.

Stores, rifles, ammunition, and every article that could be thought of, or that was likely to prove of value in the coming march were collected at Aden and then sent over to Berbera. And here, when Jim and his following passed through the town, gigantic preparations were afoot. Already the troops had begun to collect, and the garrison at Bohotle, which had been in residence for some months, and which was suffering severely from malaria and from lack of supplies, had been relieved and replaced by fresh men, while plenty of stores and ammunition for six months had been brought up.

This advance post having been placed in a condition of readiness, the eyes of those who were responsible for the movements of the troops were turned in other directions, for it is not always wise to concentrate one's forces. A division of the fighting strength which is about to invade an enemy's country often disconcerts the adversary, for then he, too, must split his followers, and send some to watch and oppose one half of the invaders, while the remainder marches to lie in wait for the other. If this precaution were not taken, it would be a simple matter for a well-mounted body of men to make a wide detour, and carefully timing their arrival and attack, to fall upon the enemy in the rear, while their comrades engaged with them in the front.

Thus was Ladysmith relieved; for when Lord Roberts, with a hastily collected force, invaded the Orange River Colony, the Boer forces, which up to then had been concentrated about the heights of Colenso and the beleaguered camp, were compelled to divide, one portion hastening across the Drakensberg Mountains to join with others about Bloemfontein, while the remainder, seeing their hopeless condition, fled before the repeated and gallant attacks of General Buller, leaving the flag of old England still proudly waving upon the Town Hall of Ladysmith.

With this thought of a diversion in view, another base was looked for, and Obbia, in the Italian Protectorate, was selected, the consent of that nation having readily been obtained. Then an arrangement was come to with the Abyssinians that they should also march upon the Mullah, getting in behind him, if possible, so that, should he take alarm and raise his camp with the intention of escaping farther into the interior until the storm had blown over, there might still be good hope of forcing him to fight, and of capturing him and a goodly portion of his men.

Many weeks had been spent in making these arrangements, and so uncertain was the mind of those who had control of the expedition, that at times it seemed likely that it would be abandoned for a space. When Jim and his friend left Berbera, the news of an immediate advance was in the air, but this was contradicted a few days later. Then it was bruited abroad again, and while he and his followers were resisting the attack of the tribesmen at the ravine, the information became public property that within a short space of time the forces would actually advance.

As the daylight increased, Jim and his friend went from side to side of the store-hut, and taking advantage of the piled-up date-bags, quickly arranged a convenient look-out, from which they could gather news of their surroundings. Some few inches of space had been left between the roof and the supporting walls, whether for the sake of ventilation, or because it was the custom of the builders of the country, it would be impossible to state. But there it was, and, by means of a pile of bags, the two Englishmen found a convenient way of reaching it.

"We'll keep watch from here all day," said Jim, peering through the opening; "then there will be no fear of a sudden surprise, while we can make up for our long vigil by a good sleep at night."

"I agree with you, my lad," was the answer. "We are in a fix here, and unless we keep our wits and our eyes sharply about us, we shall certainly fall into the Mullah's hands. But here comes the sun, and with it the life of the village will begin."

As he spoke, the street which passed from end to end of the Mullah's stronghold was flooded with the rays of the morning sun, the edge of which could be discerned rising in golden splendour over the crests of the distant hills. Scarcely had it struck upon the huts and sent long shadows slanting across the ground, when doors opened in all directions as if by magic, and out into the clear, sparkling air came the villagers. Children rolled from the dwellings, and began their chatter and play, while a few minutes later the wives appeared, some with jars upon their heads, which they carried towards the river, while others proceeded to light fires before their huts, so as to make ready for the morning meal.

"And now we can expect to see the men-folk," whispered John Margetson. "How well do I know their movements, for was not I the first to be abroad during the past three years? It was the duty of a slave, and I carried it out without failing, for, otherwise, harsh treatment was my reward. If you watch, you will see the warriors do not trouble themselves to work. The few who have failed to take part in last night's search will presently appear, strolling from their huts, and will then exert themselves so far as to lounge about the street. There is sure to be much talk about my escape, so they will collect together in groups. Only then, and when they are about to meet with enemies, will you see them roused to any energy. They will shout to one another, and discuss the question till a quarrel seems imminent. But their anger will quickly subside, and soon, when the Mullah has shaken the sleep from his eyes, and climbs aloft beneath the flagstaff, they will all turn and salaam to him, as becomes the followers of such a holy man. Then each will produce his strip of carpet, and, turning to the east, will follow the movements of their leader as he kneels and prays to Allah.

"It is a weird and wonderful sight, and their murmured 'Allah, Allah,' will enchant your ears, for the faith and devotion of these Somali warriors is very great. An infidel is an odious sight to their eyes, and were it not that the Mullah might obtain value for my life, I should long ago have ceased to exist. Often has this holy man condescended to approach me, and endeavour to change my religion. When persuasion was of no avail, he used threats, and even went so far as to starve me; but, thank God, though I was only a poor heart-broken slave, with never a white friend to rely upon, I remained resolute, and steadfastly kept to the teaching of my childhood. And through all these weary months, that alone has been my comfort. It has given me hope when all seemed hopeless, and has taught me to look forward to this day. But here they come."

As he finished speaking, the crowd of native women and children which now filled the village street was added to by the appearance of some hundred Somali warriors, who emerged in ones and twos from their dwellings, all fully armed, for none of these men dreamed of lying down to sleep, or even of walking about in the daylight, without his weapons. Staring at them through his peephole, Jim had a better opportunity of observing them than had ever occurred before, and could not but admire their height, their fine physique, and their sturdy and independent appearance.

Of those who lounged before him, very few possessed firearms, and these were obviously of a poor and obsolete kind. The remainder bore shields and spears, while double-handed swords were thrust in their waist-cloths. A few, even, carried bows and arrows.

"They are of the Midgan tribe, which have joined the Mullah almost to a man," said Jim's friend. "Should it ever fall out that you are wounded by one of their missiles, be careful to withdraw the arrow at once, and ask a comrade to apply his lips to the puncture, for it is reported that the tips are poisoned. But your revolver should keep them at a distance, while against a rifle their curious weapons should be absolutely useless."

It was at once evident that the exciting incident of the previous evening had had its effect upon the warriors, for, as John Margetson had predicted, they gathered together in clumps, and began an animated conversation. Then, at the suggestion of one of their number, they suddenly started off to search the village and its surroundings again. Fortunately, however, for the fugitives, no rain had fallen for many days, and though the mass of men congregated just outside the store-hut where Jim's knife had been found, even the sharpest eyes failed to discover a trace of them, and it never occurred to the warriors that those whom they sought so eagerly were even then listening to their words with bated breath.

"Look at the man in the centre," whispered Margetson, touching Jim upon the sleeve. "By the sound of his voice that is the scoundrel who suggested that this place should be searched. But he is evidently afraid to air his opinions again, and let us hope that the snubbing which the Mullah gave him will keep him from further investigations. Now his head is turned this way, and it is evident that he has still some fondness for his own ideas."

"I confess," answered Jim, "that I do not like the appearance of the fellow. There is no doubt that he is still suspicious, and I should not be surprised if he came here quietly to see whether or not he was right. If he does, he will have himself to thank for anything that may happen to him, for we are not going to allow one man's curiosity to ruin our hopes."

"No; nor shall fifty capture us without a struggle, my lad. Recollect what I said about my liberty. My mind is fully made up to obtain it at any price. But there they go, and all the better, say I, for it is an uncanny and an uncomfortable feeling to watch a crew of desperate men, such as they are, knowing all the while that they are searching for one's self."

Satisfied that no good was to be obtained by remaining on the spot where the tell-tale knife had been discovered, the Somali warriors went off to another portion of the village, and, having peered into every likely and unlikely place, returned to discuss the question once more. In the middle of their conversation, however, the figure of the Mullah suddenly appeared beside the flagstaff, and instantly each man, woman, and child in the village turned and salaamed deeply to him. Then they scattered to their various houses, and returning to any suitable position from which their eyes could be fixed upon their leader, while they faced the east, they discarded their sandals and reverently knelt down on their mats. For long did the Mullah remain upon his knees, and when he had finished his devotions, he rose slowly to his feet, stepped from the carpet, donned his shoes, and then salaamed deeply. A moment later he faced about, and lifting his hand for silence, just as he had done on the previous night, he began to speak to his followers.

"There is no news of these infidel dogs," he cried, "but they are as surely in our hands as are those others who have formed their zareba in the desert. Soon I hope to see those who left us last night returning, and meanwhile I command all who have not a duty to do here to leave the village and go to aid them in their search. As for the other prisoner, that one who commanded men belonging to the British Government, and who is spoken of in his own language as a colonel, he must be removed from the hut in which he now lies and be brought closer, so that he may be placed under a stronger guard. Not that there is any fear of his release, for we have taken action so early that the plans of these impudent people who have come to release him have been altogether upset."

In accordance with the orders which they had received, the Somalis who still remained in the village gulped down a hasty meal, and then mounting their ponies, set off to join their comrades. Some twenty or more remained behind and watched them depart, then, while four of them mounted guard over the Mullah's residence, the others proceeded down the street, and halted before a hovel which stood at the farther end.

"They are going to fetch their prisoner," whispered Jim, keeping his eyes fixed upon them. "Perhaps I shall be able to see him, even though to rescue him now is impossible. Ah, they have opened the door, and some have gone in."

"Your father is certainly there, my lad," answered his companion. "And you must not be surprised if you find him changed to a certain extent, for he has had a hard life of it. As I told you, he has never lost his spirit, and, careless whether he lives or dies, has never permitted any one of his guards to ill-treat him.

Once, even, when I happened to meet him in the street when carrying a message for the Mullah, he stopped to converse with me, at which the warrior who was keeping watch upon him called him an infidel and a dog, and prodded him with his spear to induce him to move on. Your father was upon him in an instant, and tearing the spear from his hand, snapped the shaft across his knee, and belaboured the man till he bellowed. Never have I seen these people so angered. Indeed, had it not been for the Mullah, who seemed always at hand at such times to guard his possessions, they would have torn him limb from limb, to revenge the insult. It was grand to see how the prisoner faced them, spear-shaft in hand, smiling disdainfully at their anger, and almost inviting them to come on to the attack. By such doings he has created a feeling of terror amongst his guards, and now, whenever he is abroad, not one, but five men follow him, ready to throw themselves upon him and bear him to the ground, should he make an attack upon them. Here they come, and you can see for yourself the truth of what I say."

As he spoke those who had entered reappeared with their white prisoner. Then the whole group retraced their footsteps, and marched up the centre of the street. Soon they were so close to the store-hut that the features of every man were visible, and with a thrill of joy Jim caught sight of his father's face. It was thinner and more bronzed than usual, and perhaps the hair was a trifle whiter, but the prisoner still wore that air of resolution to which his son was accustomed. Catching sight of the Mullah, who had again ascended to the roof of his house, Colonel Hubbard called to him in commanding tones, and would have addressed him, had it not been for the men who marched by his side. Hustling him forward, and surrounding him with a hedge of spear-points, they forced him towards a circular building, which seemed scarcely large enough to contain a human being, and motioned to him to enter.

Longingly did Jim watch his father pass, limping slightly from the wound which he had received. Had he dared he would have called out to him, or made some sign so that the prisoner should know that help was at hand. But he knew that to do so would be worse than madness.

Having carried out their orders, the group of Somali warriors separated, and all walked away, save one, who squatted down with his spear beside him and his sword on the ground at his feet, evidently having been told off as sentry. A little later one of his comrades approached, bearing a gun in his hand, which he handed over to him, together with a horn of powder, and a goat-skin bag containing slugs.

"That shows that they are afraid of your father," whispered John Margetson, who, like Jim, had watched the whole scene in silence. "No doubt that man has been given orders to fire a gun on the slightest suspicion of an attempt at escape, so that the others may come to his help. But, remembering the Mullah's words, no injury will be done to their prisoner if it can possibly be avoided."

"I've been thinking about that, too," was the thoughtful answer, "and I cannot say that my mind is over comfortable on the subject, for supposing the Mullah were to hear to-morrow that my friend, Tom Dixon, and the followers who accompanied us from the coast, had beaten off the attack of his warriors, causing them heavy loss, in his anger he might instantly give an order to have the prisoner killed. I have had little experience of these native people, but everyone tells me that they are fanatical to a degree, and that their hatred of a Christian is extraordinary. In these circumstances, it seems to me that, in spite of the Mullah's express orders to the contrary, no white man is at the present moment sure of his life while a captive in his stronghold."

"Hum! Yes, perhaps there is some truth in what you say," replied Margetson slowly. "But however great the anger of the Mullah might be on hearing of defeat, I know the rascal too well to imagine for a moment that he would allow a rash and hasty impulse to prompt him to seek revenge at once by slaying your father, for to do so would be to ruin his hopes of a hostage in case he himself were captured. He is a cunning, long-headed fellow, otherwise he would never have attained to his present position of prominence. Why, at first, when he started his depredations, he was laughed at by the majority of Somalis as a madman who would quickly come to an untimely end. But by giving out that he was a holy man, this Mahomed Abdullah gained many friends, and with these to help him, and aided by an unscrupulous nature, he punished those who had formerly jeered at him so severely as to compel them, too, to join his ranks. And thus, little by little, and because his journeyings to Mecca have taught him more knowledge of the world and more cunning than are possessed by his ignorant brethren, he has steadily increased his power over them. But not for an instant has he allowed himself to neglect to take precautions for his own individual safety. If his followers are successful, well and good, for his power at once increases. On the other hand, if the day goes against him, this crafty rogue will not grieve for the fate of his adherents, will not care how many are killed, so long as he is sure of his own safety; for with a white prisoner or more to offer in exchange, he thinks that his liberty will be assured, and then what is to prevent him from again carrying his banner far and wide through the country, and raising another band?"

"I can see your argument clearly," answered Jim, "but tell me this. However desirous the Mullah may be of keeping his prisoner alive, how can he guarantee that his followers may not, in their rage at being defeated, disobey his orders?"

"It is a danger which must be faced, my lad, and which I admit is to be feared."

"That being the case, the sooner we are out of this the better for all of us!" exclaimed Jim with decision. "It seems to me that we have now an opportunity which may never occur again, for we know that very few of the Somalis are in the village at the present moment. If the others have not returned by nightfall, I propose to slip out, and by hook or by crook to enter that hut opposite."

"But you would not attempt to escape?" whispered John Margetson, in alarm. "Listen to me, my lad, and do not misunderstand my caution. As I have said before, I owe you a debt, and as a first instalment towards repaying it I will help you in this matter to the utmost, but think of the circumstances for a moment. We know that the country outside is alive with Somali warriors in search of ourselves. It would be madness, therefore, to seek to leave the village when we have already decided that here we are in comparative safety."

"I have thought of it in that way," responded Jim quietly, his decision unchanged by his friend's argument. "And I quite agree that this is the only haven for us just now. But why should we two make use of it alone, whilst father remains over there in the hands of the Mullah, and in greater danger of his life? It has occurred to me that a method might be found for transferring him to this place, and that is what I propose to do to-night."

Some minutes passed before his comrade ventured to reply, but it was evident that his thoughts were fully occupied with the question, for though he still remained on his parapet of date-bags, and still looked through his peephole, his eyes stared vacantly at the village street, the sentry who paced up and down in front of the prisoner's hut, and the broad strip of flashing silver beyond, which showed where the river flowed. Suddenly, however, his attention was riveted upon the river, and shifting his position so as to obtain a better view, he looked long and earnestly at it, as though he had made an important discovery. Indeed, so apparent was this that Jim, too, followed his gaze, only to be disappointed, for the surface of the water was disturbed by nothing but a gentle ripple here and here as the breeze played upon it and ruffled it, or where the current washed against a sunken boulder and caused an eddy.

"What is it?" he asked in some astonishment. "Something caught your eye, but what it is I cannot imagine."

"Then I shall tell you. You say that your father must join us here, and while agreeing with that, I placed myself for the space of a few seconds in the sandals of these Somali people. When they awake to-morrow, to find their captive gone, what questions will they ask themselves, what direction will they think he has taken? They know that it cannot be that which leads towards the desert, for their comrades are watching out there, and would certainly have laid hands upon him. Then, where else could he have gone? Unless we bait a clever trap for them, they will at once come to the only conclusion, namely, that he still is here in hiding. Then they will begin to search every house in the village, and our game will be up."

"That never occurred to me," said Jim, feeling as though his hopes had received a blow. "But what trap could we prepare? How could we put them off the scent? I cannot see in what way the river can help us."

"But I can," was the ready answer, given in a voice of confidence. "There are small dug-out canoes and rafts drawn up upon the banks, and it seems to me that, were we to take one of them and ferry it across to the opposite side and land there, stamping our feet in the mud so as to leave obvious tracks, the enemy would at once take it for certain that their prisoner and those who had helped him to escape had flown in that direction. When the hue and cry is raised in the morning, someone is sure to observe that a boat is missing, and a moment's search will show it drawn up on the opposite bank. That, I feel sure, will be sufficient evidence for the Mullah and his friends, and orders will be given for instant pursuit."

"Yes, and in addition, those who have been sent towards the desert will be called in again, and commanded to join their comrades," whispered Jim in tones of exultation. "It is, undoubtedly, a splendid plan, and we will carry it out, or rather, I will do so, for one will be sufficient for the job. Having crossed the river, I shall swim back again to this side, and then creep towards the hut. If

196

possible, I will cut a hole through the wall at the back, but if the sentry is too alert, as may very well be the case, I shall floor him, and then go in through the door. What do you think of the plan?"

"Capital! It will do excellently, my lad. I was about to say that we should divide the work, but it seems to me that one of us had best remain here to keep watch, and besides, if both of us were abroad, the risk of discovery would be greater. We shall take it as settled, therefore, that you slip out to-night."

"One minute, before we leave the matter," said Jim, a thought suddenly occurring to him. "We must not be too sure of success, you know, for there is no doubt that these fellows are thoroughly aroused. Supposing, for instance, that I were discovered, and the alarm given. In that case I should make a bolt for it, and should not dare to return to this hut, for to do so would be to betray your whereabouts. I should run for the ravine in which Ali was to await me, and from there I should make an attempt to reach you both when things had settled down a little."

"Very well, then, we shall take it as agreed, that if you do not return, I am to wait here until you do. It will be lonely work, but not more so than I have had to put up with for the past three years. And now the best thing that we can do is to take it in turn to get some sleep, for we have had very little of late."

Accordingly, when they had again regaled themselves with dates and wine, Jim lay down, and was soon fast asleep. Three hours later Margetson took his place, and he again was aroused after a similar lapse of time.

"Time to be moving, my lad," said John Margetson, in a low voice, shaking Jim by the shoulder, shortly after evening had fallen. "It has been dark for an hour, and by the time you are ready the village will have settled, for these folk here keep early hours. Up you get, and make ready."

In a moment Jim was on his feet once more, and had begun his preparations for what would, in all probability, turn out to be the most daring part of his undertaking.

CHAPTER XVI

THE LAST DARING ATTEMPT

Standing in the centre of the store-hut, surrounded by darkness which was so dense that neither could see the other, Jim and his friend conversed for a little in low whispers. Then Jim divested himself of all but his waistcloth, and tucking into this the folds of linen which usually encircled his head, in case he should be delayed, and should be exposed to the rays of the sun on the morrow, he declared himself ready to set out.

"It's a good thing to get rid of all those winding sheets," he said, as he let the cotton garment drop to the ground, "for they make a man visible at night when otherwise he would pass unseen. Then, again, by discarding them, I shall have less to carry when crossing the river, and shall dry all the quicker afterwards. And that reminds me that I must carefully leave my revolvers and ammunition on this side, for, unless I do so, they will be drenched with water, and become useless."

"It's a risky thing to go without your weapons, my lad," said John Margetson, "and if you take my advice, you will tie them to the top of your head, where they will be out of reach of the water."

"Thank you, that is a better idea," answered Jim. "I shall take one of them with me, and leave the other with you as I have promised, dividing the ammunition between us. Here it is, and there are the cartridges. Have you got them safely?"

Responding in the affirmative, Margetson took one of the revolvers from him, and then placed the reserve ammunition in a fold of his garments.

"I'm ready now," said Jim quietly. "We quite understand one another, do we not? If all goes well, I return here with father; if not, I make a bolt for it, so as not to betray your hiding-place. Later on I shall return to the rescue."

"That is the arrangement," was the answer.

"Then good-bye," whispered Jim, extending his hand in the darkness.

"Good-bye, lad, good-bye, and may you have the success you deserve!"

A cordial handshake was exchanged, and then the two went to the door. The latch was gently lifted, and the wicket pushed open just far enough to allow Jim to squeeze through. Another minute and he was outside, standing there in the darkness, listening as the door was closed.

"Good-bye," he heard his comrade again whisper, and immediately after came the low sound of woodwork meeting and a gentle fall of the latch as it dropped into its old position. But Jim made no movement as yet. Standing there beside the wall, he peered into the darkness which surrounded him, and listened attentively for some five minutes, so as to make sure that no one was near at hand. Then he fell upon his hands and knees and made a complete circle of the building, halting at each corner to listen again. But nothing occurred to disturb his peace of mind, for all in the village seemed to have retired to rest. Even the dogs with which all native streets are infested had disappeared for the time, and only the gentle murmur of distant voices told him that the place was inhabited at all. Happening to cast his eyes towards the central hut, a dim solitary figure trudging disconsolately up and down attracted his attention, while still farther to the left, and enveloped in a large blanket, a second sentry squatted in front of the prisoner's door.

"One on duty at each house," said Jim to himself. "It would be a difficult matter to get rid of the man who is watching father, and if it can possibly be arranged, I shall make my way in at the back, for the other sentry being so near, he would almost certainly hear the struggle and give the alarm. Hullo! Who's that?"

As he spoke his eyes suddenly fell upon another figure of gigantic proportions, and a few moments' closer observation assured him of the fact that it was the Mullah pacing the narrow roof of his house. Up and down he went restlessly, muttering to himself as if he were ill at ease. Then with one long look round he disappeared, and soon there was no one to be seen but the men on watch.

"And now comes my time," said Jim to himself. "I'll slink away from here in the opposite direction from those fellows, and carry out the first part of my undertaking. The night is very dark, and suitable for the work. But it is very still, and the fall of a paddle in the water, the mere splash of a hand as one lifts it to swim, will be heard a long distance away. That being the case, I must float across, propelling myself by kicking out with my legs beneath the surface. Now here goes!"

Leaving the dense band of darkness, which seemed to cling to the walls of the store-house, he crept stealthily away into the night, and, taking a narrow passage which ran behind the huts, quickly placed some hundred yards between himself and the Mullah's dwelling. Then, having waited again to listen, he turned at right angles and made his way across the wide open street towards the river-bank. As he walked, feeling his way carefully before him, for the darkness was great, the ground shelved away, at first by degrees, and then more suddenly, till, happening to pause for a moment, he heard the gentle wash of water just in front of him.

"The river," he said to himself; "and now for a boat. There are several lying hereabouts, and I ought to have no difficulty in finding one."

Again he went on his knees in the mud and mire, and groped his way along by the water's edge. Soon his hand came into contact with some object, and running his fingers along it, he speedily satisfied himself that it was one of the native craft. In fact, it was a dug-out canoe, patched here and there with scraps of goat-skin, and provided with some half-dozen paddles of native workmanship, which lay on the bottom.

"I've an idea," said Jim suddenly, pausing beside the craft as a thought occurred to him. "We arranged that I should take one of these boats over, but from that it would appear that very few had had a hand in the rescue of the prisoner. Now, why should I not take half a dozen? Tie them by their head-ropes together, and then ferry the whole lot across. When I reach the other side, I'll detach one of the half-dozen, and run it up against the bank so securely that it will not be carried away by the river; then I'll land and stamp about in the mud till the whole place is marked by footprints. When that is done, I'll go elsewhere till I've got rid of all the craft, and then I'll return and go on with the other portion of my work. Yes, it sounds to me very plausible, for when they discover that their prisoner is gone, the Somalis will catch sight of six stranded boats far sooner than they will of one, and, what is of far more importance, they will think that quite a force of men has been in the village during the night, and will promptly despatch all their available followers to the far side of the river. That will be good for us, for the smaller the number we have to deal with the better."

Groping carefully about in the darkness, Jim found that three of the native craft lay side by side, and within a very short period he had loosely knotted the head-ropes together. Then he crawled still farther along the river-bank, and having discovered another, pushed it silently into the water and embarked. To grasp a paddle and use it to pole the boat along was a simple matter, and in this way, using every care to avoid making a splash, he sped silently along, till a gentle grating told him that the prow had come into contact with the stern of another craft. Five minutes later he was returning with three canoes, allowing the stream to float them noiselessly along beside the bank. When he reached the spot at which he had left the others, he stepped into the river, and, wading towards them, tied the whole six together.

Standing upright in the central one of his half-dozen captures, he thrust the paddle over the stern, and, working it as a ferryman often does when sculling with a single oar, he gradually crossed the stream. Soon the gentle sound of bending rushes fell upon his ear, and he knew that he was at his destination. Detaching one of the head-ropes, he pulled the canoe well on to the bank, and then trudged backwards and forwards in the soft earth, stamping it with the imprint of his sandalled feet in all directions. Not content with that, he walked through a patch of long grass which fringed the bank, flattening the blades and leaving obvious tracks. There was no need to go still farther, for a long stretch of rocky and hard soil ran away from the river, and upon this nothing but the hoofs of horses would have made any impression.

Six times in succession did he repeat the process, and then, having satisfied himself that the signs upon the bank were ample, he embarked again and pushed off, allowing the stream to carry him where it liked.

"There is a white line farther down," he said to himself, peering through the darkness; "and I remember that from the store-house we could see a spot where the water was broken and tumbled. If possible, I shall jam this boat among the rocks, and then it will look as if it had broken loose from the farther bank. Ah, here we are!"

Before starting out he had been careful to wrap his revolver and ammunition in the long strip of calico which usually did service as a head-covering, and this he had tied firmly in position with the weapon at the crown of his head and the knot beneath his chin. Certain, therefore, that there was no danger of damaging them by immersing them in the water, he slipped over the edge of the boat at once, and, swimming beside it, directed it towards the centre of the white line which he had observed. Soon his hand came into contact with a large boulder, which was covered with slippery moss, and upon the upper edge of which was a jagged indentation.

"Just the thing," he murmured, holding on firmly, so as not to be swept away, for the stream at this point came down with great force and rapidity. "I'll pull her on to this until she's fast, and then swim ashore."

Easy though the task seemed, it taxed his strength to the utmost, for, caught by the mass of water which swirled about her, the native craft proved a fractious thing to deal with. She wabbled from side to side, and then, just as her nose was in the right position, her stern floated out, and, being broadside on, she was borne down on to the white line of surf, where she remained for a moment jammed against the boulders. But Jim was not the lad to be easily beaten, and, realizing the difficulty before him, he waited for one moment to obtain a firm foothold in the shallow water, and then bending beneath the craft, lifted it clear from the river. Then he gently lowered it into the position which he had selected, and, having satisfied himself that it was securely fastened there, he turned and began to swim with long steady strokes towards the bank.

"And now for the second part of the undertaking," he said breathlessly, drawing himself gently from the river, and lying down upon the mud to rest. "I'll keep straight up the street, in the shadow of the huts, and when I get within sight of the one which shelters father, I shall wait a few minutes to see whether the sentry is wakeful or not. If all is quiet, I shall go to the back and endeavour to cut my way through the wall."

Accordingly, as soon as he had recovered his breath and regained his strength, for the exertion of placing the boats in position had been by no means light, he rose to his feet again, and slowly made his way up the village street. Arrived within some ten yards of the building which stood opposite to the Mullah's house, he crouched in the shadow of a wall, and remained there, peering into the darkness. At first there was not a soul to be seen in that direction, though when he looked a little farther to the right the reflection of the watch-fire, which seemed to burn continuously, caught his eye, and against it, dimly silhouetted, and looking ghostly and unreal, was the figure of the warrior who kept watch over his leader. He was a tall, athletic-looking man, and seemed at the moment to be lost in reverie, for he grasped the shaft of his long spear near its cruel metal point with both hands, and held his head bent forward. So still did he stand, and so easy and graceful was the poise of his muscular limbs, that Jim might well have been gazing at a finely carved statue of a Hercules. For five minutes his eye rested upon the man as if fascinated, and then of a sudden, as the breeze stirred the folds of the flag which flew from the roof above, causing it to flutter gently, the man awoke from his dream with a start, and began to pace restlessly up and down.

"Number one," said Jim quietly to himself; "he evidently fears no surprise, and should give no trouble at all. And now for the other fellow."

Some minutes passed before he was successful in discerning the outline of the Somali posted in front of the prisoner's door, but by turning his eyes away from the reflection of the fire, he was at length able to make out a huddled figure crouching upon the ground, and apparently slumbering deeply.

"Nothing could be better for me," murmured Jim, in tones of satisfaction. "If he will remain like that, and the other fellow continue to pace up and down, I ought to get into the hut without much trouble."

Pausing for a second or two to assure himself that his revolver was in position, he left the shadow of the wall, and slowly, and with the greatest caution, crept across the open space which intervened between himself and his goal. At last he touched the wall of the hut, and at once prepared to carry out his design. And now for the first time he realized the loss of his hunting-knife, which he had dropped when clambering to the top of the store-house. Without it, and in the absence of something with which to chip a hole in the wall, he was helpless, and at the thought a feeling of despair came over him.

"What an idiot I am!" he murmured, while tears of vexation filled his eyes. "I ought to have thought of this before, as any baby would have done. But it never occurred to me, and this is the result of my carelessness. But father shall not suffer; for if I cannot make my way to him through here, I will do so through the door, and chance discovery."

With this object in view he slowly crawled round the hut towards the place where the only entry was situated, and soon the sleeping sentry came into view as he crouched some three or four paces in front of the hut.

"What is that?" Jim asked himself the question with a start of surprise, and with a sudden feeling of reviving hope, for now again he was looking in the direction of the watch-fires, which not only aided him in locating the position of the sentry, but also showed something—a glimmer upon the ground where there should have been darkness alone.

"Was it the sword which the sentry placed beside him before he fell asleep, or was it merely some stray piece of metal upon which the firelight fell?"

Lying there full length in the shadow, Jim thought the matter out, and finally, emboldened by the fact that the man made no movement, and by the recollection that iron was a metal of great value to the Somalis, and was not likely to be flung carelessly about, he left his position, and advanced stealthily like a cat about to pounce upon its prey. It was a moment of excitement, for as he neared the man, keeping his eye fixed all the while upon him, some alteration in the reflection of the watch-fire caused him to turn his head, and there, stalking into the darkness as he walked his solitary beat about the Mullah's hut, came the warrior who kept watch there. Again his figure was silhouetted sharply, and, in spite of his dangerous position, Jim found himself vaguely wondering what was the man's height and age, and what kind of an athlete he was. Indeed, so strangely does one's mind wander in the most hazardous circumstances, that straightway Jim's thoughts carried him back to the football field at school, and in a senseless way he began to find a place for this brawny warrior in the team. But a moment later the man had vanished into the reflection of the flames again, and there was the slumbering sentry upon whose sword he had designs. Two paces forward, and Jim's fingers lit upon the handle, and began slowly, cautiously, to withdraw the weapon.

The sleeper stirred, and ground his teeth, as though his dreams were not of the sweetest, then he awoke with a start, and raised his head. But he was quickly reassured, for again, trudging from the dim light beyond into the darkness, came his comrade, head poised proudly in the air, and spear resting upon his shoulder. With a grunt of satisfaction the man behind whom Jim lay settled his head upon his breast once more, and gave himself up to sleep without restraint.

A minute later our hero was behind the hut, and with the weapon grasped in both hands was attacking the wall fiercely, as though life itself depended upon his exertions. Chip! chip! At every thrust the point of the steel bit into the hard sun-baked clay, and sent splinters of it flying. Another lunge, and a mass of the material detached itself and fell to the ground, with a sound which, though not loud, caused Jim suddenly to stop his efforts and crouch again, fearful that he had been overheard. But a glance round the corner of the building showed him the sentry still asleep, with his comrade continuing upon his round.

Chip! chip! chip! Resuming his labours, Jim kept prodding at the wall till quite a respectable amount had fallen. Then of a sudden, as he gave a still stronger thrust, he felt the mass before him give way, and the point of the weapon went through into the interior with a grating sound.

Had anyone heard the noise? Was that someone stirring? Perhaps it was the prisoner, his dear father, who had guessed that rescue was at hand; or perhaps it was the sentry.

Something fell upon Jim's listening ear, and instantly he suspended his labours, and, crouching at the foot of the wall, waited to see what would happen.

Yes, it was undoubtedly the man who had been sleeping before the door; for suddenly a stooping figure came shuffling round the building, peering suspiciously into the darkness, as if something had disturbed his rest and caused alarm.

Would he be seen? Was it possible that by lying flat there upon the ground he could have escaped the attention of the Somali warrior? And if not, then how was he to act?

Rapidly did Jim allow the thoughts to flash across his mind, and then, before an answer could come to him, indeed long before he could collect his scattered wits, the man suddenly caught sight of him, and, raising himself erect, prepared to shout an alarm. There was no time for hesitation, for had a sound escaped the lips of the sentry, flight for the prisoner, for Jim, and for John Margetson, would have been out of the question; their fate would have been hopelessly sealed. And therefore, prompted by the danger, and scarcely realizing how, Jim sprang upon the man, and, grasping him by the throat with one hand, plunged his weapon into his chest. Twice in succession did he deliver the blow, and then, still clutching his opponent, he fell with him to the ground, and lay there, overcome by his feelings and by the narrowness of his escape.

JIM SPRANG UPON THE MAN.

"If the second man has heard the struggle, we are done for," gasped Jim. "But perhaps he was on the farther side of the Mullah's house, and if so, he may be unaware of the fate which has befallen his comrade. But supposing he notices his absence and comes to find him?"

The thought set him trembling, for he was thoroughly unhinged by the events of the last few moments. As he reflected upon the matter, however, and realized how much depended upon his coolness and decision, resolution came to him at once, and straightway rising to his feet, he tumbled the body of the dead warrior on one side, and took possession of his blanket. Then casting its folds about him, resting the man's spear jauntily upon his shoulder, and carrying the sword in one hand, he began to saunter round the dwelling. A few paces brought him to the front, where he caught sight of the second man walking slowly upon his beat, and approaching him from the farther side. And now was the time when Jim's courage was tested to the utmost. Had he shown any fear, or had he turned about in the foolish endeavour to escape the attention of the sentry, all his plans would have been upset. The impulse was there to make him cast his blanket to the ground and fly for his life; he felt the longing to get away from the place, to free himself from the danger, and then, putting the temptation aside, he boldly stepped onwards, and, arriving opposite the door, paused to look sleepily about him.

"The night is dark, comrade, and it is lonely work tramping hither and thither," said the tall warrior, coming to a halt some feet away from him. "This watching is a weary trial, and my heart sickens at it. Rather would I be abroad with my brothers in search of the runaways, or, better, galloping upon my horse against the zareba which the insolent invader has erected on the fringe of the desert. It maddens me to know that our warriors are fighting there, and that at this moment they are rushing to the attack with victory before them. And then, what loot! The man who came hither from the farther side of the Hoad, and who was once a follower of the infidel, has told us of the camels and horses that accompanied the expedition, and of the rifles and ammunition. My mouth waters at the thought that one of these guns might fall into my hands, for with it I feel that I alone could beat back these British troops who are to advance against us. But an evil fate has placed me here to keep watch when there is no need for it. In these peaceful times, and when no danger is to be feared, the old women of the village could carry out the duties as well, and better than I. However——Hark! Listen to that! You hear the faint and distant sound of firing which reaches us upon the still night air. Did I not say that our comrades were even now advancing to the attack?"

As he spoke, Jim stood still, looking at him, and puzzling his brains to know how to act. That the man was addressing him he fully realized, but whether asking a question or merely making a few commonplace remarks, he could not guess, as he did not understand the language. To have attempted to respond would have been sheer madness, and yet what was he to do? Happily for him, a gust of wind swept along the village street at this instant, and, falling upon the watch-fires, sent a burst of smoke and embers whirling in his direction. A second later a fit of coughing took hold of him, and leaning upon his spear, he struggled with it till the tears were forced to his eyes. Then, as if that had been sufficient answer, he yawned loudly, and began to trudge the beat again, till the hut hid him from the sentry. No sooner was he out of sight than he ran to the other side, and, throwing himself upon the ground, crept to the end of the wall and looked out across the open space which separated him from the Mullah's residence. There was the warrior who had just addressed him, still standing in a listening attitude; but whether he was surprised at his comrade's action or not, it was impossible to state. However, that his suspicions had not been aroused was quickly evident, for, coughing and spluttering, as a second gust swept the smoke in his direction, he, too, moved away, and had soon disappeared from sight.

"Now is my opportunity," thought Jim, "and I shall never have another like it. Whilst he is behind the Mullah's house I must make a rush for the prison, and, by George, I'll do it!"

Darting round the angle of the wall, he undid the fastenings of the door and slipped into the hut. He had just time to pull the door to when the sentry came into sight again. But nothing had disturbed him, that was apparent, for he continued his leisurely walk without a pause and without a glance in the direction of his comrade.

"Father! Father! Where are you? I'm here, your son, Jim, come to help you," whispered our hero, repeating almost the same words as he had used when making the acquaintance of John Margetson.

There was a movement at the end of the hut, and he could hear someone stir, but for more than a minute there was no other sound. Then a voice broke the stillness, and a question was asked in tones with which Jim was familiar.

"Who is that? Did someone say 'Jim?' My boy whom I left away in old England?"

"Hush! Yes, I am here. Don't make a sound for your life, father! I shall come close up to you."

Creeping across the hard-beaten floor, Jim groped his way through the darkness, and very soon found himself beside the prisoner. Their hands met in a firm and loving clasp, while each kissed the other affectionately upon the cheek.

"My boy! My dear, dear lad!" was all that Colonel Hubbard could say for some minutes. "Who could have thought it possible? Who would have dreamt that such a thing could have occurred? It seems incredible, and I cannot believe that it is true. But—yes, I am pressing your hand, and I know by your voice that it is really you. Thank God that you have come!"

"I'm here right enough," whispered Jim, feeling already as though a load had been removed from his mind. "But, now about escaping. I am in disguise, and have come here from the store-hut of the Mullah, which is close at hand. There John Margetson and I have been hiding, and it is to that spot that I intend to take you now."

"John Margetson! I know him well, for we met on more than one occasion. How comes it that you have made his acquaintance, my lad? Are you, then, a prisoner, too?"

"No, father, but I found my way to his hut, thinking that you were there, and that the Mullah possessed only one white slave. It was a bitter disappointment, but this makes up for it all. Now I hope to carry both of you away with me to our zareba, which lies away on the fringe of the desert."

"Rescue us both! Zareba! I don't understand; I am bewildered!" exclaimed Colonel Hubbard, still pressing his son's hand. "But you must tell me all about it later on; for the present, let me know what I am to do, for I am completely in your hands. What is this store-house? And why should we retire to it?"

Placing his lips close to his father's ear, Jim hurriedly whispered an account of his recent doings, and told him how it was that the store-house had been pressed into their service.

"And now, father," he continued, "it only remains for us to escape from this without observation, and reach John Margetson. If we are only successful in that, we have arms and ammunition there which will enable us to protect ourselves if necessary, and make a good fight for our lives; and, in addition, I have just arranged a ruse which should send these Somalis off to pursue us in the wrong direction. If they fall into the trap, we shall say good-bye to this village, and make our way to the zareba. Are you ready?"

"Ready, ay, and willing."

CHAPTER XVII

A DASH FOR LIBERTY

For some little while Jim and his father sat close beside one another with heads touching, conversing in whispered tones, for it was necessary that the prisoner should be instructed precisely how to act when they were outside the hut.

"You must tell me what I am to do clearly and concisely, my boy, for I am entirely in your hands," whispered the colonel. "It seems strange that I, who have always prided myself upon my resourcefulness, and who have always been the leader when you and I have been together, should give place to you. But, then, you see, you have all the strings in your fingers, and know exactly which one to pull, and when to let go your hold. Indeed, so far as I have been able to gather in these few seconds, you have shown yourself to possess a master's mind. But come, let us be going, for I dread that at any moment an alarm may be given, and then we can scarcely hope to escape."

"You understand, then, father, that you follow me closely out of the hut, and slip to the back of it. I shall wrap the blanket about my shoulders and march round and round, to put the other sentry at ease. Then we shall disappear into the darkness, and I shall lead the way to our rendezvous. It will not be long before my absence will be noticed. Then, no doubt, the Somali sentry will discover the body of his comrade and your flight. But they can kick up as much row as they like, for we shall be in hiding, and even if we were discovered, we have sufficient guns with us to make a tough fight of it."

"Depend upon it, we will," was the colonel's hearty response. "Put a weapon into my hand, and I will cause them to regret the day when they first made me captive. This Mullah and his followers shall find that their slave has strength for fighting, as well as for chopping wood and drawing water."

"That reminds me, father. Here is the sentry's sword. Take it, for you may perhaps require something. I have the spear and my revolver."

Having settled their arrangements, the two rose to their feet, and silently crept to the door. Then Jim gently pushed it open a few inches, and, thrusting his

211

head out at the bottom, looked in the direction of the Mullah's house. Striding stalwartly out of the firelight, as he had done so often before, came the athletic watchman, his spear swinging easily over his shoulder, and his head held well in the air. That he was unsuspicious of the events which had happened so close at hand was evident, for as he walked he hummed a dismal native air in the sonorous tones common to these people, while his thoughts were undoubtedly far away. Most likely he was still thinking of his comrades who were attacking the infidel zareba, for he paused every now and again to listen, and stopped his song, only to be disappointed, however, and take to his lonely beat again with an impatient stamp of his foot.

Now was the time for the fugitives, for the Mullah's hut suddenly cut off the warrior's figure. The next instant Jim pushed the door open quietly, and stepping out, stood there while his father emerged. Then, as the colonel darted round the hut, Jim placed the blanket about his shoulders, and, walking some distance to the left, waited for the appearance of the sentry again. The instant he caught sight of him he began to saunter forward, and yawned deeply again, as though he had only just awakened from a sleep in which he had indulged on the farther side of the building.

Three times in succession did Jim make the complete circle, slouching round as though the effort were too much for him. Then, as he came opposite his father again, he tossed the blanket to one side, and, catching him by the arm, drew him away towards the village.

"Now for the store-hut," he said in an exultant whisper, feeling as though all their difficulties were ended. "Come this way along the dark side of the street, and when we halt, lie down in the shadow of the wall, for it will be as well to see that we are not followed. After that, all we have to do is to slip across the street, open the door, and enter."

"As simple as A, B, C, old boy. Lead the way, Jim, and you can rely upon my following your orders. Now, on you go!"

Pressing forward, Jim quickly made his way along the darkest side of the village street, and, ere many minutes had passed, had reached a spot which was exactly opposite to the store-hut. And here, in accordance with the directions which he had already given, he threw himself flat upon the ground.

"Good!" he whispered, when some little time had passed without a sound having disturbed the silence. "No one suspects us, so we may make ready to cross the street."

"Hu-s-s-sh! Keep your eyes open," came his father's voice at that moment in warning tones, while his hand gripped Jim by the arm, and steadily, and with every caution, pushed it in a direction which pointed to a spot across the street and slightly to the left. Instantly Jim's eyes turned to the place, and peering into the darkness, he quickly became aware of the fact that a stealthy figure was moving there.

"Was it the sentry who had suddenly discovered the absence of his comrade and the flight of the prisoner, or was it some other native of the village, whose suspicions had been aroused in some unforeseen manner?" Jim asked himself the question as he lay there, but for the moment could find no answer, for the stranger's figure was hidden almost completely, while his features were entirely invisible. Creeping along in the shadow of the farther wall, he soon reached a point which was exactly opposite to the fugitives, and separated only from them by a matter of a few yards. Then he crept slowly into the middle of the sun-dried road, and turning, faced the store-hut, bending his head forward as if he wished to inspect it closely. Fortunately for Jim and his father, the man had chosen a site to which a few stray rays of the watch-fire contrived to penetrate, and this light falling upon his face, revealed the fact that he was not the sentry, but the native who, when Jim's dagger was found, had suggested that the white prisoner and his rescuer had taken refuge in the store-hut. Evidently, in spite of the Mullah's derision, he had come at length to investigate the matter for himself. With a start of surprise our hero recognized him.

"Our game is up," he whispered; "that is the man who declared to his companions that we must be hiding in the village. And now he has come to set the question at rest, and so that he should not incur the ridicule of his comrades, has selected this late hour in which to put in an appearance. What can we do?"

"Do?" murmured the colonel. "We must manage to silence the fellow, or the whole village will be upon us. But I confess that it is almost an impossibility, for he is bound to discover us before we can get within reach of him. In that case, we must effectually silence him and then escape, for otherwise he would set his comrade upon us. Hush! he is looking in this direction."

As he spoke the native turned round slowly, peering into the darkness in all directions, and, as his eyes fell upon the shadow in which they were lurking, he started backwards. Then, as if uncertain of his powers of vision, he crept a few paces closer, and, shading his eyes with both hands, as though they would help him to penetrate the darkness, stared suspiciously at the two figures crouching there. A second later he had given vent to a shout, and, turning upon his heel, fled down the street, making the air ring with his calls.

Jim was utterly bewildered at the turn which events had taken, but Colonel Hubbard was a man who had faced danger in many forms, and whose wits had been sharpened upon many a field of battle. Realizing at once that this man would not only arouse his comrades, but would lead them in the pursuit, he, too, was upon his feet and dashing along between the houses before an instant had passed. Fear seemed to lend fleetness to his feet, for though the native spy sped onward at a rapid pace, he could not outdistance his pursuer. Indeed, the colonel seemed to come up with him by leaps and bounds, and then with one gigantic spring to land upon his shoulders. What followed Jim could not make out, but when Colonel Hubbard returned he knew that they were safe. The man whom he had followed had paid for his persistence with his life.

Meanwhile Jim had not been idle. Grasping the fact that the store-house could not longer afford a safe shelter, he had at once darted across the street and hurled the door open. Then, as a figure appeared to bar his progress, and he heard the sharp click of a gun-lock, he called a loud warning to John Margetson, and leapt hurriedly aside. Well was it for him that he had the presence of mind to do so, for, suddenly aroused from the slumber into which he had fallen, Margetson had seized one of the Mullah's weapons which lay close to his hand, and, hearing the door burst open and the commotion outside, had discharged the contents into the darkness.

"Steady, old man!" shouted our hero; "it's Jim, and I've come to tell you that we must make a bolt for it. Out you come at once!"

To say that John Margetson was surprised at the sudden turn which events had taken was to express the situation mildly. For half an hour after Jim's departure he had remained in the store-hut, looking out through the aperture between the roof and the wall; but, wearied of seeing nothing, and having by now no small amount of confidence in the young fellow who had so miraculously come to rescue him, he had sat down upon a bag of dates, just to rest for a few moments. Then the heavy atmosphere within the hut—the aroma of dried dates and the store of wine—had overcome him, and little by little his eyelids had drooped till he was fast asleep. Roused by the alarm and by the opening of the door, he had started to his feet, and, rushing at once to the conclusion that the natives had discovered his lair, he immediately opened fire, without thought of the harm he might have done to his young companion.

"What, you!" he exclaimed in bewilderment, appearing at the door with a smoking weapon in his hand. "Have I hurt you? Good heavens! Don't say that my bullet wounded you!"

"There's nothing wrong with me; but I'm in a desperate hurry!" cried Jim again. "Bring your gun, and come along quickly, for we haven't a moment to lose."

"But the prisoner, your father?"

"He's here. I've managed to get him safely out of his cell, and now we must fly for our lives. Ah——"

At that moment Jim became aware of the fact that a tall figure was rushing down upon them from the direction of the Mullah's house, and instantly realized that it must be the sentry who for a short period of time had claimed him as a comrade that evening. Already the man was within a few paces of him, and, with lowered spear-point, and shield held well forward so as to protect his body, came headlong towards them.

"Look out!" shouted John Margetson.

But Jim needed no warning, for, hazardous though the position was, he had never for one moment allowed his coolness to desert him. Without moving, therefore, from the spot upon which he stood, he turned slightly, and whipping the revolver from his waistcloth, levelled it at the advancing sentry. Click! Back went the lock as he gave the first pressure upon the trigger. Snap! The hammer fell; but there was no explosion, no bullet flew from the muzzle, for by an evil chance a splash of the river had damped the cap.

Undaunted, however, Jim gave vent to an exclamation of annoyance, and then, without lowering his arm, jerked at the trigger again. Bang! This time the hammer had fallen upon an undamaged cartridge. Jim heard the bullet strike the man's breast, and then, ere the flash of the powder had died down, he saw him suddenly plunge forward, with arms thrown out before him, while spear and shield were cast high into the air. A second later, with a clatter which could be heard all over the village, the muscular figure of the unfortunate sentry came crashing to the ground, where it lay motionless.

And now the Mullah's village, which a moment before had been peacefully slumbering, was suddenly plunged into a state of wildest turmoil. A very pandemonium seemed to have broken loose, for in all directions doors were flung wide open with a series of resounding bangs, while loud voices rent the silence of the night. Then, just as had happened on a previous evening, a tall figure suddenly appeared beside the flagstaff which stood upon the roof of the central dwelling, and the voice of the Mullah rang out clearly, drowning every other sound.

"Catch them!" he shouted. "After them, every one of you! For if these impudent dogs escape this time we shall be for ever disgraced. Follow them, I say! Pick up their tracks, and when you have done so, I myself will lead you."

"Come down, then, and show us the way now!" called out one of the few men who had been left in the village. "We can see no sign of them, though here, in front of the store-hut, are the bodies of two of our comrades."

"A third is here!" shrieked another at this moment, happening to stumble upon the sentry who lay behind the prisoner's hut. "It is Abdul Hamid, who kept watch over our white slave. See," he continued, appearing a moment later, dragging the body towards the watch-fire, "he is dead. Allah has taken him, and the thrust of a sword has sent him to his end. Where are these infidels? Lead us, you who are our ruler, and show us that you have those powers of which you boast."

That the incident which had so suddenly and unexpectedly aroused the village had angered the warriors there was little doubt, for they now came crowding round the Mullah's residence, and forgetting the humble manner in which they were apt to address him, demanded hotly that he should do something in the matter.

"It is a disgrace to our manhood!" cried one of them bitterly. "If these men, whoever they may prove to be, escape us, the tribes who live within touch of our camp will jeer and point the finger of disdain at us, and will speak of us as women, fit only to toil in household work, and handle the staff with which our corn is crushed, instead of shield and spear. Up, then, and lead us in the pursuit!"

That the indignant words had their due effect upon the Mullah was evident, for scarcely had the speaker ended the sentence when the door of the central hut flew open with a crash, and the leader sprang into the firelight, brandishing a sword above his head.

"Ay!" he shouted. "Women we should be, and worse! Dogs, indeed, to let these men get safely away. You have called upon me to show you how to act, and, therefore, stand still now and listen. These are the facts, as I see them. Our brothers are abroad between this and the desert, and it would be a clever fugitive who could contrive to slip between their ranks, even upon a dark night such as this is. It is clear, therefore, that these infidels have turned their faces in another direction. To the river, then! Run down some of you, and see whether a trace of their flight cannot be discovered."

At his order half a dozen of the men who surrounded him turned quickly, and rushing to the watch-fire, each picked up a smouldering brand, and ran off towards the river. By the time they had reached the banks the impact of the air upon the glowing ends of the wood had fanned them into flames, and converted them into excellent torches. Scattering with these in their hands, they proceeded to search every foot of the neighbourhood, and ere long came upon signs which rewarded them for their trouble. Then a shout rang out in the air.

"Silence!" bellowed the Mullah, who had again taken his post upon the top of his hut. "Let every man remain quiet, so that we may hear what is said."

"Our father is right," shouted the man again. "He is a wise leader, indeed, for here are sure signs of the dogs who have disturbed us. Boats are missing from the banks, and by the aid of my torch I can see them on the farther side. Wait while I go over to look further into the matter."

There was a splash as the Somali plunged into the water, and then, as all eyes were turned in that direction, he could be seen swimming sturdily by the aid of one arm and his legs, while with the other he held the flaring stake above his head. About him the stream flashed and eddied, while the light was reflected from a thousand brilliant points, and clearly showed the seething wake which he left behind him. Then, ere he had traversed half the distance, another voice awoke the silence.

"Ha! Here is another boat!" one of the searching party shouted. "I can see it stuck high and dry upon the reef which crosses the river at the foot of the village. It is stranded and empty."

"And here are five more!" called the first, who had now reached the opposite side, making a funnel of his hands, so that his voice should carry the more surely; "and by their side, and for some feet on the marshy edge of the water, the mud and grass is trampled by a hundred feet. It is clear that this alarm was caused by more than one of the enemy."

For a minute there was silence as the Mullah cogitated, and then mindful of the fact that he must not hesitate—for to do so would be to show weakness before his followers—he once more issued his orders.

"Few or many, we must follow, and that at once," he called. "Therefore, I command that the greater part of you at once cross the water and search out the tracks of these invaders. Others shall mount the fleetest horses we possess, and gallop to their brothers with the word that they are to leap into their saddles and come hither like the wind. Then, with myself at their head to lead and guide them with my wisdom, we, too, will ford the stream and take up the chase. Be sure, my men, that Allah will aid us in this matter, as He has always done, for are we not brave and deserving of His favour?"

His followers were eager to obey his words, and before a quarter of an hour had passed some fifteen of them rode down to the water's edge, and spurring their ponies into the water, swam them boldly across. Then with a forest of blazing torches held high above their heads, they took up the supposed tracks of the fugitives, and followed them to the rocky and hard ground beyond. But here their cunning and native craft were baffled, for not a scratch, not a hoof-mark could be seen upon the uneven surface, in spite of the fact that each one of the warriors was trained in such matters, and possessed eyes as keen as those of a ferret. An hour passed, and still they could make nothing of the difficulty, and were compelled to send one of their number to the Mullah with a message to that effect.

"What! No further sign of them!" exclaimed the latter wrathfully, issuing from his hut. "I will return with you and see into this matter."

Diving back into the darkness of his dwelling, he reappeared in a few minutes with a flowing robe about him and a rifle of modern workmanship in his hand.

At a shout from one of the men near at hand, a pure-bred Arab, clean of limb, and with tossing mane, was led up by a native slave, who stood there, bridle in hand, holding the finely worked stirrup for his lord and master. Scarcely had he arrived when the leader, disdaining the aid so invitingly held out towards him, leapt with a bound into the saddle. With the certainty of a practised equestrian, his feet fell into the stirrups, while his left hand picked up the embroidered reins. Then, waving his rifle above his head, he plunged the cruel rowels with which his heels were armed into the flanks of the noble animal, which at once sprang forward with a bound that would have unseated any but an accomplished horseman. With a snort, and a shout from the rider, they plunged recklessly into the river, and began to swim across. It was grand to see the manner in which the Arab thoroughbred clambered to the top of the bank beyond, and shook himself there like a dog, while the gleam of the torches shone upon his silky coat. It was splendid, too, to watch this Mullah, forgetful of intrigue and of the arts by which he maintained his authority over his followers, become a man again. Tossing the reins upon the animal's neck, he placed a hand upon the pommel of the saddle, and then leapt lightly to the ground.

"A torch!" he cried sharply. "Fools! Give me one of the brands, that I may search with my own eyes. Ha! Now follow behind me, and beware how you tread, for I wish not to be led away by the footprints which you yourselves have made."

Cowed by his fierceness, the search-party promptly obeyed his orders, falling in behind him, and following every movement he made.

"Let me start at the beginning, and then work from the river," cried the Mullah, striding to the edge of the water, where he sank to his ankles in the soft mud. "Here is the groove which the prow of the boat cut as it was run to the shore, and here, deeply impressed in the ooze, is the sandal-mark of the man who first leapt overboard. See!" He turned, and digging his heels into the ground, so as to lend power to his arms, he dragged the craft still higher. "And here are the prints of those who followed him. One, two—I count eight of them, but—what is this? Each one is broad and long and of precisely the same pattern. It is strange that all the infidels who landed here should be possessed of feet which do not differ in size. We must be careful, for this enemy of ours is a cunning one, and has already proved difficult to deal with."

Something had awakened the suspicion of this crafty leader, for, as if a sudden thought had come to him, he bent low, till his head and beard almost swept the ground, and peered at the various depressions to be seen there. Then he stalked away from the edge of the water, bearing the torch at his feet, until he came to the broken ground beyond. He did not venture as yet, however, to give his views to those who accompanied him, but, satisfied that he would learn nothing more at that spot, he trudged across to where a second boat lay drawn up on the shore. Repeating precisely the same process as before, he passed to the third and fourth in succession, and, finally, to the last. Only then, when there was no longer room for doubt in his own mind, did he permit his warriors to gain an inkling of his thoughts. But now the evidence of a ruse was so clear that there was no fear of making a blunder, and consequently of losing prestige amongst his men. Therefore, calling them about him with a peremptory wave of the torch, he addressed them in deep tones, which trembled, so great was his anger.

"Where would you be had you not myself to guide you?" he asked, staring each man in turn in the face. "You would be as children without a mother, as sheep without a herd. For, had it not been for my presence here to-night, you would have ridden your horses to this spot, and then, unmindful of the cunning of your enemies, would have galloped away into the country beyond, bent on hopeless pursuit. Listen! The dogs who came hither to-night, and disturbed the peace of our village, escaped by another way, leaving a trap behind them, in the hope that it would put you aside and give them a longer start. As I have said, had it not been for me, you would ere now have been gone on a useless mission, having fallen victims to this ruse."

"A ruse?" shouted his followers, pressing closer in their eagerness. "We are not blind; but in this we cannot follow your thoughts, and cannot agree with all that you say."

"Fools! Did I not declare that without your leader you are lost? Come with me, and I will show you the truth of my words."

Grasping the nearest man by the shoulder, with such fierceness that he would have started back had not a hand detained him, the Mullah dragged him across the turf towards the spot where one of the native craft lay stranded. From there he proceeded to the others in turn, followed closely all the while by the remainder of the party.

"Have you no eyes?" he demanded impatiently, directing their attention to the various footprints. "Measure the marks in your minds, and tell me, if you can, that they do not resemble one another. Look! The sandal upon the right foot of the infidel who planned this trap had had a portion of its inner edge cut away by some jagged stone, and the mud tells us of it as surely as could the owner. Then search about, and you will find that every print of the right foot, whether here or at the other landing-places, bears the same impression."

Following the directions of their leader, the warriors ferreted about beside the river, like so many dogs hunting for rats; and then, convinced of the wisdom of the Mullah, they returned to his side, feeling more than ever that he was, indeed, a mighty man.

"It is wonderful!" exclaimed one of them humbly. "You say truly that, had it not been for you, we should have entered upon a chase which would have been fruitless. Tell us, you who are our father, what is the reading that you gather from these signs. For my part, I could have sworn by Allah that no fewer than a hundred of the enemy had landed here."

"A hundred! I read it that one alone came here, and having settled the boats in their various positions, swam back again to the village. Then, when the trap was ready, by which he hoped to smother his trail and throw dust in our eyes, he made the attempt which has proved successful. But he shall repent. By Allah! whom we all worship, and whose slaves we are, this dog of an infidel shall suffer. Here are my orders. Cross once more to the village, and then ride hard to join your comrades. Tell them that the fugitives are in their direction, and bid them capture them alive. When the day dawns, I shall expect to see my warriors riding back triumphant."

Once more the Mullah treated each one in the party to a stern and critical inspection, and then, striding to where his Arab charger stood shivering in the cold night air, he vaulted into the saddle without touching the stirrup, and in a moment was plunging into the river again. With his rifle grasped in his left hand, and the reins hooked over the barrel, he forded the stream with the aid of the light cast by the flaming torch which he still retained. Half a minute sufficed for him to reach the opposite shore, when, turning in his saddle to take one backward glance at his followers, he tossed the brand into the river and spurred his animal on. A few paces brought him to his own dwelling, which was surrounded by a host of excited women, who were still ignorant of the cause of the uproar, and were fearful for their lives. But he thrust them aside haughtily, and springing nimbly to the ground, disappeared from view. A flickering light, however, showed that he did not seek repose, but was even then busily making preparations for the pursuit which was to be carried out on the morrow.

CHAPTER XVIII

IN THE GOLD MINE

While the Mullah is busy in the interior of his hut, making preparations for the following of the fugitives, should his men have failed to capture them before the morning dawns, let us go back to the three Englishmen, whom we last saw before the store-house of the village. From the moment when Colonel Hubbard had pursued the inquisitive Somali, and had brought him down in his tracks, events had happened with bewildering rapidity, and indeed Jim, when he had brought the sentry to the ground, seemed for some moments to be stunned.

Luckily, however, the others were fully alive to the danger in which they stood, and well knew that delay would be fatal.

"Rouse yourself! Quick! We must fly!" cried the colonel, in accents of alarm.

"Yes, pull yourself together, for you are the only one who can lead us," said John Margetson, grasping his young companion by the shoulder to emphasize his words. "Which way do we go, and where do we fly to?"

At first the words had fallen upon Jim's ears indistinctly, and as if far away. But the rough shaking he received, the reminder that the safety of all the party depended upon himself, aroused him effectually, and with a start he was himself again.

"Follow me to the ravine! This way!" he cried; and turning upon his heel, at once sped down the village street, with his comrades close behind him. When they reached the open, they swerved sharply to the left, and soon struck upon the rough path which Jim had used when coming to rescue his father. Without pause, without even turning his head to see if the others were following, Jim kept on at his fastest pace, being spurred to even greater exertions by the shouts and turmoil which he heard behind him. Not till he had put at least three-quarters of a mile between himself and the Mullah's village did he venture to come to a halt, and then it was to throw himself full length upon the grass, with which the countryside was thickly clad, and lie there breathing heavily, for the long sprint had told upon him severely. A short space of time, however, enabled all three to regain their breath once more, and then they discussed the situation in low tones.

"What is the move now?" asked the colonel shortly, in the tones of a man who demands only what is absolutely necessary, and expects to receive a concise reply.

"That depends, father. The ravine in which I left one of my followers with a couple of camels is situated barely a quarter of a mile away, and if it has proved sufficient to shelter him, it will also afford us a safe hiding-place. The question is, has he been discovered; and, if he has, then what shall our action be?"

"H'm! I understand from what you whispered to me when I was still a prisoner that the Somali natives are stationed away in this direction," said the colonel slowly, "and that another force has been despatched to attack your zareba. That being the case, we cannot hope to move during the daytime, and our only chance of safety is this ravine of which you speak. Therefore, I say, lead us to it at once, and should it prove to be occupied by the enemy, then let us go back on our trail, and while the Mullah and his following are hastening this way in pursuit, let us take post in the store-hut again. A few short moments will suffice to place it in a condition of defence. You tell me that there are muzzle-loaders there, and that there is an ample supply of ammunition, and of food and drink. Well and good; our movements are perfectly clear, and there can be no doubt of the course we must take. Failing the ravine, we'll look round as desperate men do who are cornered, and like rats who have no chance of escape; we will make for a spot in which we can die fighting, and which will give us an ample opportunity of making the enemy pay dear for their hatred of us."

"Yes, father," chimed in Jim, catching his enthusiasm. "Should it turn out that we are compelled to do as you say, I have a little plan by which we could do even more harm to these warriors; for once safely in the hut, and our defences prepared, we could set fire to the remainder of the buildings, and with a few handfuls of gunpowder, which could be easily spared, blow down any of the surrounding walls which would be likely to offer covert to the enemy. But the ravine is our object now, and I propose that we make our way there quietly and without undue hurry, for were we to run towards it at any great pace, we should, as likely as not, come suddenly upon one or more of the scouts who are posted in this direction. That would be worse than finding that the ravine was already occupied, for a shout would bring scores of the Somalis about us, and we should be hemmed in in the open. Therefore, let us take it easy. If only we can choose a defensible site in the ravine, and finally reach the zareba, we need have little fear, for at any moment one or other of the forces about to march upon the Mullah may arrive upon the scene."

"Put shortly and clearly, like a soldier!" exclaimed the colonel. "Lead on, my boy, for until we are out of this country you are in command. Not for one instant will I permit myself to interfere in your task. Carry it through by yourself, and thereby show your independence and your manliness. But when in a tight corner and uncertain how to act, do not fail to take counsel with those whose age and experience may prove of help, for that is the action of every astute leader."

By now, all were sufficiently rested and had regained their breath, and therefore were in a position to take the path once more. Springing to their feet, they stood for the space of a few seconds to listen to the distant sounds which still came from the village, and to others which could be heard away in the open country towards which they were making. Then they pressed onward in single file, each one with his hand upon his weapon, his eyes peering into the darkness on every side, and his ears listening attentively for any noise which might betray the approach of an enemy.

They had not gone many yards before Jim suddenly became aware of the fact that a couple of dim figures were advancing from the opposite direction, and instantly, without venturing to utter a word of warning, he stopped abruptly, and catching his father and John Margetson by the arms, pushed them to the right until they were in the centre of a clump of thorn-bushes, which grew thickly on either side. Neither of his companions needed an explanation of such conduct, for they, too, had caught sight of the strangers, and at once, obeying their leader's directions, crouched in the undergrowth, Jim and Margetson covering the strangers. And now as they watched, the soft call of an owl was heard, and, to the astonishment of Jim, it was repeated by the two men at whom they were looking. Again the sound broke upon the stillness, coming from a distance, and then, with the silence of ghosts, some fifteen natives filed into view, half a dozen being mounted upon ponies.

"That is evidently their signal," whispered the colonel, "and we must be careful to remember it, for it may yet be of use to us. But—hush! They are talking."

By now the group of warriors had halted upon the path within a few paces of the fugitives, and, little dreaming that the men they sought were so close at hand, began to discuss the situation in animated tones.

THE WARRIORS HAD HALTED UPON THE PATH WITHIN A FEW PACES OF THE FUGITIVES.

"We are bewildered," said one of them, "for some minutes ago a comrade reached us from the village, telling us that the other white prisoner had escaped, and had flown beyond the river. But how can that be, for we know that the zareba away in the desert is still surrounded, and there can have been no one to help the slave? And yet this man of whom I speak reports that there is evidence that at least a hundred crossed to the village on the farther side of the water, and then went their way again in a southerly direction. The orders are that we at once return, and make ready to pursue them."

"It is strange, indeed," chimed in a second. "As I stood at my post, thinking that nothing would occur to disturb the silence, I heard the report of a gun, and realized that the enemy was at work again. But I, too, cannot understand how there can be men abroad to harm us. Perhaps this is a mistake, and we shall do well to pause ere we draw in our lines, for it may fall out that this is only a ruse, and that the escaping prisoner is even now making his way in this direction."

"Hark!" cried a third at this moment. "I think the sound of a galloping horseman just now fell upon my ears. Stand still, brothers, and be silent while I signal to him. If it is not answered, we shall know that it is this infidel for whom we are waiting; and then——"

"Ah!"

Each one of the group gave vent to a guttural exclamation, which denoted the delight he would feel should his long watch prove successful in the end. Then all waited in silence, while the man who had last spoken did as he had suggested. It was weird to hear that low cooing noise vibrating upon the midnight air, and still more wonderful to note how accurately the cry of the owl was reproduced. Twice in succession was it sent out from the throat of the warrior, and then as they listened, hoping against hope that it would not be repeated from the stranger, the distant splash and clatter of hoofs striking upon the path and upon the springy turf at its side ceased suddenly, and a wailing cry came shrilly in response. Then once more the galloping hoofs could be heard and very soon a horseman dashed up to the party. Not till he was almost upon them, and ran the danger of riding them down, did he attempt to pull in his steed, for the Somali loves a brilliant equestrian, and rather than save pain and distress to the animal he rides, prefers to pull upon its mouth until the bit cuts into the flesh, and the poor beast is dragged upon its quarters.

"The order is reversed," cried the horseman, flinging his reins upon the neck of his mount and springing to the ground. "Our father, the Mullah, has with his great wisdom discovered a ruse, cunningly planned by the enemy. He finds that they have not fled beyond the river, but in this direction. He commands, therefore, that you set a careful watch, and bring the captives to him by dawn. If you are not successful, he himself will come out in the daylight and lead you. Those are his orders."

"And we will see that they are carried out at once," cried one of the group. "Listen, comrades. It is useless for us to wait here expecting these infidels, for they would never dare to come by the path. It is in the bush that we shall find them, and in all probability nearer to the village than we are now. Let us separate from here, therefore, and ride away to right and left."

The remainder of the natives hastily expressed their approval, and as time was of much importance, and they could not afford to indulge in delay, they at once parted with one another, and melted into the darkness as silently as they had come.

"Things look brighter for us," said John Margetson, in a whisper, hastily interpreting all that had passed. "These men declare that it is useless watching the path along which we came, and that is a fact which will serve our purpose admirably, for, if I remember rightly, the ravine has its opening close beside a turn in the road, and it, too, should escape observation. Lead on, Jim, and let us make a run for this hiding-place."

Springing to their feet, the trio emerged from the thorn-bushes, and taking the beaten track again, pressed on at a rapid pace, for, now that it was certain that their ruse had been discovered, it was of great importance to them to find a lair at an early moment. Otherwise, however carefully they hid themselves in the undergrowth, the search-parties would be certain to discover them at the first streak of daylight, and then their fate would be settled. Having traversed a few hundred yards, Jim, who was again leading the party, broke into a walk, and began to study carefully the left-hand edge of the road. Then he suddenly turned away on to the grass, and striding forward, halted, as the pale glimmer of water caught his eye.

"The well which lies at the entrance to the ravine," he explained in a whisper. "We pass it by and then sweep round to the right until we are out of sight of the path. Then I shall give the signal arranged upon between Ali and myself. Follow closely, and be ready to come to a stop at any moment."

He pressed forward, and gradually inclining towards his right till he judged that the path would no longer be visible had it been daytime, he stopped and gave vent to a low cough. Again he repeated the signal, and waited in silence for the answer. So long an interval elapsed that at last it appeared as if Ali Kumar must have been forced to leave his post, or as if he had fallen into the hands of the enemy. But just as Jim was about to repeat the signal for the third time, there was a cough close at hand, and someone seemed to start from the darkness and stand beside him.

"I am here, master, and rejoice at your return," was said in a voice which was undoubtedly that of Ali Kumar. "Speak! Are you unhurt, and sound in wind and limb? And is one of the two who accompany you the Mullah's white slave, the father for whose rescue you yearned?"

"I am strong and well, and my father is here, Ali. In addition, I have brought with me a second prisoner, the one whom you saw when you went to the village, and whom you took to be the colonel. But we have no time to chatter here, for the Mullah's followers are hotly in chase. It is a relief to find that you are still in the ravine, for it shows that it has escaped the search of the enemy. Take us farther into it, and show us a spot where we can defend ourselves, for you may be sure that these Somali people will go over the road again, and hunt each corner of the land as if they were dogs."

"We have a grand hiding-place, master," was the answer, "though I cannot say that the ravine will escape a further search. However, there is that within these walls of earth which will aid us, should we be discovered, and from which we should be able to drive away every follower that this tyrant possesses. But, come, follow closely, and do not hesitate to hold out your hands on either side, for the path is rugged and dangerous, and in the dark it may well happen that one of you might strike his head against a rock, or tumble and break a limb."

"Right! Push on like a good fellow! We'll look to ourselves."

Ali at once turned about, and pushed on into the ravine at a swift pace, which taxed the efforts of those who came after him. Striking to the right, he soon came to a part which was shrouded in even denser darkness, and then began to mount slightly, following a track which seemed to cut its way along the side of the tiny valley.

"Have a care, my masters," he whispered suddenly, turning round when he had traversed some forty yards of this path. "At this point our road bends abruptly to the left, and comes to an end at the entrance to an ancient mine, which your servant discovered by the merest chance. It is faced outside with hewn blocks of stone, and from that point runs back for some little way, widening as it does so. Then it divides, and numerous galleries pass away into the hill, but how far I dare not say, for I would not explore one of them to save my life. The opening is close at hand, and when we reach it, I warn you to bend low, for the archway is of no great height and would injure men of your stature."

This news was a surprise indeed, and in other circumstances would have almost taken their breath away. But the excitement of the past few hours, the numerous incidents which had been crowded into their lives whilst in the Mullah's village, had left but little room for wonder. With scarcely a murmur, therefore, at the strange tidings which they had just heard, they demanded to be led on again, and followed the native, with only one thought in their minds—the longing to find themselves in some hiding-place, some haven in which they could take refuge, and, if necessary, defend themselves against attack.

Pressing swiftly forward, Ali Kumar swung to the left, and ere long came to a halt for the second time.

"We are here, my masters," he said. "Take heed of my words."

Once more he advanced into the inky darkness, Jim and his two companions following without hesitation. It was soon evident to all that they had entered some underground chamber, for each felt a rough archway of hewn stones above his head, while his surroundings suddenly became even denser and less visible. Then the pungent smell of smouldering logs fell upon their nostrils, and in the distance they saw the faint glimmer of a fire. At the same time they noticed that camels were in the place, for the irregular outlines of two of these animals could be seen upon the floor away on the right, while, closer at hand, was a large pile of newly cut grass with which to feed them.

Striking across the large entrance-hall of the mine, Ali strode to the fire and seized a brand, then he raised it above his head, and bade his followers look about them.

"I have seen places like this elsewhere," he remarked, "and a hunter whom I accompanied from the coast informed me that they were the work of an ancient people who lived and throve hundreds of years ago. They discovered by their wisdom that gold lay hid among the hills and rocks, and straightway set their slaves and captives to labour in the mines. But these races of which my master spoke must have died out, and become almost forgotten, though the tribes who live in Africa still have legends which tell of their existence."

"He speaks the truth," said Colonel Hubbard, going to the fire and helping himself to a piece of flaring timber, with which the better to inspect his surroundings. "I, too, have seen such works as these elsewhere in the continent of Africa, and so greatly has my curiosity and interest been aroused that I have explored some of the mines, and have gone to the trouble of hunting up literature upon the subject. It is currently reported, on the strength of an old legend, that Queen Sheba herself set sail from a point on the northern coast of Africa, not far removed from Berbera, and made her historic journey to the court of Solomon. No doubt her wealth was derived from mines like these, and it is even possible that as soon as this country is opened up, others may become rich from the same source, for an expert, who accompanied me when searching the old workings of which I have spoken, assured me that many of them were still capable of producing gold. But I must not forget that we are fugitives, and that even now the Mullah's followers are hunting for us. The question arises as to whether we should remain here or push on for Jim's zareba. I shall not venture to offer my opinion until I have heard him speak, for this is his adventure, and it is my wish that he should carry it through to the end."

"And mine, too, colonel!" exclaimed John Margetson.

"What you say is fair and right, for our young friend has shown most admirable coolness and a ready wit. We must remember that it was he who thought of entering the country on your behalf, and that he has already been the leader of a small following. To deprive him of that post at this moment would be mean indeed, and would cast a slur upon him. For myself, I have the utmost faith in his decision."

At the words Jim flushed red with pleasure, for there was no doubt that they were said in earnest.

"It is more than kind of you both," he began, after a short pause, during which he looked sharply about him. "As you have left this matter to me, I will settle it, if possible, but I ask you to correct me should you consider my decision unwise or unreasonable. When I consider that the surrounding country is overrun by enemies, and that to venture from this curious place would mean capture, I say at once that we should be fools even to dream of quitting such a spot. Why, look at it! That low and narrow arch is just the position which four desperate men should be able to defend so long as food and drink lasted, and it is my advice that we at once make plans to keep watch at the entrance, in case of discovery. Our future actions absolutely depend upon the existence of sufficient supplies."

"Then you may call it certain that we have flesh and water to last us for a month," interposed Ali Kumar. "Look there, master! There we have a store of food, while yonder, in the corner of this great chamber, is a pool of clear spring water, into which a stream drains from the hillside continually, while the overflow disappears through a crevice in the floor."

Turning suddenly upon his heel, the native shikari pointed to the two sleeping camels, and then away to one side of the entrance-hall. Looking in that direction, and by the aid of the torches, Jim and his comrades at once caught the reflection from the surface of a large pool of water, while a moment later, as they stood there listening, the gentle splash of a falling stream came to their ears.

"Good!" said Jim, in tones of pleasure. "I reckon that, if we were to slay one of the beasts, we could cut the flesh into strips, as the Boers and Red Indians do, and cure it by placing it outside in the sun, or by drying it over a smoky fire. Yes, in my opinion, that absolutely settles the question. Our game is to stick to this place through thick and thin, and resist all attacks; and meanwhile two of our number can easily be spared to explore some of these workings which I see lead from this hall. Indeed, the more I think of it, the more certain am I that Ali's find will prove to be the very thing for us; for, supposing the Mullah and his men rush the entrance, we can still retire into one of the tunnels, and make things hot for them."

"I fully agree with you, my boy," said Colonel Hubbard heartily. "So long as powder and shot last, we four men—for I count you equal to ourselves in strength and pluck—should be able to keep the enemy out. Then, if things get too hot for us, we shall retire, with food, and water too, if we can carry it, into the old workings and defy the Mullah's army. Indeed I doubt whether one of them would have the courage to pursue us underground, for these natives are superstitious fellows, and fear all kinds of imaginary things. Had it not been for that, they or their ancestors would have quickly investigated these mines, and would have turned them to account. But for generations they have been little better than savages, and have been pleased with an existence which has been spent partly in agricultural pursuits, and partly in raids upon their neighbours. And now, how are we to defend the position?"

"I've an idea," cried John Margetson, suddenly snatching the torch from the colonel's hand and advancing to the entrance. "But, first of all, I should like to know from Ali the condition of affairs outside, for I confess that, though I have been for three years a slave to the Mullah, I have never been in this ravine. Indeed, amongst the Somalis, it is scarcely known, and I doubt whether a single one of them has ventured into it; for it is considered to be haunted, and that is quite sufficient to keep all inquisitive people away. But answer my question, Ali, like a good fellow."

"The valley is a narrow one, and, indeed, when looked into from the hills above, is more like a deep pit with steeply sloping sides. A well stands at the opening, which is but a few yards in breadth. But, farther in, the walls give back quickly, and then slowly approach again, till a sharp angle is formed, in which this mine is situated. In the old days, of which my master's father has spoken, a paved road led down the centre of the ravine, and ascended easily to this entrance, and by that, no doubt, the slaves were wont to come to their work. But the store of water in this chamber has cut its way through the floor, and, issuing upon this stone, has, in course of time, cut a deep and wide furrow across it to its bed beyond, from which it flows to the well beside the village path. For that reason, my masters, I led you by a track which ascended the slope of the hill."

"Then my plan should be of service to us," said John Margetson, who had closely followed Ali's explanation. "It seems to me that when the morning comes, and we have daylight to help us, we shall have an uninterrupted view of the whole ravine from this low-arched entrance of the mine, and shall be able to cover every foot of it with our rifles. But we must remember that these Somalis possess many firearms, and if they happen to discover us, and can get rid of their fears of the supernatural, they will lie upon the slopes about us and pour in their fire with certain aim, for the range will be a close one. Only then should we learn that to lie at the entrance would be impossible, for it would cost us our lives. Do you follow me, my friends?"

"Quite easily!" exclaimed the colonel. "Had you had the training of a soldier, you could not have seen the danger more clearly. I am waiting impatiently to hear how you propose to get over the difficulty, which, there is no doubt, is a very real one."

"Then listen, colonel. My idea is a very simple one, and had I not thought of it, you or your son would quickly have done so. Since life to us would be impossible, even though we were to lie flat upon the floor, my suggestion is that we set to work with what implements we have and dig a trench of sufficient depth just within the opening to allow us to obtain shelter. The earth which we remove can be thrown up in front, so that the hole need not be more than three feet in depth."

"It seems a splendid proposal," cried Jim, who had been listening attentively. "I notice that the floor here is also paved with slabs of stone, but the earth beneath is soft, and quite loose, as you will see for yourself if you look at this large patch here, where the covering has been removed. That being the case, the sword which I took from the sentry who was watching over father's prison should be sufficient to thoroughly turn it up, and the remainder of the work can be finished with our hands. If we were to set to at it now, the job would be finished by daylight, and then all would be in readiness in case of attack."

For some little time the fugitives stood thoughtfully considering the question, and then, taking care that the torches should not be brought too close to the entrance, they went there in a body and closely inspected the ground. Thrusting the long native sword into a crevice between two of the paving-slabs, the colonel rapidly levered one of them up, and lifted it out of its place. Then he put the point of the weapon upon the bare earth, and pressed firmly upon the handle, with the result that the blade sank into it easily until the hilt stopped its farther descent. A gentle tug released it, and, when it was held up to the light, they saw that it was not even stained.

"We're in luck!" cried the colonel. "The soil beneath is composed of pure sand, and can be removed with the greatest ease. Look here!"

Dropping upon his knees, he thrust his hands into the opening which he had made and drew them out filled with shining particles.

"That explains the reason for these slabs, and for the paved road outside," he said; "for if they were not here, movement would have become most difficult, and the slaves, as they trudged to and fro with their bags of quartz or of gold-bearing sand, would have had a weary time indeed. Let us get to work at once, for the sooner the task is finished, the better."

Placing their weapons upon the pavement close at hand, the party at once began to tear up the square slabs of stone. They found that, when one had been removed, the rest gave little trouble, and ere many minutes had passed they had cleared a long and narrow track across the opening of the mine. Then they began to shovel out handfuls of sand, and did not desist from their labour until a deep trench had been dug. And now, at Jim's suggestion, the slabs were relaid at the bottom, while a few were used as a narrow coping on the summit of the bank which they had thrown up in front of the trench. Through this four narrow embrasures were left to accommodate the muzzles of the guns, and were cut so deeply that the weapons could be fired whilst the heads of the defenders remained completely under cover.

Two hours later the arched opening became more visible, and soon the rays of the sun were pouring down upon the land.

"I vote for a meal," sang out the colonel cheerily. "We may as well have it now, while we are undisturbed, for we may not have the opportunity later, and besides, you remember the old tale that men fight better and more bravely when they have had all their wants satisfied."

Nothing loth, for their exertions during the night had sharpened their appetites, the remainder of the party hastily agreed, and turned with questioning eyes towards Ali Kumar. The shikari was by no means disconcerted, and instantly crossing the entrance of the mine to where the camels lay, he returned with one of the saddle-bags, in which was stored the greater portion of the food which he and Jim had thoughtfully brought from the zareba.

The fugitives had barely done justice to the meal when a low cry from Ali alarmed them, and, looking out through their embrasures, they caught sight of a group of dusky figures standing at the mouth of the ravine. That their eyes were fixed upon the old mine-workings was evident, and soon there was little doubt that the sight had attracted their attention. They remained close together, talking and waving their arms, and then, to the consternation of the defenders, they were seen to be searching for marks upon the ground. That success was likely to attend their efforts was without question, and indeed but a little time had elapsed before one of them gave vent to a shout, and called to his comrades to join him. An instant later the party separated, scrambling like so many monkeys up the steep slopes of the tiny valley, and, when they arrived at the top, each man instantly began to wave his arms aloft, and shout the news of the discovery to all who were within hearing.

CHAPTER XIX

A STRATEGIC RETREAT

There was no doubt that the hiding-place of the fugitives was now discovered, and that they must prepare to defend their position and their lives; for, knowing the character of the Mullah, they could not hope to escape from attack. Sooner or later, and as quickly as they could overcome their fears of the spot, the fierce followers would advance into the ravine and pour their bullets into the entrance to the mine. Indeed, in view of the fanatical hatred in which they held the infidels, it was more than probable that they would gather together in a body and throw themselves with the utmost ferocity upon the fugitives. But we must leave the little party for a few moments and once more fly to the coast and see how the preparations for invasion were progressing.

The reader will recollect how a force had collected at Berbera, and, following in the wake of Jim's expedition, had marched across the lowlands and reached the highlands by the very pass in which the latter had so severely defeated the tribesmen. The rendezvous of the British troops had been Bohotle, which had already been strongly reinforced, and filled with supplies calculated to last at least six months. As a strategic base, this was the very best that the country offered in these parts, for it was practically on the fringe of the Hoad, and guarded the wells at which the last store of water could be obtained. From that point onwards a march of at least six days must be contemplated, across a waterless desert, before the invading force could reach the Mudug pasture lands in which the Mullah had made his home. From the farther fringe of the desert, two days at most would be occupied in marching upon the Mullah's stronghold, and after that much depended upon circumstances. If the enemy stood and faced the troops boldly, as he had boasted he would, there was every hope that short work would be made of his army, and that the same fate would befall him as had happened to the Khalifa in the Soudan. On the other hand, he or his men might suddenly become fearful of this small band marching against him, and might fly into the interior. If that were to happen, much would depend upon whether the force which had already set out from Obbia, and that which had left the Abyssinian frontier, were able to cut off his retreat and compel him to come to action. For the moment, no one could tell how the affair would turn out, but the troops at Bohotle were in the finest spirits, and confident of success. Making little of the privations before them, therefore, they welcomed the notes of the bugle which sounded the reveillé on the morning selected for the advance, and fell into their ranks with faces which showed their enthusiasm. Had their leader but known the precarious position of Jim's zareba, and the fact that our hero himself, together with three friends, was at that moment awaiting the attack of the Mullah's whole force, he would have pushed on with even greater haste, for his men were fit and ready for any exertions. But though he was aware of the marching of a small expedition into the interior, and knew what its object was, he had received no tidings of the fortune or misfortune which had befallen it, and therefore, in accordance with the arrangements which he had so carefully drawn out, he did not venture to begin his march across the Hoad before the date which had been agreed upon. Now, however, the time for action had arrived, and with a feeling of enthusiasm which was not less than that displayed by his officers and men, he gave the order to march, and, having seen the advance guard leave the camp, sat there upon his pony in the glare of the morning sun, watching critically as each battalion and each portion of the transport corps passed him. Then waving a farewell to the unlucky ones who were to remain behind to garrison Bohotle, and who gave him a ringing cheer in return, he set his beast into a canter, and in due time took his post at the head of his men.

The expedition which had been gathering at Obbia and elsewhere on the Abyssinian frontier had also set out on the date agreed upon, and were even then pushing forward as rapidly as possible in the hope of coming to close quarters with the Mullah.

With this knowledge, let us return to the fugitives in the mine. Seated upon the edge of their trench, with their faces glued to the embrasures which perforated the low bank of sand in front of them, our hero and his comrades had kept their eyes intently fixed upon the Somali scouts, and had seen, with a thrill of excitement, that these men had already guessed their whereabouts.

"They are signalling to the others," said Jim with an effort to keep his voice steady. "I suppose we must soon expect to have a large force attacking us."

"That just depends upon how long it takes for the news to spread," remarked the colonel, his calmness quite unruffled by the sudden excitement. "Unless those fellows who are waving and shouting from the top of the hill can be seen a long distance away, it seems to me that it may be many hours before the others are informed of our discovery, and consequently no serious attack will be made upon us for the present."

"The deduction is a good one, but, unfortunately, the facts are not precise," interposed John Margetson, in tones which showed that the turn events had taken had not been without its effect upon him. "I am quite an old resident in this country, you must remember, and I shall tell you one of the many things which I have learnt. It is the power these natives have of transmitting news to one another across long distances. Those beggars whom you see up there, apparently waving their arms in a reckless manner, are, nevertheless, fully alert and quite aware of what they are doing. Just as we in the Navy use semaphores to convey our news to distant vessels, so do these Somali fellows roughly send their messages to one another by means of their arms. Look at that chap up there! He is standing alone on the summit of the hill, so that his figure is against the sky-line, while his comrades are taking care to keep well away from him, so that those who are looking on at a distance shall not be confused. You may take it from me that there is another native, a mile or more away, upon a second hill, and still another elsewhere. By their means the order to concentrate at this ravine will flash across the country, and the swift ponies which these Somalis possess will quickly bring them to the spot."

"Then we must make up our minds for an early fight," said Jim calmly; "and, so far as I can see, we are fully prepared, and have no need to do more than sit where we are, awaiting developments. We've fed, and feel contented. For my part, having so recently had a brush with the native tribesmen, I feel confident that our chances are good, and that, so long as our ammunition lasts, we can defy these people."

"That's just the way to take it, my boy," sang out Colonel Hubbard cheerily. "Recklessness in a soldier is, as a general rule, inexcusable, for he should take good care to count the odds. But I freely admit that the forlorn hope has on many occasions gained us a victory, though it is not advisable. But there is nothing like going into an engagement with full belief in yourself, for then you have every determination to be successful. As to the power these beggars have of signalling, it is an interesting piece of information, and one of which I was quite unaware. But the news does not absolutely astound me, for I have met with a similar thing elsewhere. For instance, look at the Kaffirs, who inhabit a land in which we have been so recently fighting. They have some extraordinary means of conveying tidings to one another. Indeed, the result of large engagements, and even of small skirmishes, was known by these people a hundred and more miles away long before our telegraphists had been able to send it over the wires. But we must not occupy our attention with these matters at the present moment, for there is no doubt that we are in for a struggle. I therefore propose that we inspect arms at once."

Acting on this suggestion, all the available weapons were brought forward and their merits discussed. Then the ammunition was carefully counted out and put in a convenient spot. It was found that the party owned two modern rifles which Jim and Ali Kumar had brought with them from the zareba, and for which a large store of cartridges was available. Then there was the muzzle-loading gun which John Margetson had thoughtfully carried away from the store-hut, together with a quantity of powder and a bag of slugs, while in his belt he still retained the revolver which Jim had handed to him. As for the colonel, his son had presented him with the second revolver, so that each one of the party was fully armed, while there was one firearm over in case of accidents. In addition, they possessed the long double-handled native sword, in case of attack at close quarters.

"It seems to me that we are excellently provided," remarked Jim, when the inspection was completed. "If we are careful not to throw away a shot, our ammunition should last for a considerable time. The bag of slugs will be the first to require replenishing, and in that case I should imagine a few chips from one of these stone slabs would answer the purpose just as well. But—I say—look at those fellows!"

The group of Somali warriors, who had been standing upon the hill-top signalling to their friends, had become greatly enlarged, and within a very short space of time some two hundred men were stationed there, staring down into the ravine, and looking with suspicion at the entrance to the mine. But as yet not one had dared to enter the haunted valley, though they did not hesitate to crowd together at the opening, as if in the act of doing so.

An hour later their numbers had increased to quite double, while a movement amongst them showed that some leader was expected. That it should prove to be the Mullah himself was not wonderful, for he had promised to help his followers to capture the runaways. His charger was soon seen upon the sky-line, while a figure stood with the reins hooked over his arm, listening to the words of his scouts.

"Now something will happen," said the colonel calmly. "That rogue will find some means by which to quiet his followers' fears, though I doubt whether he will dare to lead them in person. See! He is haranguing them, and to show that there is no danger to be apprehended, he is descending into the valley alone. By Jove! With those rifles we could knock him over to a certainty. But fair play's a jewel, and for myself, I confess that I don't care to fire at a man unless I know that he is about to do the same to me; it's too much like murder to sight a weapon for a native clambering down the slope of a hill and pull the trigger on him. All the same, the prejudice is a silly one, for were we to drop him in his tracks, the chances are that his followers would decamp, and in that case the expeditions which are about to march into the country would find that they had little work to do. Look at the ruffian!"

Clambering down the steep slope of the hill, it was not long before the Mullah had gained the centre of the ravine, where he stood for some few moments, observing the paved road which traversed it. Then he turned to his followers, and called loudly to them to come and join him.

"Slide down, and have no fear!" he shouted in reassuring tones. "The story that this place is haunted is an old woman's tale, made only to frighten the children. But you are brave men, and there are your enemies, the infidel dogs, who have had the insolence to come hither. By Allah! I swear to you that no harm shall befall you, and I call upon you once more to join me, and then to rush with all your fury upon the mine."

For a short space of time it was clear that his followers hesitated, but on the Mullah's repeating his assurances, they began to descend one by one, and then came sliding and running down in a body. Very soon they were collected together in the centre of the ravine, and at a shout from their leader they advanced towards the mine.

"Now, Jim," whispered the colonel, "we're in your hands, for you are the senior officer at present."

"Then hold your fire till I give the word," was the calm response, "and then you can blaze into them for all you are worth."

Standing on the stone pavement at the bottom of their trench, each of the defenders carefully adjusted his weapon, Jim and Ali taking care to throw open the catch of their magazines, while John Margetson placed the spare revolver close at hand, so that, when his gun was discharged, he would still have something to fall back upon. Then, in absolute silence, and without allowing any portion of their figures to be observed, they waited with fast-beating hearts for the attack of the enemy. It came even sooner than they had expected, for, spurred on by the Mullah's words of encouragement, and by their own fanatical hatred of the infidel, the mass of Somali warriors came bounding towards the mine, those on the outer edge crushing towards the centre in their desire to take a part in the battle. As a result, they became closely jammed together, and arrived at the arched entrance in this formation.

"Fire!" cried Jim, when they were only a few yards away.

Instantly the guns of the defenders rang out and poured a perfect hail of missiles into the enemy. At such a close range it was impossible to miss one's aim, and therefore the losses sustained by the Somalis were very great. Indeed, so unexpected was the volley, and so disconcerted were they at the fall of their comrades, that all at once stopped their mad rush at the mine, and stood there aghast at the slaughter, and hesitating how to act. The breathing-space thus afforded was taken full advantage of by Jim and his friends, for, instantly reloading, they sent a second volley into the attackers. Its effect was excellent, for, finding that more of their fellow-warriors were falling, and that as yet not one of them had caught sight of the enemy, the Somalis gave vent to a howl of dismay, and retreated at the top of their speed. Nor did they pause until they had clambered from the ravine to the top of the slope outside.

"That will make them think twice about the matter," said the colonel, with a chuckle. "And just look at their leader! He took particular care not to join in the attack, and was the very first to scramble away to a safe distance. However, a humbug, such as he is, will soon stir up the tribesmen again by reminding them that we are few in numbers, and that the score against us is a heavy one. Then, no doubt, we can expect a second attack, and, if I know their wily commander at all, he will adopt different tactics."

How true the prophecy of the colonel was destined to be was soon found out, for, after retiring out of sight for a short period, the Somalis again appeared on the surrounding heights. Then they dropped silently into the ravine, and, lying down in the long grass at the foot of the hills, began to pour a hot fire into the mine. Soon, indeed, the air was alive with their slugs and bullets, which came whistling in through the opening. But, thanks to the trench which John

Margetson had suggested, the defenders ran no danger of being hit, but sat down at the bottom, placidly listening to the uproar. For half an hour the fusillade continued without cessation, and, indeed, at the end of that time, became even louder and fiercer.

"It sounds as though they had been strongly reinforced," remarked Jim, whose coolness had never for a moment deserted him. "I'll just take a look through one of our peep-holes and see what is happening, for it would never do to make the sudden discovery that they were rushing upon us again."

Accordingly, taking every precaution not to expose himself to the bullets, he cautiously raised an eye to one of the embrasures, and closely inspected the ravine. He found that what he had thought had just occurred, for even then scores of men were climbing over the hill-tops, to slide at once into the valley beneath. Down below a large force of Somalis was gathered, and these, it was easy to perceive, were filled with excitement, and eager for the attack. They were shouting to one another, and brandishing their weapons.

"We can expect a second rush in a few moments," said Jim, sinking into the trench again; "there are scores of the enemy, and it seems to me that we shall be wise if we at once take steps to arrange for a retreat. I cannot think that our four weapons will be sufficient to keep them out. No doubt we shall kill a number of them, but all are in such desperate earnest that those who survive will come on, in spite of their losses, and once they get to close quarters with us, we shall be done for. I suggest, therefore, that a couple of us go and investigate those passages, while the others keep watch here. Then, as soon as the advance begins, a shout will bring us together again."

"A good soldier should always arrange for an orderly retirement," remarked the colonel thoughtfully, "for it is not always wise to burn your boats behind you, or destroy your bridges. I must confess that in this case we shall be wise to do as my son suggests, for it will help us to fight the harder if we possess the knowledge that retreat is possible. At the same time, I am quite sure that we are men enough to stand to our guns to the very last, and, in spite of a means of retirement, to stick to our position so long as it is tenable."

"Hear, hear!" sang out John Margetson, who, as the danger increased, seemed to become more cheerful. "Both of you have made most excellent proposals, and, as they do not need seconding, I shall show my approval by at once volunteering to form one of the exploring party."

"Then Jim had better go with you, my friend. I will remain here with Ali, and when you hear a shout, come back to us as fast as you can."

The question having thus been settled, and it being evident that there was no time for delay, the two who had been selected for the enterprise left their weapons on the edge of the sandbank, and, crawling from the trench, crept to the left, where they were quickly out of the range of the bullets. Then they sprang to their feet and ran to the fire, which still smouldered, and, snatching a couple of the largest brands, stepped towards the many openings which ran from the entrance-hall into the workings of the mine.

"Which one?" asked John Margetson, holding his torch aloft. "All are of exactly the same size and appearance, so that it is difficult to make a choice."

"Then I vote for the central arch," cried Jim. "Come along."

Darting across the intervening space, which was swept by a cloud of bullets, they plunged into the dark opening, and then, with firebrands held well in front of them, advanced at as rapid a pace as possible. They found themselves in a tunnel, which was of sufficient height to allow them to stand easily. A glance on either side showed them that the walls were composed of bare rock, or of sandstone, while the roof was supported at short intervals by buttresses of stone on either hand, and by a girder of the same material stretched from summit to summit. Like the hall and the ravine outside, the floor was paved with square blocks, but in parts these had caved in, and the recesses were filled with dark pools of water. Elsewhere falls of the roof and of the sides had taken place, and obstructed the passage, but in no place did it close it completely. Indeed, in view of the fact that hundreds of years had probably passed since the workings had been constructed, their condition was marvellous, and reflected the greatest credit upon those who had slaved at their construction.

But Jim and his comrade had little time for observing all these points, for they were conscious that their pressing needs would admit of no delay. Avoiding, therefore, the depressions and crevices in the floor, and clambering over the mounds formed by fallen rocks and *débris* from the roof above, they pushed on at a pace which brought them many a bruise from projecting obstacles. But they never seemed to heed them, and, scrambling along, had quickly traversed some two hundred yards of the tunnel. At this point they came to a crossway, where a passage ran to right and left.

"I should think that our best plan will be to take the direct road," said Jim, coming to a halt. "However, we will just see where these two tunnels lead to. You take that on the right, John, while I go to the left. If after walking some twenty yards you find nothing extraordinary, return at once, and meet me here."

Without discussing the question further, they separated at once. When they met again in the space of a couple of minutes, each reported that the crossway opened into a parallel tunnel a few yards away, and into still another farther on.

"Then it looks as though the openings from the entrance-hall ran on into the hill, diverging slightly, and connected at this point by a cross-cut. Evidently our path lies right ahead."

"You've hit the right nail this time, without a doubt," answered John Margetson. "Forward is the word."

When they had advanced some two or three hundred yards farther, the explorers suddenly came to a spot where the workings converged, and here they found a chamber which was larger even than that at the entrance. From it again there were many exits, into which they dared not venture. However, they had already gone far enough to learn that, should the enemy prove too strong for them, they had a way of retreat which would enable them to elude pursuit for some time.

"I doubt even whether these Somali beggars would dare to follow us as far as this," said John Margetson; "and if they do, I think we can guarantee that they shall be thoroughly scared. But I am firmly of belief that by pushing on we should come to an exit on the other side of this enormous hill, for the air here is perfectly pure and good, which is wonderful, when you come to consider the age of these workings. It looks, in fact, as though there was a perfect system of ventilation, a precaution which the ancients were too wise to neglect. Hullo! That was a shout."

At that moment a loud cry reached their ears, the sound, indeed, seeming to be collected together and enlarged by the solid walls of the mine. There was no doubt that it came from the two defenders who were watching the Mullah's followers, and at once Jim and his companion took to their heels, and raced back at their fastest pace. Arrived at the entrance-hall, they flung their brands into the fire and darted across the floor to the trench, in which they at once took their places.

"You have returned in the nick of time," remarked the colonel, in unruffled tones, "for those fellows outside are on the point of attacking. You can hear for yourself that the firing has ceased. But tell me, what luck have you had?"

"Splendid, father. We've explored the central tunnel, and find that it runs on for a considerable distance before coming to a meeting-place in the centre of the hill, from which a second series of workings emerge. If we have to fly, there will be plenty of room in which to play hide-and-seek, and always a chance of turning upon our followers and punishing them."

"Then we put the command in your hands as before, my boy, and leave it to you to give the word to retire. But, remember, all of you, that ammunition is valuable, and that you must not forget to carry every cartridge away with you."

His last words were interrupted by a perfect babel of sounds which came from the ravine, and each of the defenders at once sprang to his position, and, looking through the embrasure, saw that the enemy had begun to advance. This time they had taken the precaution to observe some order, and collecting together into a long, tongue-like band, came rushing up the central road towards the entrance of the mine. As before, Jim waited calmly until they were within easy range, and then gave the word to fire. Immediately a volley flashed from the sandbank, and a number of the natives fell. Then the defenders emptied their magazines into the closely packed ranks, and set to work with all haste to load again. For the second time they repeated the process, causing great loss to the enemy. But, in spite of that fact, the latter still rushed forward with marvellous pluck, and with loud shouts. Leaping over the bodies of the fallen, shrieking with pain, and tumbling headlong to the ground in their haste, they struggled fiercely to get at the infidels. Arriving at the deep cutting which the stream had made through the pathway, the foremost leapt it successfully; but those behind were not able to see it till right upon its edge, and, pushed by those who followed them, fell into the abyss with wild shrieks. Soon some thirty of them had met with this fate, and the gulley was full to overflowing. But their comrades never paused, never even hesitated, but, roused to fury by the loss of their friends, and by the stinging hail of bullets which still swept amongst them, came on with fierce determination, and in such huge numbers that it quickly became clear that there was no stopping them.

"Give them a last volley!" shouted Jim, raising his voice above the din. "Now, all together, and afterwards let us bolt."

Waiting till all were prepared, the four defenders rapidly emptied their magazines into the enemy, until the barrels of their weapons were so hot that they blistered their fingers. Then snatching up the piles of ammunition which they had placed close at hand, they scrambled from the trench, and, running swiftly across the entrance-hall, dived into the central tunnel, for all the world like rabbits taking to their burrows.

"Halt!" cried Jim sharply, at this moment. "Without a torch we shall be lost. Wait here till I get one."

Returning, he ran to the fire, and quickly secured four flaming brands, then he rejoined his comrades, noticing as he was about to enter the workings that the cries of the attackers had suddenly ceased, and that they had all come to a halt outside the mine, as if too fearful to enter it. But scarcely had the fugitives traversed more than a hundred yards of the tunnel, when loud shouts and cries again rent the air, and being magnified by the enclosing walls, came echoing and reverberating into the working. Indeed, the natives had at last overcome their superstitious terrors, and, rendered desperate by the baffling tactics of the infidels, had flowed into the entrance-hall till it was packed with humanity. Then a second pause ensued, for the passages which led on into the hill looked dark and forbidding. However, a leader was forthcoming, who, imitating Jim's example, snatched at one of the fiery brands, and, having peered into each one of the tunnels in succession, finally waved to his comrades to divide and search all of them.

Meanwhile the fugitives had sped on without a pause, and very soon arrived at the large chamber, which seemed to be the heart of the workings. And here they halted to listen for sounds of the pursuers.

"It is perfectly clear," said the colonel, seating himself to regain his breath, "that these fellows have overcome their fears, and are in hot chase. It occurs to me at the same time that the movement we have made was a most excellent one, for the very fact that there are so many channels leading into the hill will cause the Somalis to divide up into parties. Then in the darkness they will lose one another, and in that way will fall easy victims to our rifles, if they happen to come up with us. My advice is that we sit here for a little while, and then take matters more easily, for we shall require all our powers later. Perhaps we shall find an exit, and in that case we shall be obliged to travel fast to the zareba."

Accordingly the party crossed to the other side of the chamber, and entered the tunnel which stood opposite to that from which they had just emerged. Then lowering their torches, so that the flames could not be easily observed, they sat down to await events. Presently they became aware that some, at least, of the natives were close at hand, and prepared to push on, or repel the pursuers, as circumstances should dictate. But there was no need for interference on their part, for as they peered into the depths of the chamber, the glowing end of a firebrand suddenly appeared, the feeble light enabling them to perceive that five men only accompanied the bearer. They were on the point of levelling their rifles at these intruders when there was a shout from one of the side tunnels, and before the onlookers could realize what was about to happen, a second party of Somalis rushed into the open space, and mistaking the first for the flying infidels, threw themselves with spear and sword upon them.

"I almost expected a catastrophe of that sort," whispered the colonel; "and it is very probable that it may occur elsewhere, for our pursuers are too angry to be cautious. I think we may safely leave them to themselves and push on now deeper into the mine."

Acting upon this advice, the party stole silently away into the darkness, leaving the Somali warriors struggling desperately with one another. A trudge of nearly half a mile brought them to a point which seemed to be the farthest limit of the mine, for here galleries ran in every direction, and a glance at the rough surfaces of the walls showed that the workings had been deserted in a hurry, and not because gold was no longer to be found. Indeed, had it been possible, the three Englishmen would have gladly stayed to investigate the matter, for there were numerous interesting relics scattered about. But to delay then might have brought disaster to the party, and, therefore, they at once began to search for an exit.

"I feel sure we are not far from the open air," cried Jim, suddenly coming to a stop in the centre of a wide space, from which the tiny galleries cut into the hill.

"Come here, and you will feel quite a draught blowing upon your heads, and——By Jove! Look at my torch!"

He held the brand above his head, and as he did so the dull red end began to glow brightly, and then, fanned by an invisible stream of air which played upon it, it burst into a brilliant flame, which effectually lit up the surroundings.

"A grand find, my boy!" shouted the colonel, for the first time showing some trace of excitement. "By the aid of that flaring brand we shall find our way to liberty. Push on, and when you see the light die down, you will know at once that we are moving in the wrong direction."

Jim needed no further encouragement, but, with his rifle grasped in one hand, strode forward, keeping his eye fixed upon the torch. And all the while he could feel the cold air blowing upon his face as it rushed into the workings through the ventilating shaft. Soon he came to a large square orifice, and entering it without hesitation, he went on till almost stopped by the pressure of the atmosphere. Following him closely, his companions were struck with wonder at the draught and watched in amazement as their torches kindled even brighter and sent long flames to the roof above.

"It is almost beyond belief," murmured John Margetson, breaking in upon the silence, "and I cannot realize how it is that the ventilation of the mine is managed. In a coal-pit there would be an up-cast and a down-cast shaft, with some arrangement at the former to cause the air to rush in that direction. But here we have come across nothing of the sort."

"It would take a week to discover the cause," answered the colonel, "but I have been through similar mines, and have come to the conclusion that the people who constructed them were most capable engineers. Hullo! What's that?"

As he spoke, the party came to an abrupt halt, and gave vent to cries of delight, for away ahead of them was a square patch of light, the goal for which they had been aiming.

CHAPTER XX

BACK TO THE COAST

"The exit! A means by which we may make good our escape from the mine, leaving the enemy utterly baffled!" shouted the colonel, as the square of brilliant light suddenly came into view, permitting, for the second time since his rescue from the Mullah's village, his usual composure to give way to the excitement of the moment. "Phew! What a breeze! It is as much as one can do to force a path towards the opening, for the draught comes singing in like a magnified gale, and fairly makes one stagger."

"Clever beggars, those old fellows who engineered the concern," gasped John Margetson, turning his face from the stream of air, so as to breathe more freely. "This is undoubtedly their ventilating shaft; and, George! how fond they must have been of a breeze. The hottest day in the tropics would be cool if spent in this tunnel, while in the winter——"

"A case of freezing," laughed the colonel. "The gale fairly sweeps and rushes in, and the atmosphere must reach to the farthest corner and nook of the mine, and clear it thoroughly. It is marvellous."

"It is fine, I admit," said Jim at this moment, joining in the conversation curtly; "but talking will not help us to get away from those fellows—will it, father?"

"Quite right! The lad speaks the truth, and we deserve to be reproved," was the smiling answer. "There is a time for everything, and at the present moment we have to think of our lives, and of the comrades whom we hope to join. But I will return here one of these days, when the Mullah has had his licking; and then how I shall enjoy exploring every inch of this place! But forward! What is the next move, Jim?"

"Let us get to the opening and take a look out, father. Till then I cannot say. We may find that the Somalis are already there, expecting our arrival, and in that case we shall have to retire to the workings again. If not, we must hold a council, and discuss what we must do to get to the zareba. Of course, we might make for the coast alone; but, then, that would be leaving my friend in the lurch, for he is waiting for us patiently."

"It would be the act of cowards," cried the colonel. "Our duty is to save ourselves, and to join hands with this gallant young fellow who has accompanied you into the country. Let us get ahead, my dear lad, for I must admit that this tunnel, at first so cool and invigorating, is now somewhat too cold for my liking. And then, the breeze comes in with such a rush that it is difficult to breathe, and talking is no easy matter."

"Then on we go," said Jim shortly, turning to the opening at once, from which, like his companions, he had been glad to keep his face away.

With torches held aloft, and spouting long streams of brilliant flame from their glowing ends, the little party sped on up the incline which led to the patch of daylight, their thoughts all the while bent upon the possible chances of ultimate escape. All realized that they had perhaps a thousand fanatical foes to deal with, and that many, many miles of rolling country intervened between themselves and the zareba away in the desert. Could they hope to make their way there without discovery? Was it not more than likely that before their weary feet had carried them more than a tenth of the distance, these fierce warriors would be upon them? But there was little use in imagining such things, and as nothing could be known for certain till the opening of the air-shaft was reached, they all hastened forward at as fast a pace as possible, gasping for air, with bodies leaning forward upon the column of wind pouring into the mine, fighting their way through its very centre.

"Hurrah!" cried Jim at length, as his hand came in contact with the solid arch of masonry which marked the entrance. "The open sky again. And now for a look round."

"Be cautious, master," came Ali's voice at this moment. "You have told me that these men who cry to Allah have scattered in search of the runaways. It may well be that some are even now close at hand, and will see you the instant your head appears. Be careful, therefore, I beg of you, for we cannot hope for such good fortune a second time."

"He needs no warning, this leader of ours," said John Margetson, halting beside our hero. "Has he not already shown his cuteness? Leave him to manage the matter alone, friend Ali."

"The words are filled with truth, sahib, and I am sorry," answered the native follower humbly. "I should know of his caution and wisdom even better than you do, seeing that I have marched beside him for many a day. But this danger has made me nervous. Never in my life before have I been in such peril, not even when the tribe attacked us in the pass on our way hither. Let my fears be my excuse, and forgive me. From this moment I shall maintain silence."

Jim very cautiously looked about him, pushing the blades of grass aside to enable him to see clearly. As there were no trees or bushes to obstruct the view, he was soon able to inform his comrades that not a single one of the enemy was in sight.

"They are all on the other side of the hill, rushing into the workings," he said with a smile of relief; "and now it becomes a question as to whether we should move in the direction of the desert, or whether we should remain here till matters have calmed down. This is too serious a decision for me to arrive at alone, and therefore I call all of you in to help me."

"Hum, a very difficult situation," said the colonel, pushing his way to the front and carefully surveying the surrounding country. "I see hills and valleys for a few miles, and then, as you have told me, a dead level extends to the zareba. This is the most dangerous point in our escape, for if we leave the mine, we throw comparative safety away. On the other hand, we cannot hope to remain here for long. Our provisions will soon become exhausted, and, moreover, once having overcome their fears, and having dared to enter the workings, these Somali warriors will penetrate to its farthest corners in search of their prisoners. Be sure of this: if the news of an advancing English column has angered the Mullah, this impudent and successful attempt to rescue prisoners from under his very eyes will rouse him to fury, and he will turn aside from the invading force in order to capture us. I confess that I hesitate. Here is a haven for a time. Out there, sunny and sweet as the country looks, it promises disaster."

"He who hesitates is lost," whispered John Margetson in his ear. "Listen to me, colonel; and you, too, Jim. To remain here is impossible. That is how I read it, for in an hour we shall be discovered by the searchers. Therefore, there can be no question. That is our way. Forward, my friends."

He pointed across the rolling expanse of grass, and would have emerged from the shaft, had not Jim detained him.

"Steady," he said quietly. "To hop out there into the open may be to commit the greatest of errors. A glance at you would convince one of the enemy that you are the escaping sailor; and then what a shout there would be!"

"Well? That would be the end of the matter."

"Quite so," responded Jim coolly. "But look at me. Am I not like the average Somali warrior?"

"Jove! The lad has a way to help us," shouted the colonel. "Silence while we listen to him. A Somali, my boy? Why, your disguise is undoubtedly excellent."

"Then I shall take advantage of the fact, father. Stay here, all of you, while I slip out. If I am seen, I shall be just one of the Mullah's followers, and all the while shall be on the look-out so as to see how we can best escape. Ta, ta. Wait till I return."

Before they could stretch out a friendly arm to detain him, Jim was outside the shaft, and was running up the slope of the hill. Anxiously did his comrades await his return, and more than once they were tempted to throw caution to the winds, and, giving way to their impatience, to rush into the open in search of their leader. But the calmness of the colonel held them back.

"Trust the lad," he said, his head held proudly in the air. "He has done as well as any man, and has shown that he has pluck and plenty of brains. Give him a full half-hour before we make any movement. Ah, what are those sounds?"

"The dogs in search of us," said Ali, placing his hand to his ear, and facing down the shaft. "These walls carry the sound as does the tube which they have in Aden. Have I not listened at one end to hear the sound of a comrade's voice? Have little fear, masters, for those men will hardly dare to follow us into this shaft."

"Hush! Here is someone coming towards us!" exclaimed the colonel, in a warning whisper at this moment. "I think it is Jim; but it may not be. He is evidently hunting for the entrance."

"It is the lad, sure enough," cried John Margetson, staring out of the shaft. "Look at the condition of his linen clothing. No self-respecting follower of

Allah would dare to go abroad in such a dress. He is travel-soiled, and there can be no mistake as to his identity. I shall call to him."

Thrusting his arm clear of the opening, he waved it, and called gently to Jim. A second or two later Jim appeared at the entrance of the shaft, his dusky features radiant with smiles.

"Good news!" he cried eagerly. "Not one of the enemy on this side, so far as I have been able to observe, but all are in the ravine beyond, trying to screw up their courage to enter the mine as some of their comrades have done."

"Then they do not suspect that we are on the farther side," said the colonel, in tones of relief. "Nevertheless, the question of escape is still one of difficulty."

"I think not, father," answered Jim quietly. "We have a clear field before us, and scarcely forty miles to cover."

"But, good gracious! that will take us a day and a half at least," cried his parent.

"On foot—yes," said Jim gaily. "But on horseback, say a day at the most."

"Horseback! What do you mean?" burst in those who were listening to him, eagerly pressing about their young leader.

"Listen," was the smiling rejoinder. "I said that the followers of the Mullah were on the farther side of the hill, but I did not tell you that they had taken their animals to the ravine. Obviously, in such a small place, there would some overcrowding, for there is not too much room for the warriors themselves."

"Then where are they, my boy?" demanded the colonel.

"Come with me," was Jim's quiet answer, "but be careful not to show yourselves over the corner of the hill. The horses are grazing quietly in a little nook, a small valley which cuts into this long hill, and they are practically unwatched. That was a point about which I took a deal of trouble, and I ascertained without a doubt that only one man was stationed as a guard over the beasts. He, like his comrades, is all eagerness to help in our capture, and as I watched him, he was for ever staring into the ravine, and shouting words of encouragement to his fellows. He is the only man we have to fear at the present moment."

"Then he is the only one who shall taste one of our bullets," said John Margetson brusquely. "This fellow must not be allowed to give the alarm, and though I do not like the action, still it is imperative that we should shoot him. Otherwise he will give the alarm, and we shall have the whole host galloping after us."

"Running, you mean," replied Jim, with an easy laugh. "You see, we want more than a few ponies. A dozen are useless to us, for the remainder would carry the enemy in the same direction, and a long chase is a hard one, you know."

"But you don't propose——" gasped the colonel, staring at his son in bewilderment.

"Oh, yes, I do, father! If we are to escape, we shall have to take the bulk of the ponies for a few miles with us. A mile would not do, for these natives can run very fast. But after, say five miles, all but a very few would have fallen off, and the remainder we could easily account for. If we ride away, and leave the animals to the enemy, we shall be captives before the afternoon."

For a minute all stared at their young leader in amazement at the daring of his plan; then smacking his thigh, as if to give expression to his thoughts, John Margetson broke the silence.

"The Mullah will die of rage!" he gasped, while a smile of delight lit up his sun-tanned features. "Never before has he been so treated, and now to see his prisoners ride away, taking every horse he possesses, well——"

Evidently the thought was too much for the gallant mate, for he lapsed into silence, and writhed, as if his feelings were too much for him. As for the colonel, with the keenness of a trained soldier, he at once grasped the importance of the proposed movement.

"It is a capital plan," he said, with decision. "Every pony must come with us, and this fellow who watches them must be shot without mercy. Give me your rifle, Jim. I am too old a campaigner to have any qualms, and in such a case as this the act is justified. Now, what next?"

"Forward," said Jim quietly. "When we reach the top of the hill, Ali will stop where he is, and we others shall turn to the right. Thirty yards from Ali, John Margetson will come to a stop; another interval, and father will do the same.

All will wait till I am in position. I shall wave my arm, and then we shall all move to the ponies. Select a couple of the finest, and tie their halters together. Then mount, and set the remainder in motion. They are well-trained beasts, and will give us no difficulty."

A glance was sufficient to show that his comrades comprehended his words, and at once turning, Jim led the way to the top of the rise.

"Ah!" an exclamation burst from all of the fugitives at the sight of some two hundred horses grazing in a small valley below.

"All the mounted men that the Mullah happens to have within call," murmured John Margetson. "No doubt the remainder are at the attack of the zareba. Now for the fellow who is looking after the horses."

"He has gone to take a look at his comrades," said Jim. "Forward again. Ali, you stay where you are."

Turning to the right, the three Englishmen at once hurried forward, and obedient to the orders of their young leader, John Margetson and the colonel halted when they had gained the correct distance. Jim kept on till he was at a point slightly beyond the horses. Waiting only to make sure that the animals were now surrounded, he waved his hand to his comrades and at once walked quietly towards two spirited-looking ponies, which promised to be amongst the strongest and swiftest there.

"Likely little beggars," he said to himself. "If they will allow me, I will become their owner for the time being."

A few paces brought him beside one of the animals, and with a bound he was in the saddle. Then grasping the halter of the other, he made a turn with it through the bridle of the pony he rode. Then he began to round up that part of the troop between him and his comrades.

"Look out!" came a shout in the colonel's voice; and turning swiftly, Jim saw a figure bounding across the grass towards him. Snap, bang! went a rifle, and a bullet discharged by the colonel whistled past the head of the pursuing Somali warrior. Bang! A second had no better effect, and ere a third could be attempted the man was upon our hero. Quick as lightning Jim dived his hand into his waistcloth, only to discover that his father had his revolver. He was apparently unarmed, while the Somali bore a flashing spear, and a huge sword at his girdle. "Ah, the sword!" thought Jim, and instantly recollected that he had thrust the weapon into the belt tied about his left forearm.

How it happened Jim never knew, but in the shortest space of time he was riding forward, driving part of the troop before him, while behind, huddled upon his face upon the grass, was the Somali warrior, a murmured "Allah" on his dying lips.

"A great stroke! Bravely and coolly done!" shouted the colonel, who had looked on anxiously, expecting the worst to happen, and blaming himself for his want of skill. "A running man is no easy object when one is mounted upon a fresh pony such as his; but all's well. It was a stroke! The lad has a head, and can look well to himself. I thought the spear was through him, and almost shouted, but he ducked at the very instant, and then—ah, I saw the blade go well home. But those fellows may have heard the shots, and if so, we shall soon be followed."

"Forward!" came Jim's voice at this moment; and instantly all began to urge the troop of animals into a trot. Leaping from their saddles, they picked stones from the earth and then pelted the beasts, shouting at them till their trot broke into a gallop.

"Now keep them to it, and if they try to stop, make a rush at them," shrieked John Margetson, sitting his pony in an attitude which showed clearly that he was no horseman. "Forward! To the zareba!"

It was a time of wild excitement, and each of the fugitives entered into the spirit of it thoroughly. Exhilarated by the quick movement over the rolling hills and valleys, with the smell of the horses in their nostrils, and the dust of four hundred heels in their eyes, they raced over the grass, driving the frantic animals before them. A thunderous sound filled the air as the animals galloped, but loud as it was it failed to drown that shout which came from behind.

"Allah! Allah! They have escaped us, and are riding away! Back! Leave the mine, and run! Money and a high place will be given to those who come up with the infidel!"

It was the Mullah who had heard the shots aimed at the sentry, and had climbed to the top of the hill to ascertain the cause.

"Our friend, the Mullah, my late master," shouted the colonel, looking grimly over his shoulder. "Let them run, for to those who happen to come in touch with us we will give more than the Mullah can promise. Death to them, my friends! Forward, for liberty and comrades are there."

Waving his weapon in the air, he looked at each of his comrades in turn, and smiled at them encouragingly. Then, with a shout at the animals directly in front of him, he sent them ahead at an even greater pace.

An hour later, when the little band of fugitives turned in their saddles, and brought the horses to a standstill, not one of the Mullah's followers was in sight, all having fallen out from the chase.

"We'll give the poor beasts a breather now," said Jim, dropping to the ground and going to his father's side. "We have put a good ten miles between us and the enemy, and I fancy we can say 'good-bye' to them."

"But there must be no delaying," burst in John Margetson. "Though we have prevented immediate pursuit, there will be other horses in the village, and by now these are tearing in this direction. I advise that when we have waited for some ten minutes we select the best of these animals, and then press them forward. They are fine and wiry beasts, and will make little of the forty miles if ridden fairly. We will loosen the girths, and throw away all but the saddle and bridle, so as to relieve them of any unnecessary weight. Then, by changing from animal to animal, say every half-hour, we shall be able to reach the zareba without more than an occasional halt."

Acting upon his words, the little band at once set about discarding those of the ponies which seemed to be in bad condition. Twenty of the finest were kept, and having been relieved of all forage-bags and other impediments, were driven ahead of the others.

"The tracks will be plain to the enemy," said Jim, looking at the wide trail of trampled grass which the troop had left behind it; "so it will be useless to hide these remaining animals by driving them into a ravine. After all, till someone can escort them back, or the Mullah's men can run as far as this, the horses will be of no service to them. Are we all ready? Then on we go."

Leaving the bulk of the horses panting upon the road, they set off again, and did not draw rein save to change from one animal to another, or to give the beasts a few moments' rest. By evening they were cantering over the sandy stretch of desert, and ere long they were in sight of the oasis where Tom and the remainder of the expedition had been quartered.

"Now what shall we find?" said Jim, coming to a halt, and shading his eyes. "The falling sun makes it difficult to see, but everything seems quiet over there, and I can catch sight of none of the enemy."

"An ominous sign," whispered John Margetson. "What if these fanatics have butchered every one of those who accompanied you from the coast?"

"Then we must act alone and for ourselves," said the colonel.

"There will be no need, my masters," came a voice at their elbows at this moment. "Your servant, Ali Kumar, is used to these desert sunsets, and can see where others are blinded by the glare. A flag flies from the summit of one of those trees, and men are coming out to greet us. They are friends. Yes, our comrades are safe and well."

"Then forward to meet them," cried Jim. "I can place full reliance on what Ali says."

Riding on again, it was not long before the fugitives met Tom and the native followers. Shouts and cries of welcome greeted them, and they were at once escorted back to the zareba.

"And now tell us the news," said Jim quickly. "We have little time to rest, and if the enemy are not near at hand, we shall push ahead at once."

"Then you have nothing to fear," answered Tom, with assurance. "The Mullah's followers have left us, and I have just been able to ascertain that they had had news of the approach of the English forces, and had been withdrawn to repel them. Meanwhile, I am glad to say that we have given an excellent account of ourselves. Thanks to the preparations made, when the enemy advanced we beat them back with ease. Time and again they rushed to the attack, but the barbed wire kept them at a distance, and our rifles mowed them down. How many we accounted for I cannot say, but large numbers were killed. In fact, they soon began to lose heart, and I fancy they were glad when the order suddenly reached them that they were to withdraw. And what of you?"

"That you shall hear later," said Jim. "The order now is to retire. Strike camp at once. Load the beasts, and prepare to march in an hour at most."

So rapidly were the orders carried out, and so eagerly did the natives fly to obey them, that within the time mentioned the whole of the expedition was marching north, *en route* to the coast. Camels staggered along with tanks of sweet water upon their backs; others carried fresh-cut grass; while the remainder were laden with ammunition and food for the men. Ten days later all arrived at Berbera, where they attracted a great deal of attention. Having rewarded the followers with gifts of camels, and having taken farewell of Tom and of Ali Kumar, Jim, his father, and John Margetson took ship for England, where they arrived in due time.

"Back, and alive!" gasped Mr. George Hubbard, when the colonel and Jim put in an appearance at his house. "It is astounding! I had expected to hear nothing more of you, and your arrival lifts a weight from my heart. How could it be otherwise when the news just comes to hand that a portion of the British expedition was hemmed in a few days ago by the Mullah, and, falling short of ammunition, suffered very heavy losses? However, though this reverse has put a stop to the campaign for a moment, it is certain to be renewed again, and then this Mullah will be crushed. Indeed, the cables have told us that, since the disaster to our own troops, the Abyssinians have come in contact with this host of Somali plunderers and have inflicted severe losses upon them. But sit down and let me have the yarn. Dear, dear! I declare that Jim is as brown as a berry, and looks quite a man."

That the colonel was of the same opinion was evident, for very few days had passed ere he paid a visit to those in authority, and returned with smiling face and a big blue official envelope.

"Open it," he said, handing it to Jim. "It is your commission in my old regiment, given you for the information which you were able to gather in Somaliland. In two months you and I will be on our way to India, there to join our brother officers."

To say that our hero was delighted is to express the matter mildly. He was almost more excited than he had been when planning his father's rescue. From that moment all was bustle, for his uniform and many other things had to be obtained. In due time, however, the two set sail for India, and entered the Suez

Canal. At Aden they left the ship for a few hours to find Tom and have a chat with him. As for John Margetson, he soon settled down to the routine of life in charge of a ship. Neither he nor the colonel, however, will ever forget those days when they were in the grip of the Mullah.

The End

www.ingramcontent.com/pod-product-compliance
Lightning Source LLC
Chambersburg PA
CBHW060615290526

45793CB00001B/36